Trend Trading

Founded in 1807, John Wiley & Sons is the oldest independent publishing company in the United States. With offices in North America, Europe, Australia, and Asia, Wiley is globally committed to developing and marketing print and electronic products and services for our customers' professional and personal knowledge and understanding.

The Wiley Trading series features books by traders who have survived the market's ever changing temperament and have prospered—some by reinventing systems, others by getting back to basics. Whether a novice trader, professional, or somewhere in-between, these books will provide the advice and strategies needed to prosper today and well into the future.

For a list of available titles, please visit our Web site at www.Wiley Finance.com.

Trend Trading

Timing Market Tides

KEDRICK F. BROWN

WILEY

John Wiley & Sons, Inc.

Published by John Wiley & Sons, Inc., Hoboken, New Jersey.
Published simultaneously in Canada.

For general information on our other products and services or for technical support, please contact our Customer Care Department within the United States at (800) 762-2974, outside the United States at (317) 572-3993, or fax (317) 572-4002.

Wiley also publishes its books in a variety of electronic formats. Some content that appears in print may not be available in electronic books. For more information about Wiley products, visit our Web site at www.wiley.com.

Library of Congress Cataloging-in-Publication Data:

Brown, Kedrick F., 1975–
    Trend trading : timing market tides / Kedrick F. Brown.
        p. cm. — (Wiley trading series)
    Includes bibliographical references and index.
    ISBN-13 978-0-471-98021-6 (cloth)
    ISBN-10 0-471-98021-8 (cloth)
    1. Investments. 2. Stocks. 3. Futures. 4. Risk management. I. Title. II.
Series.
    HG4521.B695   2006
    332.6—dc22

                                                              2006009334

Printed in the United States of America.

10 9 8 7 6 5 4 3 2 1

For Ivana, Jacob, and Natalie

Contents

Preface   xi

Acknowledgments   xvii

PART I   TREND TRADING PSYCHOLOGY   1

CHAPTER 1   Elements of an Edge   3

CHAPTER 2   What Can an Equity Trader Learn from
                a Futures Trend Follower?   31

CHAPTER 3   Equity Trend Following in Action   57

PART II   TREND TRADING TACTICS   75

CHAPTER 4   Three-Dimensional Technical Analysis   77

CHAPTER 5   Structuring a Trend Trade   117

CHAPTER 6   Structuring a Trend Trading Portfolio   153

CHAPTER 7   Out of the Box: Further Possibilities   171

Epilogue   195

APPENDIX   Trend Trading Worksheets and Checklists   197

Notes **204**

Bibliography **209**

Recommended Reading **211**

Additional Resources **212**

Index **213**

There is a tide in the affairs of men,

Which, taken at the flood, leads on to fortune;

Omitted, all the voyage of their life

Is bound in shallows and in miseries.

On such a full sea are we now afloat;

And we must take the current when it serves,

Or lose our ventures.

—William Shakespeare,
Julius Caesar, act 4, scene III[1]

Preface

WHAT THIS BOOK IS ABOUT

I recently decided to write down my many insights about trading equity trends, which I share with you in this book. This book, made possible only after a great deal of toil in real world situations, explains how to trade equity trends—in the real world and not just on paper. Some of the strategies and ideas I present are based on my actual trading experiences, and others are theoretical in nature. I may also be invested (or may invest in the future) in some of the markets or strategies that I mention. You should rigorously test and explore all the ideas (here and wherever else you come upon trading strategies) before putting your own money on the line.

The trading and money management methods I present in this book are meant to be illustrations of the kind of detailed thinking that any investor will need to increase his trading efficiency. My intention is thus not to give the reader a fish, so to speak, but to teach him or her how to fish. There is no holy grail in investing, because the only constant thing about markets is change. Therefore, I hope you take from this book the skills that will enable you to develop your own enhancements to the presented methods, as well as to continually take your research in new directions that will enable you to remain profitable over the long run.

As an equity market maker, I often found myself long in declining markets and short in rising ones because one of my roles was to add liquidity to the market. I absorbed short-term risks so that others could enter or exit longer-term risks, and dealt with risk on a continuous basis. By nature I like to quantify my risks as precisely as possible, and so the trading methods I present in this book arose from my innate need to specify the risks that I expose myself to in the market in more detail, along with some of my insights for trading the market.

There are numerous sources of risk in trading. I developed an instinctive grasp of volatility related risk very quickly, which was crucial when I traded tech stocks through the 2000 peak in the NASDAQ Composite. During this time, the importance of volatility related position sizing was crystal clear. A 1,000-share position in a volatile fiber optic stock might mean a $20,000 intraday swing, while a 1,000-share position in a super-liquid semiconductor stock might be unusually volatile if it had a $4,000 intraday swing. It was obvious that I had to size my positions sensibly compared not only to the typical volatility of a stock I was trading, but also according to what I was willing to risk personally. Over time I was able to distill my insights into simple techniques that now help me to size my personal investments with ease.

I was also struck by how closely the positions in my book moved with the broader market. I watched the Dow Jones Industrial Average keenly each day, and scrutinized how my individual stocks reacted to it. Did a stock rocket up $2 on a 40-point move in the Dow? Was a stock struggling to stay positive in a market up 100 points? How was the NAS-DAQ performing relative to the Dow, and how did that impact my stocks? How was the industry leader in a sector I was trading behaving? Over time, I found myself focusing a great deal on the relative motion of stocks I was trading. When I first began my trading career, I had been fascinated with single stock technical analysis, focusing on indicators like moving averages, trend lines and the like, and even trying to create and construct some of my own. I soon realized that by paying attention to the live action of multiple stocks *simultaneously* rather than a myriad of single stock technical indicators, I could gain a much broader perspective than I could by analyzing the price action of individual stocks. As I matured as a trader, I began to focus more strongly on the aggregate and relative motions of stocks in the marketplace to give me clues about timing my trades, while making sure that my positions were properly sized to limit my risk.

Although sizing positions properly is critical, proper management of open position profits and losses is also extremely important. I struggled many times with underwater positions, occasionally adding to them and fighting through an entire day or two to achieve little better than breakeven at best. I repeatedly cut profits short on winning trades that would have gone much further in my favor had I had another hour or two of patience. I often entered at wonderful price points based on my instincts but then failed to hold my position for a period of time in which it would have made me serious profits. I often dumped the bulk of my position right after surviving through a choppy market drift in my favor, but right before the clean, powerful secondary move that would have made me much happier. I realized through my market studies that my mistakes were those of all investors and traders and resolved to improve my hold times on winning positions. My problem was not in cutting losses quickly, which I was fortunately skilled at, but rather in failing to press my winners correctly, the key to capturing large profits.

My studies to improve this area of my trading led me to the methods of the master trend following traders in the futures markets, some of which were recently popularized by Michael Covel in his excellent book *Trend Following*[2] and on his Web site www.turtletrader.com. I became attracted to trend following trading methods because I admired how objective and disciplined their practitioners in the futures markets are about trading their ideas. I also found parallels between their position management philosophies and those of equity traders such as the great Jesse Livermore, immortalized in Edwin Lefevre's *Reminiscences of a Stock Operator*,[3] who I refer to many times in this book. Many of these large futures money managers trade the markets in a completely systematic manner, often buying rising financial instruments and selling or shorting falling ones. My studies into the level of rigorousness these traders applied to their work[4] inspired me to improve my own trading by mimicking certain aspects of their methods. I detail in this book how I view these methods and how I have adapted some of them for my personal use in equity trading.

I find the methods of these systematic traders most useful for their rigorous application of exit timing and position sizing techniques, and it is these areas that I have adapted the most to my own trading. I also use technical indicators to define market trends in an objective manner, which can provide a filter for putting on or exiting certain types of trades. I do not have anywhere near the research and back testing capabilities of the major funds but have found their trade planning discipline worth emulating. I make investment decisions based on personal insights gained from observing market conditions and reading a wide variety of material, rather than after rigorous back testing, which makes my approach to research different from that of a purely systematic trader. However, I then execute on some of my insights by planning my trade executions in a manner similar to a systematic trend follower. I have found this hybrid of unsystematic research and well planned trade execution suitable for me.

The major futures trend followers, on the other hand, use extensive and very sophisticated back testing software to analyze the profitability of their insights. They are also generally diversified across multiple asset classes besides equities. A full application of their back testing and diversification methods is beyond my scope and likely to be beyond the scope of many individual equity investors as well. However, I have adapted what I find useful in their methods to my own trading, and am certain that other traders and investors can benefit by doing the same. In this book I refer to traders and investors interchangeably, as there is no way to invest without trading.

An equity investor might mistakenly think that since some futures trend followers have been so successful that they can just apply the same

trend following methods to an individual asset class, like equities, and re-
tire rich. This is of course not the case, and I have also written this book
to provide the reader with information that I have found important to
know in my trading of equity trends specifically. The process of planning a
trend following trade or structuring a portfolio in equities is not trivial.
There are also vast differences between applying trend following techniques in a futures portfolio versus an equity portfolio, such as the high
level of correlation between equity instruments. I explain in this book my
take on these issues.

Planning my trades in detail is one of the most important disci-
plines that I have developed in my many years of trading. Let me walk
you through a scenario to show you why. Imagine that you decide to
buy 1,000 shares of a stock after doing your own due diligence. All of a
sudden, a talking head comes on financial television and before you can
take a deep breath, the stock has plummeted $1. Do you cut your posi-
tion? Buy more? Did you plan for this contingency when you decided
how much to buy, or have you bet the farm? Does the broader market
give you any clues about the state of sentiment out there? What if the
stock that you bought goes on to rally $2 after falling $1? Most people
would be content to flatten out for a profit and call it quits. But what if
the stock is about to move $5 higher? Are there any rules you can use to
participate in some of this upside? How do you press your winners
while keeping your losses limited? Each trader must answer questions
like these over and over again while trading. This book helps you to define your answers to all of these questions in a logical, simple, and relatively quick manner *before you enter the market*, allowing you to spend
more time finding great investing ideas and to streamline your trade
planning process.

Trend following in which you chase prices on both your entry and exit
is often a very volatile strategy and cannot be blindly applied to equities,
especially since so many equities tend to move in unison. I thus use this
kind of trend following very selectively, and only with risk capital. Since I
have found the trade planning process of trend followers very useful,
however, I use similar methods to help me manage my open position profits and losses on individual trading ideas. Trend followers in the futures
markets follow price trends in a variety of asset classes after rigorous
back testing, which I lack the resources to do in equities. However, I have
found that what I can do as an equity trader is to plan my trades in detail
before I enter them, allowing me to cut my losses short and let my winners run without emotion. In short, if there is a trend in my favor in my
open position profit and loss (P&L), I want to follow it to its full potential.
In order to do this properly, I have to define the conditions that constitute
its full potential in advance.

I thus believe that you can still be a trend follower if you exit the market with trend following techniques even though you may enter it by buying a dip instead of a rally. You can be a trend follower if you go long a sideways moving stock during a period that you perceive as a broader market uptrend. You can be a trend follower if you resemble a buy and holder during a period that you perceive to be a decade long bull market (as long as your positions are profitable on paper). In short, whether you are a trend follower is determined by how you react to your open profits and losses once you have entered the market, rather than by whether you use the completely systematic research, testing, and trading strategies of the trend following market wizards. I thus write this book to show you in detail how to rigorously plan your trades in the spirit of these master traders, and also to suggest new areas in the equity markets to apply technical analysis to aid you in your search for an edge.

The main questions this book answers are:

What are the major differences between trading trends in the equity markets versus the futures markets?

How do you plan an equity trade using trend following techniques?

How can you structure an equity portfolio to trade ideas with trend following or technical trading techniques?

How might you use trend following techniques to rotate from an investment in one instrument to another?

WHY THIS BOOK IS IMPORTANT

Many investors sustained tragic losses in the bear market years from 2000 through 2002. I can imagine that it was especially tough for those who held falling mutual funds whose strategies they did not fully understand, or held falling stocks they had bought with no plan of action. This book gives you some easy to apply ideas about how to take more control over the investment process and better estimate your risks when trading. In this way whether you win or lose in the markets, you will at least have an idea of what you are getting yourself into.

In my market readings, I noticed a lack of material that discusses trading equity trends on the very detailed level of position sizing and other risks. As a result, I have written this book to appeal to a wide range of investors, and so its scope runs from the simple to the more complex. Many market participants trade on every urge, using undisciplined money management and rapidly switching strategies without giving them a chance to work. These traders panic out of winning positions and stubbornly hang onto losing ones, without a proper understanding of the risks they are exposing themselves to. As a trader, you need to know how to plan specific trades well enough that you could leave your instructions with someone else to trade them and be comfortable that every contingency would be covered. I want to convey some of my ideas about how to do this to the reader. If you have the patience to follow my reasoning through these pages, I am confident that you will find this book an excellent investment of your time. To know that I have been able to help even one investor approach the markets more intelligently would make the writing of this book entirely worthwhile to me.

KEDRICK F. BROWN

East Brunswick, New Jersey
January 2006

Acknowledgments

I would like to extend special thanks to several wonderful and generous people who helped to make this book possible. To my wife Ivana—I could not have completed this book without your love, patience, amazing editing help, and unwavering support. Thank you from the bottom of my heart. To Stephen Engst—Your frank advice and help on this work has been invaluable. Thanks for being a true friend, and for sharing your wisdom about trading, trend following, and life so generously. To my brother Baika, a true genius with computers—Your help has made a big difference. To my editors Pamela van Giessen and Jennifer MacDonald—Thank you for giving me this chance, and for your wonderful support along the way. To Dave Goodboy—Without your encouragement, my writings might still be only on my computer. Thank you. To my attorney Kevin Pollock—Thanks for all you have done to make this possible. To my cousin Annis—Thanks for introducing me to the world of equity trading. There are also many others to whom I am grateful for having reached this point in my life, from family to teachers to colleagues to friends. Thank you all so very much.

K.F.B.

PART I

Trend Trading Psychology

CHAPTER 1

Elements of an Edge

THE EFFICIENT MARKET HYPOTHESIS

The efficient market hypothesis contends that "the rewards obtainable from investing in highly competitive markets will be fair, on the average, for the risks involved."[1] This definition says that it is very difficult to *consistently* achieve abnormally large returns in exchange for taking normal risks. The tremendous amount of competition from investors of all types struggling to do this in the stock market helps to push the market toward efficiency. The efficient market hypothesis doesn't mean you should give up trying to outperform the market, but it is good to be aware that it is not a cakewalk. A primary tool to be equipped with in this quest for superior performance, which many traders lack, is the discipline to plan your trades properly.

Investors are not always well compensated for the risks they take on. If you had shorted the Standard & Poor's (S&P 500) at any time prior to 1997 and had held to the present (early 2006) you would have lost a great deal of money. Taking on risk does not always mean that you will be compensated for it, because then it wouldn't be real risk. No matter what has happened in U.S. stock market history, we may one day find ourselves in an extended bear market such as Japanese equities during much of the 1990s. I for one would not be able to hold the bulk of my money in a falling mutual fund through an extended multiyear period, regardless of what the efficient market hypothesis implies about how difficult it is to outperform the market. What if I suddenly need the money when my capital is down 50 percent from its peak? I might have faith that the fund would rebound but would have to exit because of necessity. It would be unbearable not to know how the portfolio manager was allocating and managing my money. When I invest or trade, I prefer to know what I am getting myself into so that I can sleep at night. This requires me to believe in my reasons for investing and use reasonably objective estimates of the downside risk I am taking on in my trades. Technical analysis is a powerful ally in accomplishing this goal.

Any rational trader would want limited downside exposure and the chance to capture open-ended profits if a position moves in their favor. However, few take the time to plan out exactly how they will trade individual situations. Technical trading forces you to think in exact terms and objectively plan your trades. If you are skilled at identifying outstanding profit opportunities, timing your trades with technical methods can enable you to perform very well in the markets.

PLACING TECHNICAL ANALYSIS IN ITS PROPER CONTEXT

Countless books have been written about stock charting. In addition to trend lines, which are well-known, there are a host of technical indicators that are widely used in attempts to predict the future although their effectiveness in doing this is often questioned. Although traders often try to use technical analysis as a crystal ball, this is by no means its only use. A much more important use of it is to objectively size and time investments in potentially profitable situations. Thus, technical trading is worth understanding because it can be used to trade unfamiliar market situations— volatile tech stocks, sudden breakouts in previously quiet industries, and so on. However, since technical analysis is so often used in attempts to predict the future, it pays to briefly discuss some of the pitfalls that can arise from using it in this manner.

Trend Line Issues

Even in a price signal that moves up and down unpredictably, or "randomly walks," chart patterns such as double bottoms are often present. Since people see pictures in clouds, we should naturally expect that they will see stock prices bounded by imaginary lines and curves on stock charts. Randomly walking data can easily be used to create trend lines, moving averages, moving average convergence/divergence (MACD) oscillators, and a host of other indicators that are usually derived from historical prices. This is a fact that needs illustrating. Figures 1.1 and 1.2 show randomly walking charts generated using two different methods.

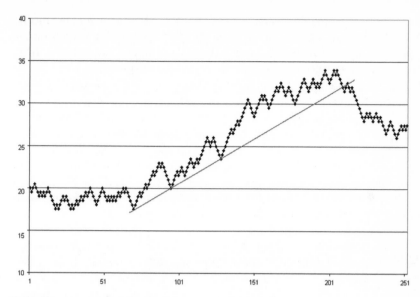

FIGURE 1.1   A random walk with equal step size.

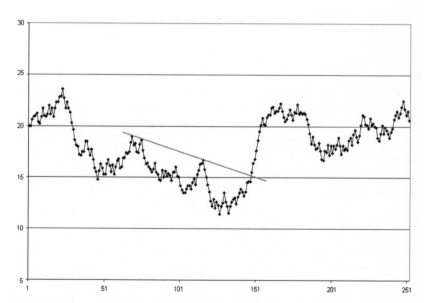

FIGURE 1.2   A random walk with variable step size.

Figure 1.1 shows a randomly walking pseudo-price series that has been generated using steps of equal size (0.5 in this case). Even in this very simple chart, there is a very obvious trend line. A commentator might describe the action by saying, "As soon as price broke through the support provided by the long-term trend line, support became resistance. Resistance was then briefly tested but the valiant attempt failed and prices rapidly moved lower."

Figure 1.2 shows a randomly walking series generated using steps of variable sizes between +1.0 and –1.0, rounded to the nearest 0.1. This chart looks a little more like a standard stock chart, which also has day-to-day movements of varying sizes. I've also drawn a trend line on this chart with little effort. In this case a commentator might describe the action by saying, "As soon as prices broke up through the downward trend line, they rapidly moved higher."

Now let's look at a third chart of real stock prices, in this case Intel Corporation (symbol: INTC) in 2002 through 2003, which is shown in Figure 1.3. Once again, I've drawn a trend line on this chart, but you must be asking by now, "Why would trend lines have predictive power on a real stock chart if they lack predictive power on a randomly walking simulated stock chart?" This is a great question. Since there is such a strong visual similarity between real and random prices, and since the effectiveness of

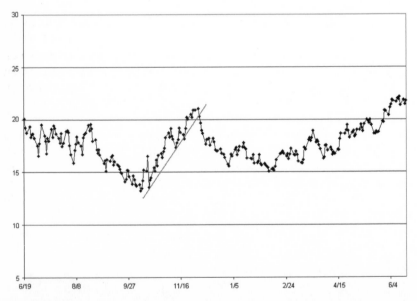

FIGURE 1.3 A real stock chart—Intel Corporation, 2002–2003. (*Source:* Stock price data from Yahoo! Finance.)

technical trading methods to predict the future is so fiercely debated: *I prefer to approach each stock that I invest in as if its short-term price movement will be completely unpredictable once I am in the stock.*

This approach forces me to look at factors *other than the stock's price alone* for relationships or ideas that support my decision to invest in it. In other words, it is much easier for me to buy a stock if I believe there is an underlying theme that will cause the stock to drift upward over the intermediate to long term, as opposed to only looking for profitable patterns in past price data.

William Gallacher expounds on the weaknesses of using trend lines for real world trading in his book *Winner Take All*. Trend lines, although very famous as technical indicators, are often obvious only in hindsight.[2] Two short-term peaks occur in a descending stock, so a trend line is drawn that connects them, with the obvious implication that if price breaks above the trend line, a "breakout" has occurred that should be bought. If the breakout succeeds, it "confirms" that trend lines work. However if the breakout immediately fails, the small breach of the trend line is often overlooked—maybe "price failed to break *decisively* through resistance." If price does break decisively through resistance and then makes a new peak, a new trend line is drawn between one of the old peaks and the new peak, and the process starts all over again. To each his own, I suppose, but this is too much ambiguity for me to trade with.

Many traders use trend lines to see what they want to see, or to justify holding existing positions after they are already in. As a general rule, I draw only basic conclusions from my examination of individual stock charts, because the future can change dramatically and unexpectedly. Of course, I take note if a stock's chart appears very bullish (sustained upward movement, perhaps accompanied by unusually strong volume) or very bearish. I have found that it can be dangerous, however, to draw conclusions about whether a stock is too "high" or too "low" based on how a chart presents the data. High stocks can always move higher and low stocks can always move lower. Whether I buy at what appears to be a high price or what appears to be a low price is based entirely on the context provided by factors *other than the stock's price*. These factors are continually subject to change but may include the price action of the overall market or the stock's industry, articles that I have read or anecdotes that I have observed, and fundamental data about the company.

Chart Scale Issues

Most computer charts today tend to take price data within a certain time frame and automatically scale the data around the limits of the price movement. This means that if a stock moved between $17.52 and $24.60 over the period of a chart, it might be scaled so that the lowest price on the scale is $17 and the highest price is $25. Thus, if the stock happened to be trading at $24, you would see its price as "high" on the scale you are using. If the stock happened to be trading at $18, you would see its price as "low" on the scale. Of course "high" and "low" are all relative; if the stock proceeds to move rapidly up to $48.42, so that its range over a similar period is now between $18.26 and $48.42, the chart might be rescaled to show prices between $15 and $50. Looking back to the period where it was scaled between $17 and $25, you would notice that all prices at that time would appear to be vertically compacted, and the breakout past the top of the $25 range would appear obvious, and possibly even like a textbook trend line breakout! Figures 1.4 and 1.5 are examples of this phenomenon (using artificial data).

In Figure 1.4, prices move largely sideways, and several rally attempts are made that all fail. Based on the chart, it might seem likely that the final rally attempt (with the last price in the time frame circled) will fail as well.

In Figure 1.5, which pictures an identical time frame, we see that the final rally attempt resulted in a breakout. The final "price" from Figure 1.4 is circled again for comparison. Looking back at Figure 1.4, we see that

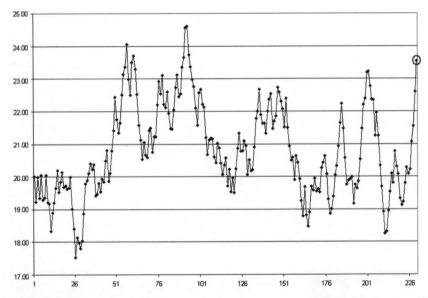

FIGURE 1.4 Chart of an artificial, sideways moving stock. Rallies fail multiple times and no imminent breakout is obvious at the end of the time frame.

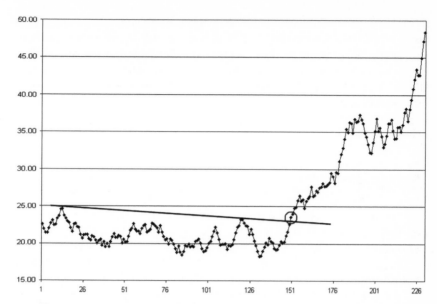

FIGURE 1.5 The same artificial stock after a breakout occurs. In retrospect both the trend line and the circled breakout point seem obvious.

the breakout above the top of the range seems obvious, as does an easily drawn trend line.

To guard against scale related subjectivity entering your trading, you should look at all charts with a skeptic's viewpoint, and spend less time concentrating on charting than on coming up with profitable ideas. When you look at a chart that shows what appears to be a clear breakout or clear breakdown, try to imagine what the chart would have looked like before the breakout or breakdown occurred and the chart was rescaled. Scroll back in time on the chart if possible, to observe how it looked before the big move occurred. Were there truly any clues about the future present in the existing price data? Imagine when you scroll back that price moved in the opposite direction from what you know to be true. How could you have prepared for this? If you look at a chart in which price appears to be high or low based on the scale, imagine that the last price is midway between the top and bottom of the screen, rather than close to the top or bottom. Would this perspective make you behave differently?

Look also for areas where you would have made *poor* decisions based on how the chart looked at the time, rather than for textbook patterns that would have been wildly profitable. I think of textbook patterns on charts like textbook moves in the martial arts—interesting phenomena to get you thinking about the subject matter, but far secondary to the ability to think on your feet. Real time combat demands real time thinking. So do not look for textbook trend line breakouts; look for poor trend lines that you might have drawn or other technical indicators that you might have used in a certain way that would have led to losses. Then ask yourself, "How would I have reacted to these losses if I were in an actual position at this point?" You need to unlearn what you have learned to be able to take yourself in a new direction, and gaining skepticism about the right way to apply the charting methods you have learned can help you in this regard.

The Right Questions to Ask

Above all, the primary problem with charting as it is commonly used is its lack of a rule-based framework. Unhelpful statements like, "If price breaks through resistance, it is going to go higher" should bring to mind several questions instantly:

1. What percentage of my capital should I allocate to this opportunity if it occurs?
2. If price does move in my favor, how would I exit profitably?
3. If price moves against me instead, how would I exit with a loss?

These questions are all variations of the question, "How would I exploit this inefficiency?" Professional money managers must be able to answer these questions for each of the positions they hold or contemplate holding; otherwise they are leaving themselves at the mercy of the markets. In some cases, they may be able to answer the relevant questions for their portfolio as a whole, which may be a completely different animal from its individual components. The bottom line is that money managers are always cognizant of their risk, and to correctly quantify one's risk requires the use of more advanced methods than simple charting.

The Unexpected Is Always Possible

Even though I have many years of trading experience, I use only the simplest technical indicators in my trading, and understand *exactly why* I am using them and what they are showing me. As Leonardo da Vinci said, "Simplicity is the ultimate sophistication."

Using simple indicators gives you the flexibility to plan complicated trades with simple building blocks.

Rather than using technical indicators to time your entries, you may prefer to pore through historical prices, economic numbers, fundamental company statistics, and so on to uncover exploitable numerical relationships. For example, perhaps you find that after each peak-to-trough drop of more than 10 percent on an index within a week, its return over the next month ranges between +12 percent and –4 percent. Let's say that you make 100 observations and discover an average return of +4 percent. You might consider this an exploitable pattern. To exploit this inefficiency consistently, assuming that your analysis of the situation was done properly, you must still go on to answer:

- What percentage of my capital should I allocate to this opportunity?
- If price does move in my favor, how would I exit profitably?
- If price moves against me instead, how would I exit with a loss?

You must also be able to answer a more challenging question, namely:

- How will I recognize if this apparent market inefficiency is breaking down rather than performing within historical parameters?

For example, if you entered the market following a one-week drop of 15 percent, and the market proceeds to drop a further 8 percent in a month (which is a larger percentage drop than you have seen in your studies of the past), is this a sign that the relationship you are trying to exploit is changing? This is a tough question to answer, but I would approach it by trying to study the behavior of price during the prospective holding periods. It is always helpful to try to understand how your equity curve would have behaved if you had taken certain trades; would you honestly have been able to stomach the volatility?

Putting your money at risk in the markets is a trying experience. Paper trading, or trading with negligible amounts of money, cannot do it justice even remotely, and I do not much recommend it for several reasons. The first reason is that the process of actually trading involves minutiae like deciding exactly how to enter orders, waiting for fills, dealing with slippage, and so on, that paper trading cannot adequately do justice to. The second is that it is always more instructive to risk real money on your opinions and then experience how you respond emotionally. If you risk an amount that matters to you for one day and document your experiences, you will be much better for it than making 10 paper trades. It thus behooves you to be aware of as many nuances as possible of the equity curve that could have occurred during the periods you would hypothetically have been positioned. You must endeavor to have an excellent understanding of the risks you are taking on, so that you can properly envision the psychological effects you would undergo. In this way, if you encounter a stock drop in the course of your trading that has occurred before, you will be somewhat mentally prepared. Solid preparation is absolutely essential to being able to survive as a trader in the long run. Without it, you run a very serious risk of either panicking out of a normally behaving position midtrade, or hanging stubbornly onto a losing position that rapidly deteriorates further, leaving you with a catastrophic loss.

Catastrophic losses have wiped out or demoralized many traders, and are often the result of a trader's two deadliest enemies:

1. Overtrading: Trading with too large a position size for your account, trading with any position size or strategy that you are uncomfortable with and may cause you to panic, or in extreme cases, trading with gigantic size relative to the liquidity of an instrument. If you can't sleep at night because of a position, or find yourself constantly glued to the computer screen or missing meals, you should reduce your position size until you are comfortable. Then work on planning your trades to prevent a similar level of discomfort with your positions in the future.

2. Trading without a plan: Losses in the market can come rapidly and unexpectedly, and if you have not planned your course of action in advance, you run the risk of being steamrolled or freezing up like a deer in the headlights. Liquidity might dry up, or terrible news might be released, sending a stock into a tailspin. Be ready to react to as many situations as possible in advance, so that you can honestly be able to tell yourself afterward that you did the right thing.

One of the most prominent examples of overtrading was the Long Term Capital Management debacle of 1998. Long Term Capital Management used tremendously sophisticated data mining techniques and extremely high leverage. After several years of stellar returns they were subjected to a very rare confluence of events that yielded rapid, massive losses on many positions they held across multiple markets.[3] Their story illustrates that no matter what trading method you use, the unexpected is always possible. Thus, you can always benefit from excellent trade planning discipline over the long run. Let's discuss in more detail some elements that you must understand to extract money from the markets intelligently, the elements of an edge.

EXTRACTING MONEY FROM THE MARKET

There would be no reason to enter the market if you didn't think you would make money (or at least save money versus some other alternative). You can either make money by arbitraging a price discrepancy in the present or speculating on a future price change. For example, what if you can buy gas at a local station for $2 a gallon and sell it immediately to a next door station for $3 a gallon? This is profiting from an arbitrage opportunity. Alternatively, perhaps you can buy gas at a local station for $2 a gallon and sell it to any station in the area at whatever the market price happens to be. However, you anticipate that a local shortage of gas will occur in about a week (possibly driving gas to at least $3 a gallon), so you buy gas today and store it in containers, in the hope that you will be able to sell it back soon at a higher price. In this case you are speculating on a perceived opportunity based on your *assumptions* about the future availability and future price of gas. Your assumptions could of course be wrong, so risk is involved, requiring strict rules to define when you will take a loss (e.g., if gas falls to $1 a gallon in a week). Conversely, if gas moves higher than the $3 a gallon you had anticipated (e.g., to $6 a gallon), you ideally also want to be ready to capture some unforeseen profits.

Regardless of whether you are an arbitrageur or a speculator, *all opportunities for profit are fleeting*. They may be fleeting on a scale of minutes, months, or more, but they do not last forever. In my first example where two next door gas stations are selling and buying gas at dramatically different prices, it is clear that as soon as another person discovers this discrepancy, he will act along with you to exploit the profit opportunity until it disappears. The gas station paying the higher price will eventually get all the gas it needs from sellers trying to profit from the price discrepancy, or it will lower the price it is willing to pay. On the other hand, the station with the cheaper gas will soon realize that it can sell at a higher price due to all the demand from buyers trying to profit from the discrepancy. In my second example, if other speculators begin to share your view that the price of gas will move up due to an imminent shortage, they will bid the price of gas up with you until the potential profit from participating in the opportunity becomes much slimmer.

The same logic goes for all other market opportunities. You may uncover opportunities in your research that other members of the investing public seem to be oblivious to. Your acting on these opportunities of limited size works to reduce the size of the opportunities, and it also adds liquidity to the markets, making it easier for others to trade. As soon as enough people join you in taking advantage of an opportunity, it will shrink or even disappear entirely. The market can subtly adjust its behavior because people can subtly adjust their behavior. This truth applies no matter what trading strategy you are using. Always keep it in mind as you trade the markets; work on being prepared for the future in your trading, not the past. By the time an idea becomes widely popular and accepted as common sense, it is time to start thinking seriously about whether you should continue trying to profit from it.

I strive in my research to identify long-term investment themes and profit from them. I believe that the main thing an investor has to do to generate excellent long-term returns is to identify and invest in these macro themes with prudent risk management tools. My thinking has been directly influenced by the writings of Jim Puplava, creator of the www.financialsense.com Web site. His thinking on this subject is profound:

> *[I]nvestors need to make only a few key investment decisions in their lifetime. If they can get on board a primary trend in its initial stages and then have the patience to ride that trend until it is discredited, they would do very well as an investor. In the last half century, there have been four key primary trends and investment themes where an investor could have done exceedingly well as an investor. They are listed below:*
>
> *1. U.S. stocks 1952–1966.*
>
> *2. Gold/silver and commodities 1971–1980.*
>
> *3. Japanese stocks 1980–1989.*
>
> *4. U.S. stocks, especially technology 1990–2000.*[4]

More recently, if you had moved back into commodities (or commodity stocks) in the early twenty-first century, this would be a picture perfect example of investing in line with this philosophy. Investing in emerging markets like India or Brazil over the past three years would also have produced stunning outperformance compared to the S&P 500. True bull markets in which wealth is created take years to form and accelerate to their full potential, when the public is shouting about them from the rooftops. The rewards for early investors in a bull market cycle can be tremendous, but finding the bull market is the challenging part. I have found the following general guidelines useful in trying to accomplish this:

1. Identify a long-term investment theme through research that appears to have tremendous *potential to excite the public imagination* in the future. You don't have to be an expert in the area, but may partially rely on well written arguments from other experts in the area to come to your conclusions. These themes do not come along every day or even every month; they are uncommon and take time to develop fully.

2. You do not have to go all in immediately. You can dabble a little and/or wait for signs of aggregate movement in your favored direction in the investments under scrutiny. For example, if you have identified a par-

ticular industry that you are interested in investing in, you may wait for signs of industry-wide price strength to confirm your hypothesis before increasing your exposure.

3. If a bull market is already underway in an area that you have researched, but you still believe in great future potential, go ahead and participate in it.

4. Whenever you enter the market, use the appropriate risk management tools and either *hold* or trade in the general direction of the trend until you see clear signs that it is exhausted. By planning your exits objectively, you can remove emotion from the process, because the chatter around you as the market moves will be very compelling.

5. Repeat the process.

In other words, find the bull market in which you see far more potential than the public does (but are certain that they will catch on later), enter, and hold or trade in the direction of the trend until it shows clear signs of exhaustion. Real secular bull trends don't occur overnight, and finding one and holding patiently for the long-term ride is much less stressful than frequently trading in and out of the market.

Trade Only When You Believe You Have an Edge

If each stock in the stock market moved in a completely random and independent fashion, there would be no way to make money over the long term with *any* trading strategy. Once any hypothetical commissions or slippage are factored into trading, anyone who attempts to apply a trading strategy to such a random market will end up a long-term loser by definition. In reality, however, the U.S. stock market has drifted upward dramatically over long periods of time. Imagine for a moment, though, that the market instead randomly walked with an equal probability of moving up or down by a fixed amount, with no upward drift. You might then invest with a strategy in which you hold a position until you either lock in gains of $1,000 or cut off your losses at $9,000. With this strategy you would likely win $1,000 about 90 percent of the time, but this would mean losing $9,000 the other 10 percent of the time. Conversely, you might choose to hold all trades for a period of 10 days and then exit them, stopping yourself out at a loss of $1,000. If you locked in losses of $1,000 80 percent of the time, this would mean average gains of $4,000 the other 20 percent of the time. Thus, you could vary your win percentage almost at will, but you would still make no money in the long run before fees, and you would lose money after fees. This thought experiment shows that your percentage of wins in a purely random market with no drift is largely irrelevant. You need an edge to make your aggregate winnings larger than your aggregate losses and be net profitable.

Many people naively believe that if their percentage of winning trades exceeds their percentage of losing trades, profits are guaranteed. This is a dangerous fallacy, because this analysis does not take the sizes of your *net* wins and *net* losses into account. Of course it is very tempting to think well of a high percentage of winning trades; due to our education we probably equate high win percentages with great test scores like *A*s and *B*+s. However, in trading it does not work like this. If you rarely win but make gigantic net profits when you do that overwhelm your aggregate net losses, you will be profitable overall. In short, your aggregate net profits *must exceed* your aggregate net losses for you to be profitable. Once you include commissions and slippage in your calculations, it becomes clear that you should put your money only in ideas that you are reasonably confident will be winners. The patience to wait for these ideas to come along before speculating is a mark of top traders and investors. As Jim Rogers says in *Market Wizards*:

> *I just wait until there is money lying in the corner, and all I have to do is go over there and pick it up. I do nothing in the meantime . . . That is why I don't think of myself as a trader. I think of myself as someone who waits for something to come along. I wait for a situation that is like the proverbial "shooting fish in a barrel."*[5]

To summarize:

- Having more winning trades than losing trades does not necessarily mean that you are a profitable trader.
- Instead, (aggregate net profits) > (aggregate net losses) means profitability.

Of course, it seems to be hardwired in human psychology to want to win more frequently than you lose. But what is necessary to be profitable over the long run is to win *more money* than you lose. To win more money than you lose, especially after costs like commissions and slippage, you must have an edge over random good luck. Of course, since the future is unknown, no edge is truly guaranteed. However, the only way to achieve a *perceived edge* is to do your homework. For example, perhaps you focus on reading macroscopic economic and market conditions. You come up with a thesis about where market prices are headed, and if there is an exploitable discrepancy between where you believe they will be and where they actually are, you jump in. Regardless of what you do, it's imperative that you *do not trade for the sake of trad-*

ing, or because you are bored and need something to do. As Jesse Livermore says in *Reminiscences*:

> *The desire for constant action irrespective of underlying conditions is responsible for many losses in Wall Street even among the professionals, who feel that they must take home some money every day, as though they were working for regular wages.*[6]

Livermore reinforces this statement in his book *How to Trade in Stocks*:

> *Remember this: When you are doing nothing, those speculators who feel they must trade day in and day out, are laying the foundation for your next venture. You will reap benefits from their mistakes.*[7]

This is a lesson that took me years to learn, and Livermore's articulation of it highlights his wisdom. It is much less costly to leave your trading room and go running for an hour than to trade a situation that you do not believe in because you need the adrenaline rush. There are times to be aggressive and times to be patient, because odds of winning in the market shift. As a trader, you must speculate only when you believe that conditions are in your favor, because only with this kind of conviction will you have the mental strength to weather difficult times in your portfolio.

CASINOS AND STATISTICAL EDGES

Casinos make money because they have a statistical, rather than a perceived, edge over their customers. The fact that numerous people are willing to play games in which they have no edge is very instructive about human psychology. To explain my point, let's go over a simple example of how a casino might make money. Imagine a simplified roulette wheel with 36 slots. If the ball lands in your slot, you win $30 net per $1 bet. In other words, you win $30 for every $1 you bet and your bet is returned to you. Since the table has 36 spaces, the house should win over the long term (as long as it has sufficient funds to cover payouts to winning customers). In this example, a player who bets $1 has a 35/36 chance of losing $1 (a 100 percent loss) and a 1/36 chance of winning $30 net (a 3,000 percent gain). This means that the house can expect to make:

$$+35/36(\$1) - 1/36(\$30) = \$(5/36) = \$0.139 \text{ per bet}$$

Over 1,000 bets of $1 each, the house could thus expect to pocket about $139.

Conversely, imagine a modified roulette game where you must bet in increments of $40 to play. On 35 of 36 slots, the game pays you $1 net (a 2.5 percent return). However, on 1 out of 36 spaces (i.e., the space the ball lands on), the house collects your $40, and you lose 100 percent. There might be a lot of happy winners of $1, but the house would still win overall with the same expectation per bet of:

$$+1/36(\$40) - 35/36(\$1) = \$(5/36) = \$0.139$$

In the market, the odds of winning are certainly not as fixed as in a casino. Instead, market conditions and odds of profiting from various strategies change over time, and it is the investor's job to continually scour the market for conditions in which he or she has a favorable (and hopefully tremendous) expectation of making money. Let's return to the first roulette example. If you discovered that on each Monday, the house paid out $40 net for getting the winning slot on a $1 bet, but every other day it paid $30 net per $1 winning bet, it would only make sense for you to play on Mondays (i.e., when you have an expectation of being profitable). Conversely, it would make sense to stay out of the casino on all other days (when you have an expectation of losing money). In this case, the house can expect to *lose* $0.139 per bet on Mondays, but can expect to *make* $0.139 per $1 bet on all other days. As long as the general public is not aware of this recurring pattern, and similar numbers of people play and bet similar amounts of money on each day, the house will *still* be profitable overall. The house's losses on Monday will be more than offset by their gains from the less informed players who play on the other days. If the public starts catching on, and Mondays become too popular at the casino, they can simply shift the day on which the customers have an edge to another day like Wednesday, effectively luring the public along endlessly with a carrot on a stick.

Analogously in the markets, it only makes sense to invest your capital during periods when market conditions indicate a higher than random probability of making a worthwhile profit. I don't mean by this that you need some sophisticated method of calculating probabilities to four decimal places; I mean that you need to have strong convictions before you put your money at risk. To identify profit opportunities that you are strongly convicted about, you must diligently study as much about past and present market and economic behavior as you can, and try to interpret current market conditions in this light. This is an endless learning and adapting process. Although some of the research methods used by large investors are prohibitively expensive for small investors, this does not mean that small investors cannot make significant sums in the market. On the contrary, it means that small investors should focus on maximizing their successes with the research methods and trading styles that are most accessible to them. The exact odds of winning in a potentially profitable market situation are rarely ever known, even by the pros. At best, they can only be estimated, and this is why rigorous trade planning discipline is absolutely crucial to protecting and growing your capital over the long run.

FINDING YOUR EDGE

Everyone sees the world differently, and everyone who trades applies his or her own worldview to the market, nudging it ever so slightly in the directions of their beliefs. Some professionals look at fundamental analysis, and at creating their own models that link fundamental metrics to price movement. Others swear by fully mechanical trading systems, and spend their time sifting through mountains of data to find exploitable anomalies that they believe will continue. Others watch the same stock trading on different exchanges and arbitrage the stock if there is a profitable discrepancy. In all cases, however, true professionals try to do a few things well rather than many things poorly. Similarly, by focusing your investing in a style that you feel comfortable with, you may be able to take money from the inefficient traders who feel it is necessary to donate to the market by being a jack-of-all-trades.

Bruce Lee had some powerful words about adapting martial arts techniques to real world situations that are also applicable in your quest to adapt spontaneously to real world market conditions:

> *Empty your mind, be formless, shapeless. Like water.*
> *Now you put water into a cup, it becomes the cup.*
> *You pour water into a bottle, it becomes the bottle.*
> *You pour water into a teapot, it becomes the teapot.*
> *Now water can flow or creep or drip—or crash!*
> *Be water, my friend.*[8]

Rather than wasting time dictating to the markets how they *should* behave, spend your time observing how they actually behave. Then formulate your opinions or theses and have the courage to act on your convictions. I give a recommended reading list at the end of this book that can help you further on this journey.

The Mathematics Behind an Edge

To be profitable in the markets, your aggregate winnings must exceed your aggregate losses. Even in a completely unpredictable, randomly walking market with equal step size and an equal probability of each step being up or down, it would be relatively simple to create a trading strategy that has nearly any winning percentage you may want (although this does not necessarily mean that you will be profitable). Simply vary the ratio of the size of the open profits where you cut your winning trades off to the size of the open losses where you cut your losing trades off.

William Gallacher discusses an analogous issue in detail in his book *Winner Take All*:

> *Risk to trading equity* cannot *be reduced by reducing the amount risked on each trade. You can drive from Toronto to Miami in one day, or you can spread the driving over three days; it still takes the same amount of gas to get there. The small amounts risked with very tight stops will be balanced by the higher frequency of occurrence of losing trades. And if amounts risked are reduced to absurdly low levels, the commission and slippage charges will begin to eat heavily into whatever trading edge existed in the first place.*[9]

To overcome this obstacle in your trading, it is imperative to limit your trading to situations where you believe that you have a positive expectation (i.e., an edge). In one simple type of trading strategy, you may limit your average gross loss per trade to a maximum amount. This means that if your percentage of winning trades is fixed, your average net profit per trade must be large enough for you to have a positive expectation. For example, take a look at Table 1.1, which shows a hypothetical trader with a 40 percent winning percentage on his trades, and thus a 60 percent losing percentage (both of which I assume to be fixed, for simplicity's sake). Different average gross losses per trade are shown along with the respective average profits per trade that would be required for this trader to break even in terms of expectation (i.e., to have a zero expectation). Both gross and net profits are also shown to illustrate the effects of trading costs. For example, a trader with an average gross loss of $100 per trade requires an offsetting average gross profit of over $150 per trade to have a positive expectation if no costs of trading are present. However, once we factor in commissions and slippage of, for instance, $10 per trade, this trader has an average net loss of $100 + $10 + $10 = $120 per trade, which requires an average gross profit of over $200 per trade and thus an average net profit of over $200 − $10 − $10 = $180 per trade to have a positive expectation. Note that $200 is 33.33 percent *larger* than the average gross

			Breakeven (in terms of expectation) profit requirements for a trader
TABLE 1.1			with varying average gross losses per trade, varying expenses per trade, and a 40 percent winning percentage. In this table, GP = Average Gross Profit and GL = Average Gross Loss.

Average Gross Loss	Expense Per Trade	Average Net Loss	Average Gross Profit Required to Break Even	Average Net Profit Required to Break Even	Breakeven GP/GL Ratio
$ 100	$ 0	$ 100	$ 150	$ 150	1.500
$ 100	$ 5	$ 110	$ 175	$ 165	1.750
$ 100	$10	$ 120	$ 200	$ 180	2.000
$ 100	$15	$ 130	$ 225	$ 195	2.250
$ 500	$ 0	$ 500	$ 750	$ 750	1.500
$ 500	$ 5	$ 510	$ 775	$ 765	1.550
$ 500	$10	$ 520	$ 800	$ 780	1.600
$ 500	$15	$ 530	$ 825	$ 795	1.650
$1,000	$ 0	$1,000	$1,500	$1,500	1.500
$1,000	$ 5	$1,010	$1,525	$1,515	1.525
$1,000	$10	$1,020	$1,550	$1,530	1.550
$1,000	$15	$1,030	$1,575	$1,545	1.575

profit of $150 that must be exceeded to achieve a positive expectation in a cost-free environment. It is also twice the magnitude of the average gross loss of $100, and this is only the minimum that the trader must achieve to break even in terms of expectation! The realities of trading costs make it imperative that you trade only when you believe you have an edge.

To achieve a positive expectation with a fixed 40 percent winning rate and the costs shown in Table 1.1, your GP/GL ratio must exceed the respective breakeven GP/GL ratios shown. If your trading costs are high, it may thus be difficult to repeatedly find trades that are able to both make up for these costs *and* make you significant net profits beyond that.

Even if you can't identify these types of abnormally large profit opportunities, there is a second method of attempting to achieve a positive expectation in your trading. This method is simply to trade only when you believe that your probability of winning on a trade is sufficiently high for you to have a positive expectation on that trade. So in the next simplified trading example, let's assume a fixed gross loss size of $500 per trade. What are the winning percentages required to break even for fixed

gross profit sizes per trade of $500, $750, $1,000 and $1,250, respectively?
Table 1.2 examines this question, for different expenses per trade of $0,
$5, and $10.

Table 1.2 shows that you can only overcome trading costs if your percentage of winning trades exceeds the breakeven percentages shown.
This means that it makes sense to trade one of these situations only if you
believe that your probability of winning exceeds the respective breakeven
percentage shown! Since your estimate of your probability of winning on
any trade could be wrong, it is prudent to trade only situations that you
strongly believe in so that you allow yourself some room for this. Of
course even with probability in your favor, you will still experience both
losing and winning trades.

In Table 1.2 I assume that you cut your gross losses and gross profits
off at the exact amounts shown. Even an actual winning percentage that is
as little as 5 percent above any of the breakeven winning percentages
shown in the table is capable of generating decent profitability over the
long run. For example, look at the case in the table where expenses are
$10 per trade and the fixed gross profit size is $750 per trade (i.e., you cut
off your open profits at this level). The winning percentage required to

TABLE 1.2 What winning percentages are required to break even if you hold gross loss per trade constant, and vary gross profit per trade and expense per trade?

Fixed Gross Loss Size	Expense Per Trade	Net Loss	Fixed Gross Profit Size	Net Profit	Win % Required to Break Even
$500	$ 0	$500	$ 500	$ 500	50.0%
$500	$ 0	$500	$ 750	$ 750	40.0%
$500	$ 0	$500	$1,000	$1,000	33.3%
$500	$ 0	$500	$1,250	$1,250	28.6%
$500	$ 5	$510	$ 500	$ 490	51.0%
$500	$ 5	$510	$ 750	$ 740	40.8%
$500	$ 5	$510	$1,000	$ 990	34.0%
$500	$ 5	$510	$1,250	$1,240	29.1%
$500	$10	$520	$ 500	$ 480	52.0%
$500	$10	$520	$ 750	$ 730	41.6%
$500	$10	$520	$1,000	$ 980	34.7%
$500	$10	$520	$1,250	$1,230	29.7%

break even in this scenario is 41.6 percent. This is 1.6 percent higher than the 40 percent winning percentage required to break even with no trading expenses. Let's first see what the trader's expected profit would be if he achieves a winning percentage of 40 percent on a group of trades with $10 costs per trade. This winning percentage would enable him to break even in the absence of costs, but would yield losses with costs present. Next, let's examine what happens if the trader manages to achieve a winning percentage of 45 percent, which is 3.4 percent higher than the winning percentage required to break even with $10 costs per trade. His average net profit per trade would increase

$$\text{from: } (40\% \times \$730) - (60\% \times \$520) = -\$20.00 \text{ per trade}$$
$$\text{to: } \quad (45\% \times \$730) - (55\% \times \$520) = +\$42.50 \text{ per trade}$$

If the trader can maintain this 45 percent winning percentage going forward, he can thus expect to make approximately $42.50 per trade, a dramatic improvement over a $20.00 loss per trade. Note that if your probability of winning on a particular trade truly provides you with a positive expectation, anyone taking the *opposite* bet from you will have a negative expectation. Clearly, there are instances in the markets where those who do their homework profit at the expense of those who do not.[10]

HOW CAN TECHNICAL TRADING HELP?

I use technical trading strategies to help me plan how I will objectively trade ideas that I have previously researched. The future is unknown and unknowable. How many people foresaw around the early 1980s that the Dow was due for a rise to above the 10,000 level? How many people foresaw oil trading over $70 a barrel just a few years ago? Believing in future price strength before these dramatic moves would have been a remarkable accomplishment to begin with. However, to simultaneously anticipate the future direction of a financial instrument *and* the ultimate price target in that direction *and* the price patterns it will exhibit along the way to reaching that price target is a stretch even for the best of speculators.

Planning your trades in detail enables you to trade uncertain situations with confidence, because you can never know in advance exactly how a situation will play out. There is no rule that says that you always need to enter a position with a technical strategy, but technical analysis can always be used to objectively time your exit from a position. By using trend following strategies to trade a situation, for example, you can position yourself to capture open-ended upside in exchange for limited downside. There is no single right way to participate in a move you believe strongly in while managing your risk. To trade a situation in the correct way, however, you must first answer the following four questions in detail:

1. Instrument Selection: What will you invest in?
2. Position Sizing: What percentage of your capital will you invest or risk in it?
3. Entry Timing: When and how will you invest in it?
4. Exit Timing: When and how will you exit your investment in it?

Think of the answers to these four questions as the four legs of a "Well Planned Trade" table, which I illustrate in Figure 1.6. Without solid support by all legs, your table will be unstable. Although it may stand for a while without all four legs, a light push may be all it takes to tip it over in the long run. Although authors of the bulk of popular books on investing spend their time on Instrument Selection and Entry Timing alone, focusing exclusively on these areas may leave your investment table with a shaky foundation. Instrument Selection and Entry Timing determine your *potential* for profit, but Position Sizing and Exit Timing determine your *actual* profits. Solid coverage of all four elements is necessary for a well planned trade.

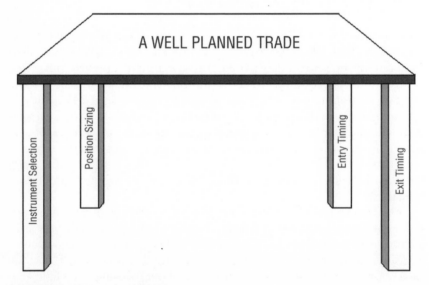

FIGURE 1.6 The well planned trade table.

I like to plan my trades in such a way that even if I buy at the top tick of a market move, my losses will be limited to an acceptable amount. I also like to plan them in a way that allows me to capture additional profits from a move in my favor that is much larger than I may have anticipated. Similarly, if you buy a stock at $40, thinking it will reach $50, but it unexpectedly moves higher, to $60, $70, $80, or even $100, you ideally want a trading plan that will allow you to capture some of that extra move in certain circumstances, as it could mean multiples of the original profit you had envisioned. Of course, no one can anticipate the full extent of a move, so this means that your trading plan may entail waiting for a reversal in prices before locking in profits. If you get whipsawed out of a stock by exiting on a reversal in prices, you also want your trading plan to instruct you on how to reenter that stock in a logical, objective manner if conditions still warrant doing so.

Your trading plan should also specify the exact amount of your capital that you will invest in an opportunity. Imagine, for example that you buy two stocks, stock A and stock B, and hold them both for a year. Stock A increases in value by 50 percent while stock B falls in value by 50 percent during this year. The percentage of your capital that you invest in the respective stocks can have widely varying effects on your ultimate portfolio return, as shown in Table 1.3.

Table 1.3 shows that a 50/50 balance between stock A and stock B, respectively, produces no profits, while a 25/75 balance produces a 25% loss, and a 75/25 balance produces a 25 percent profit. Clearly, the amount of capital that you choose to allocate to each position in your portfolio can have a significant impact on your ultimate performance. Position sizing/capital allocation decisions are a crucial element of any trading plan.

With all this said, instrument selection and entry timing are the elements of your trading plan that will produce a substantial portion of

TABLE 1.3 Overall portfolio returns for different weightings of stock A (which returns +50 percent) and stock B (which returns –50 percent).

Stock A Weighting	Stock B Weighting	Overall Portfolio Return
0%	100%	–50%
25%	75%	–25%
50%	50%	0%
75%	25%	+25%
100%	0%	+50%

your edge, so you should focus a great deal on these areas as well. In my research for personal investments I strive to identify time periods in which certain types of trades are likely to be profitable. I may study both a stock's price and a variety of external factors, such as the market's overall direction, the basic fundamental metrics of the company, the opinions of newsletter writers, and so on to form an opinion about when upward *drift* may occur in a stock, industry, or market. This is a three-dimensional thought process (price, time, and external factors). I often read the opinions of newsletter writers (by which I mean electronic newsletter writers), because many of their analyses tend to be sophisticated but also understandable to a nonexpert. I reason that if a nonexpert can understand their reasoning, than the public will eventually be able to as well.

Analogously, your edge in trading will come from your proprietary ideas, and your proprietary ideas will in turn come from your study of markets and the world around you. As an individual investor with limited resources you have two main methods by which you can diagnose whether a stock or group of stocks presents a profitable trading opportunity:

1. Qualitative: Read (and listen) voraciously, and try to develop big-picture *opinions* about future stock price action in certain industries or countries. This may be based either on evidence in the present, or analogies drawn from similar situations in the past. Note your insights and study *if possible* how they might have performed in the past.

2. Quantitative: Focus your attention on uncovering and *quantifying* historically profitable inefficiencies in the behavior of stocks or combinations of stocks that you believe are likely to repeat.

Since my research resources as an individual investor are rather limited, I focus mainly on the qualitative method in my trading, but I am also aware that the latter method has produced vast profits for a wide variety of traders. Trend following commmodity trading advisors (CTAs), statistical arbitrage fund managers, and other systematic traders tend to focus on the latter method, using large amounts of computing power to uncover and exploit market inefficiencies. The main inefficiency that trend following CTAs try to exploit in the market is the fact that markets have a tendency to periodically *trend*. Their instrument selection, position sizing, entry timing, and exit timing on all trades are well planned to profit from this tendency of markets. They try to latch onto trends in a *wide variety* of financial instruments in the hope that the potentially unlimited gains from their winning trades will offset the limited losses from their losing trades. Trend following CTAs probably profit primarily because the distributions of the markets they trade are not as simple as theoretical bell curves. Since their profitability is based on the continued existence of a market inefficiency, however, it has the potential to be further reduced if competition in this area increases in the future.

When formulating a qualitative opinion about future market action, keep in mind that the current market situation may often not be an exact match for a past situation. However, perhaps components of the current market situation occurred individually in the past, which can allow you to study these components individually (or in any combinations that did occur) and form an opinion about future market action. At other times, for example if you happen to be trading a newly public company, there might simply not be a lot of price history to go by. Be aware that:

- Not everything can be *perfectly* back-tested, and not every back test may be fully relevant to current market conditions.
- There will always be room for differences of market opinion even in the presence of clearcut historical facts. This is of course what creates risks and opportunities for reward.
- You do not need to know all the information possible to put on a trade. An educated opinion based on the fraction of the information that you deem the most relevant will often have to do. Finding the right situations to trade is as much about filtering out irrelevant information as it is about studying relevant information in detail.

Once a potentially profitable opportunity is discovered with either a qualitative or quantitative approach, it can then be traded with a mechanical plan similar to those used by systematic trend followers on their individual trades, which removes emotion from the process. You must uncover the opportunity *first*, which requires toil. Don't think for a second that you can just jump into the market today, mechanically buy rallies and sell dips till the end of time and end up being wealthy. A get-rich-quick mentality may put you on a fast track to disaster.

Technical trading methods can be useful for extracting profit from the market *after* you identify a potentially profitable opportunity. Technical trading methods are not panaceas in and of themselves; they are simply tools. Furthermore, if you uncover unique, high potential profit opportunities in your research, you should be able to use very simple technical strategies to trade your ideas, simply because the relationships you are studying will be largely unexploited. In other words:

> *It is better as an individual trader to uncover high potential opportunities that you can trade with simple strategies rather than questionable opportunities that you can trade only with complicated strategies.*

A WORD ON LONG SIDE EQUITY INVESTING

The U.S. stock market (as measured by the major averages) has drifted upward dramatically over the long term. This upward march has of course been interrupted by multiyear periods when the all-time high values of the averages have not been exceeded. On the positive side, a considerable number of stocks pay dividends, and reinvested dividends have added significantly to the total return of market participants throughout history. Price charts of the averages generally do not show "total return" from immediately reinvested dividends.

Conversely, the short side has been the side with considerably weaker odds of *long-term* profit. Pure short sellers of stocks also have returns structurally capped (even when they borrow on margin) due to the fact that no stock can fall below zero. Short sellers also have to pay dividends and may not receive good interest rates on their short balances (depending on their brokerage arrangement). Conversely, long holders of stocks have unlimited upside and limited downside without having to resort to margin borrowing. In the futures and options markets, market participants can trade equity indices with higher leverage than that available in the stock market, but this also brings with it increased risk of loss. In order to sell individual stocks short, the stocks must also be literally borrowed, and sometimes there are availability issues. All of these complications can make short side equity trading a questionable undertaking for an individual investor. To me, the successful history of long side equity investing contrasted with the complexities and lower odds of short side investing provides excellent incentives to invest in stocks mainly from the long side (especially if I intend to hold for the intermediate to long term). I thus focus specifically in this book on long side investing in cash equity portfolios.

Of course, stock market averages do not and can not give information about the behavior of all stocks. The composition of major averages like the S&P 500 are altered over time to reflect only the crème de la crème of stocks and the darling industries of the day, based on fundamentals, market caps, and so on. Stocks that don't make the cut are ignored in the indices, and the fact that some are de-listed after they are dropped means that the averages contain only survivors. The averages also do not take into account any costs of rotating out of one stock that is being removed from the average into another that is being added. Furthermore, the market has substantial swings from year to year even though it has drifted up over the long term, and individual stocks don't move exactly like it. Some are much more volatile than the market, while others have comparable or smaller volatilities. Depending on the stocks you choose, your portfolio can thus have dramatically different results from a major index portfolio.

The major indices thus only provide a generalized snapshot of possible investment results.

DEFINING YOUR TRADING/INVESTING GOAL

One possible goal of a trading account is to time your trades in a manner that enables you to achieve better returns after trading costs and taxes than buying or holding a major market index like the S&P 500. There are different ways to try to outperform the benchmark. You may decide to dart in and out of the market, holding cash in between your trades. If this is your goal, you will have heavy lifting to do, as the *net* returns from your trades (i.e., after fees and taxes) must not only beat the market during your holding periods, but also beat the market *in between* your holding periods (to justify trading rather than holding an index fund). On the other hand, you may believe that the historical upward drift of the market indicates that holding the market portfolio for the long term is a great strategy that already has a built-in edge. You are also aware that it is difficult to outperform the market portfolio. In this case, you may decide to trade *only* when you believe that you can outperform a broader market index like the S&P 500 (by making more or losing less), and hold the S&P 500 at all other times. You thus aim to outperform the market short term, and equal its return during other time periods. This is a mix between technical trading and buying and holding that I talk about in some more detail toward the end of this book. The sole purpose of each trading account may not necessarily be to beat the market portfolio, however. For example, if you have a lot of your investment capital in mutual funds already, you may want to use some additional risk capital to make selective trades, which diversifies you somewhat from a buy and hold strategy. In this case, your goal would simply be to make as much as possible whenever you trade rather than beat the S&P 500 outright.

Before I get into trading methods, let me mention some of the habits of professional futures trend followers that I find most worth paying attention to and emulating in my own trading. Before you go about trading with similar methods, it is good to know whether these habits fit your personality and to decide in advance exactly how you want to apply them.

CHAPTER 2

What Can an Equity Trader Learn from a Futures Trend Follower?

WHAT IS A TREND FOLLOWING TRADING STRATEGY?

No one invests without an expectation of future profit. Even professional CTAs invest with the hope that strategies they employ after back testing will be profitable over the long run. More generally, they often believe that the financial markets they trade will continue to have exploitable trends for their foreseeable existence. Thus, trend followers have intelligent assumptions about the future backing up their application of their strategies. They often make the entire trade planning process completely mechanical, from choosing which instruments they trade to timing their entries, sizing their positions, and timing their exits. However, there's no rule that requires you to time all of your entries with a trend following strategy in order to size your positions and time your exits with such a strategy. You can easily mix a fundamentals based entry with a trend following exit method, for example. For this reason, I broadly define a trend following trading strategy as in the box.

> Any *preplanned, rule-based strategy* for managing *open position* P&L in which open profits could hypothetically grow indefinitely under a *limited* set of circumstances, while open losses are limited under *all* circumstances.

Note that this definition is independent of your reasons for entering the market and your timing in doing so. The fact that a trend following trading method is both preplanned and rule-based means that decisions about how to react to all possible scenarios are made before entering the market, and thus a trader using a trend following method simply reacts to prices unemotionally once in the market rather than trying to predict what prices will do next.

Note also that I define trend following as a method of managing *open position* P&L, that is, exits and position sizes specifically, rather than both entries and exits. This expands the universe of what are commonly thought of as trend following strategies, because it means that you don't always have to chase prices when entering the market in order to employ a trend following position sizing and exit strategy.

Trend following entries are not the only method of entering markets that can provide an edge, and neither are they always the best method of entering markets. However, you may certainly chase prices on your entries if your overall strategy calls for it. Managing open position P&L with a mechanical trend following strategy allows you to concentrate the bulk of your time on finding situations in which you strongly believe in a sustained directional move. You can then trade these situations unemotionally.

Note that in my definition, I say that in a trend following trading strategy, "open losses are limited under *all* circumstances," while "open profits could hypothetically grow indefinitely under a limited set of circumstances." Since the user of such a trading strategy simply reacts to market prices, he has no way of knowing how much open profit he will eventually lock in, but he always has the peace of mind of knowing the maximum open loss he will allow before liquidating.

Clearly, then, a trend following trading strategy can be employed to time exits in any market situation in which sustained future movement in a particular direction is expected. Correctly anticipating sustained future movement in a financial instrument is difficult enough. Correctly anticipating the exact form that this sustained movement will take is impossible. For example, the market could drift up with a lot of choppiness, move up steadily, or rocket up and then plateau. Trading an idea with a mechanical strategy can make you equally comfortable encountering any of these situations, because your strategy will enable you to react to market fluctuations of any form in an unemotional and logical manner.

PHILOSOPHY OF A TREND FOLLOWER

In my studies about the philosophies of trend followers, it became clear to me that trend followers do not believe that they can truly predict the future of the markets. Think about this fact for a minute. A trend following trader can still use back testing or other methods to *estimate* whether a trade or strategy will be profitable going forward, as his only reason to invest is because he *believes* he will earn a positive return on his money. However, this is a far cry from believing that he can predict the future. Furthermore, no matter what his method for selecting positions, once in a position he is subject to the same uncertainty and risk as everyone else with a similar position. Since you cannot know what the outcome of holding a position will be, isn't it logical to use objective tools to estimate and control your risk? Trend followers understand that the unpredictable short-term fluctuations of the market are *normal*, and prepare for this when planning trades. This is a sensible way to approach the trading process.

Trend followers also believe that a financial instrument's price is the most important piece of information about that instrument.[1] Price is a powerful indicator with unique qualities. It directly affects your pocketbook when you are invested, and so it pays, especially when you are in a position, to take it seriously and literally at face value. Sometimes using a trend following strategy may entail buying rallies, selling dips, entering or exiting the market right before a major reversal, or being repeatedly whipsawed (i.e., buying highs and then selling lows repeatedly). However, failing to catch the exact top or bottom of a move is not as bad as it sounds when you think of how a high or a low in a stock really comes about. Jesse Livermore wisely stated:

> *One of the most helpful things that anybody can learn is to give up trying to catch the last eighth—or the first. These two are the most expensive eighths in the world. They have cost stock traders, in the aggregate, enough millions of dollars to build a concrete highway across the continent.*[2]

On an intraday basis, a high may be a price where only a few hundred shares briefly traded before the market plunged lower. Consider if you had to sell 10,000 shares in such a market—this high would likely be impossible for you to catch. Highs and lows are simply artifacts of temporary (and unpredictable) supply and demand imbalances in a stock. How can you know whether an order will be coming in even as little as 10 seconds from now to buy 500 shares or to sell 50,000 shares? It is impossible to know this, so why waste time trying to peer into the future? In fact, if the size you are trying to move is relatively small, it is almost a guarantee that your order will be a drop in the bucket compared to larger orders that are actually moving the markets substantially. This is why I protect myself by planning my trades as if the markets will behave unpredictably once I'm in (although I may believe otherwise). Many novice traders feel that they are able to trade by the seat of their pants, literally believing that they know better than the market what it is going to do immediately next. You may have more luck guessing whether a flipped coin will land heads or tails, or guessing the direction a flying butterfly is about to turn, than guessing the short-term fluctuations of the market. There is literally no use getting angry at the market for behaving according to its nature. You will never be able to control the market, but you will always be able to control your own actions, so work on doing that. In the words of Jesse Livermore:

> *That is why I repeat that I never argue with the tape. To be angry at the market because it unexpectedly or even illogically goes against you is like getting mad at your lungs because you have pneumonia.*[3]

It is dangerous to believe that you can call tops or bottoms in a stock consistently over time. The faster you can abandon this belief, the better.

Regardless of whether you trade exactly as a trend follower does, the trade planning discipline of a trend follower is definitely worth emulating. No matter when you enter an investment, it is how you size your positions and time your exits that determine your actual profits or losses in it. Your trading strategy should thus be robust enough to protect you whether you buy the very top of a move or the very bottom of a move. You have to be comfortable no matter when you enter an investment that you will not get badly burned. This allows you to concentrate on the bigger picture instead of worrying about market minutiae.

I believe that a sound trading plan should provide you with a mechanical method of cutting your losses short while giving your profits room to run. Experts often talk about doing this but rarely specify exactly how to go about doing it. If you have already entered the market after doing your homework properly, a mechanical trading strategy can perform as an autopilot that manages your position according to your instructions rather than your emotions.

In my experience, I learned that in certain types of short-term trading situations, I would cut both losses and profits short based on market feel, limiting my profitability. On rare occasions, often after I had been completely right but had failed to adequately capitalize on a move, I would then overtrade my next idea, and my position would of course start to move against me. This position would then rapidly transform into a loss, which I would reluctantly liquidate, wiping out a few sessions of gains and being forced to fight back from a psychological low point.

Thus, although I may have been right more times than I was wrong, my method of trading my opinions *occasionally* led to larger losses than a completely emotionless trader might have had. I now know that many traders make similar mistakes. Trading without a plan can be dangerous to your financial health. Returning again to my coin flip example, if you can't anticipate whether the next flip will land heads or tails, you are better off learning about how to manage your money according to strict rules. Timing my exits with mechanical trend following methods has helped me to trade positions with dramatically less emotion. It gives me peace of mind knowing that I will exit the market either with a limited loss or after capturing a profit that has been allowed to grow according to objective guidelines.

The Bigger Picture

Trend followers see individual trades as part of a larger strategy,[4] sort of like individual points in tennis or basketball (you win some, you lose some). They often expect more losing trades than winning trades, but work toward achieving larger *aggregate* profits than losses over the long run. As a trader you must realize that there is no such thing as a trade without an exit, or a one-sided trade. All trades eventually have an exit, either planned or unplanned in advance. Professional trend followers plan their exits (and all other aspects of their trading process) in advance. They may find that their trading plan reacts to the actual price action of the market terribly, but they know that this is far worse than the alternative of trading without a plan. They also expect losses to occur rather regularly or even frequently, as part of the cost of doing business. You must be able to take and move past a loss if you want to be successful at trading. Can you imagine a basketball player being furious because his team gave up 95 points but won the game with a score of 96–95? What if you had to update the scoreboard after the opposing team scored a point before you could continue with the game? Would you hesitate to update the scoreboard because you don't want to see a point scored against you in lights? This would be unthinkable, but for some reason when money is on the line, humans feel that they should never lose. Trading has its share of setbacks, just like any other business, and you must expect to lose many points on the way to winning overall. Think of it as the cost of doing business.

SOME THOUGHTS ON APPLYING TECHNICAL TRADING STRATEGIES IN EQUITIES

"Know Thyself" (Socrates)

A widespread investment strategy among many mutual funds is to continuously hold the bulk of their portfolio in stocks but occasionally rebalance, switching old stocks for new ones. In this way they always have exposure to the stock market and any upward drift it may have. The major indices are also periodically rebalanced. This ensures that they contain a majority of quality companies that are likely to continue as going concerns, making it very unlikely that a major index portfolio would ever drop to zero. However, constant exposure to stocks can certainly lead to protracted drawdowns from time to time, just like any other trading strategy. Furthermore, although the market portfolio might drop by a limited amount such as 25 percent in such a drawdown, individual stocks may fall twice or three times that percentage. Clearly, it is prudent if you are going to trade individual stocks to take steps to protect your capital from taking major hits in one sitting. Theories about the long-term resilience of the market may not bring you back quickly from a top tick purchase of Internet stocks.

Some serious questions thus arise for a prospective investor. What equity curve behavior can you tolerate, and do you find recovering from an open loss more painful than giving up an open profit? In my personal experience, I have found that being exposed to a large open loss and recovering back to even from it is a dramatically more harrowing experience than giving up a large open gain and returning to even. The latter can be shrugged off, as none of your capital is lost—the former might cause you sleepless nights. Volatility in open losses is more nerve-racking than volatility in open profits, and an attractive characteristic of a trend following trading strategy is that it mechanically limits volatility in open losses while allowing greater volatility in open profits. The tradeoff for this, however, is generally a higher percentage of losses than you would experience if you were to limit the sizes of your profits and losses to roughly the same amount. No matter how you choose to trade, the most important thing overall is to plan your trades well so that you are prepared for any market conditions. Risk is part and parcel of gaining a reward, but not all equity curves are equally palpable to all investors, so you must choose strategies that fit with your market philosophy. Since many investor portfolios are less diversified than the market portfolio, and may contain more volatile stocks than it, these investors have to be nimble in reacting to the behavior of their investments. If you plan every aspect of your investment process, this nimbleness will be built into your reaction to the market.

You must know yourself as an investor. Do you prefer taking your losses in small doses, without constant exposure to the markets? Or are you willing to always be exposed to the markets and endure occasional 2002 style drawdowns without any direct control? Rationally or not, many investors balk when faced with an actual protracted drawdown. Some panic out of positions, others swear off stocks, and others wait helplessly for a recovery that may or may not come. In the stock market, not all stocks are as well behaved as the indices, and a lack of quick reaction in

Internet stocks might have left an investor with several single stock losses in the neighborhood of 90 percent or even more. As of this writing the NASDAQ Composite is still more than 50 percent below its 2000 peak. Since many of my years in the market occurred during the last stages of a massive bull market and the beginning stages of a subsequent bear market, the experience certainly reinforced in my mind the necessity of planning my trades in advance and employing strategies to limit my downside losses. It is certainly conceivable that a trader whose career began around a market bottom might think differently.

One of the advantages of trading with a preplanned technical strategy is that it provides you with a logical method of timing an investment in a market whose prospects you may not be completely sure about. It limits your open losses if you pick individual stocks (as many investors do) that can help limit your exposure to unknowable factors such as the timing of the Internet bubble crash. If as an investor you were to sit on the sidelines any time a questionable investment came along, you might never invest, and over the long run this would definitely be more harmful to you than being exposed to volatility in your investment returns. Planning your trading strategies in advance allows you to trade in and out of a market even if you hear that price-earnings ratios (P/Es) are dangerously high or hear doomsayers about the economy saturating the airwaves.

Some Limitations of Back Testing

> *Past performance is not necessarily indicative of future results.*
> —Typical mutual fund disclaimer

If you come up with an investment idea, it is great *whenever possible* to study or test how it would have worked in the past. This is analogous to doing a feasibility study if you want to enter a new business venture. Undoubtedly, any business environment can change overnight, which is a caveat to any feasibility study, and a possibility that you should always be aware of. Walking backward down the street does not help you avoid obstacles in the road or navigate upcoming turns, but seeing some detailed information related to a strategy you want to employ (even if it is old) may be better than walking completely blind. Rigorous testing of how mechanical trading strategies would have performed in the past can also be a useful tool, but it must be viewed in its proper context. There is no substitute for action, and an obsession with obtaining profitable back tested results in a strategy may also lead you to analysis paralysis. Remember, you do not trade the known past. You trade the unknown future.

There are numerous ads for systems that would have performed admirably over such and such period had one used them. Some questions often overlooked are, "Would anyone have realistically chosen to use this miracle system at the beginning of the period in question?" and "Would anyone have realistically stuck with this miracle system exclusively for the period in question?" For example, let's say a hypothetical system has performed well over the past 10 years. Would it have performed equally admirably over the 10-year period before that? Chances are you would have used the system only during the beginning of its testing period if this were the case! But how many systems perform admirably well for such long periods of time, and would they still be relevant today? It can be tempting to focus today on those systems that would have done well had you just had the foresight to use them at some time in the past. However, you should keep in mind that the entire picture of the markets back then would have been different, and you might not have been as receptive to those miracle systems as you might be tempted to be today.

Let's look at this concept in more detail in stocks. Let's say you pick a portfolio of 10 stocks using a special fundamental and technical filter. You intend to back-test a mechanical trading strategy in these 10 stocks over the past five years. If the results are favorable, you plan to invest in the strategy. So let's say that you use your filter to identify profitable listed companies with market caps more than $5 billion and average volumes of more than 1,000,000 shares per day. You run a filter search today and it yields you 300 companies out of a universe of 6,000, of which you pick the top 10 by market cap to use in your five year back test. Although this may seem sensible, a problem with this approach is that although the stocks you pick might be great companies, the universe of 6,000 stocks that you picked them from would have been completely different five years ago. Certain mergers and acquisitions had not yet occurred. Certain companies that trade today were not yet public, while certain companies that existed then might be out of business now. Average volumes, market caps, price to book ratios and other characteristics of various stocks were completely different. So what would be the use in picking the stocks with your current filter as back testing candidates when there is a reasonable likelihood that you would *not* have picked them in the beginning of your back test period?! Although you may be able to purchase filters that would tell you what the available universe of stocks would have been at different times in the past (so you can see if your filtering methodology is profitable over time), this would be very specialized information, and not likely to be cheap.

I hope my point is clear by now. For example, how many individuals would have picked Microsoft (symbol: MSFT) as a trading candidate a year after its initial public offering (IPO) date? It is only now that Microsoft has become a very prominent stock that it is likely to show up on many filters. The next Microsoft may be under the radar right now. This is something to keep in mind when looking at back tested results in equities. Be skeptical about the underlying assumptions and keep your eyes trained for situations *today* that have the potential to develop into very profitable trades, situations whose full potential the public does not yet appreciate. Of course, one way to keep your back testing consistent is to confine your universe of stocks to the components of a major index like the S&P 500, the Russell 2000, or a periodically published list like the *Investor's Business Daily* 100. The components of these indices/lists are periodically updated, but their creators keep historical records of what they are. Trading index stocks exclusively will exclude a large number of other stocks from your studies but may at least make it possible for you to pick stocks from a group about which detailed long-term records are kept.

All of this goes to show that even if you can produce great back tests of how your portfolio would have performed if you had traded certain stocks a certain way, even your method of identifying those stocks may be questionable. Furthermore, the more complex the phenomenon you are back testing, the more likely it is to be a transient phenomenon, or at least a phenomenon that is difficult to distinguish from the market's upward drift. Relevance of results is a difficult thing to determine. For example, if you see great back test results of a buy signal that occurs every time a stock drops 17.3 percent below its 150-day moving average—as long as 20-day average volume exceeds 200,000 shares; as long as you hold for exactly 37 days, you may have observed a fluke. Each component that determines the signal you are testing, for example, the 17.3 percent, the 150-day moving average, the 20-day average volume, the 200,000 share cutoff, and the 37-day holding time, is a separate degree of freedom of the phenomenon you are back testing. The phenomenon may also be largely a result of the market's upward drift. The more degrees of freedom in the phenomenon you are back testing, the more likely it is that you observed a profitable coincidence.[5] You should thus be very wary of the possibility of such a phenomenon changing its behavior in the near future.

By definition, the fewer the degrees of freedom that a completely mechanical trading system uses, the less variables there are that can alter the behavior of the system. If you use complex systems with many degrees of freedom, you may have to change systems rather frequently, as relationships that existed in the past begin to deteriorate. This requires a method for detecting the breakdown of these relationships, which introduces new complexities. In any case, few individuals would have the confidence to commit all their capital to any miracle system with great back tested results (unless they could see an almanac from the future telling them in advance how the system is going to behave). Realistically, most traders will probably doubt that a black box system works as soon as it begins to lose money. Realistically, they will likely ignore signals they find questionable, or allocate too much capital to others. Realistically, unless they believe in the principles underlying the system, they are likely to abandon it at some point. Clearly, it can be risky to rely too much on back tested results to give a proper road map of tomorrow's market action. In the long run, people stick with investment strategies based on principles and ideas they believe in. A healthy sense of skepticism should prevent you from blindly investing in a black box created by someone else because it happens to spit out great back tested results.

Another area in which you must question the relevance of back tested results is when they depend on clearly unrelated phenomena. For example, if lunar eclipses have preceded five-day negative NASDAQ returns for each of the past 10 years, does this mean that a relationship truly exists? When you move on to forms of financial data like economic data, determining the long-term relevance of what you are observing becomes less clear-cut, and this is where interpretation of back tested results becomes more art than science. For example, perhaps you think you've observed a relationship among stock market activity, unemployment data, and national real estate prices. You must then decide how relevant it is. I prefer to read the opinions of multiple experts in an area when I am out of my depth and come to my own conclusions, however imperfect they may be.

In summary, back testing can be very useful for some traders, but it is not a panacea, because not every potentially profitable idea can be properly or thoroughly back tested. Furthermore, there is always a degree of uncertainty present in trading because if there were not, prices would already have moved to a new equilibrium. Some of the greatest trades possible would have been the right thing to do when the consensus thought them to be highly questionable (like buying the S&P 500 in 1979). Back testing does not provide good insight into the future in certain scenarios and can be expensive to do completely rigorously in equities. Regardless of whether you use back testing or not, you will need the courage to trade your convictions with discipline, although the crowd might ridicule your decisions and although you may have only partial information about the situations you choose to invest in. As long as you plan your trades in a disciplined manner, your capital should be reasonably well protected.

The Importance of Long-Term Discipline and Patience

Many new traders fail to realize that the bulk of profitable trading, or managing money, is waiting. Trading simply gets you in and out of the market—like walking through a doorway into a house. You wait for the right time to enter stocks that you think will be profitable for you. You wait until the time when your trading strategy tells you to exit your open positions, which may be minutes, months, or more. Making a trade is a relatively simple process compared to the research and preparation that should underlie it. Since trading is the visible tip of the iceberg, as illustrated in Figure 2.1, people tend to focus on it a lot more than their *preparations for trading*. The particulars of executing an order in the market do matter, but this process is only one component of your research and planning. While the crowd focuses on a boxer's punches, the trainer focuses on his strategy, execution, and behind-the-scenes preparation.

As a speculator you will sometimes have to wait for large profits to grow larger. You will also sometimes have to wait through nerve-racking drops in your account equity (if these drops are within the parameters of your investment plan). Most people do not have the patience to stick with a long-term viewpoint or strategy, and this is to your advantage—if you actually have that patience. Many people are impatient. They want to be in the best performing funds, make a quick buck in the hottest stock, live in the most attractive areas, and drive the most beautiful cars—yesterday. They are confident that they can outperform George Soros and Warren Buffett by trading with the same tools as everyone else, and without

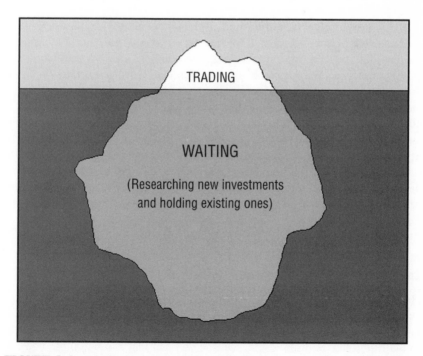

FIGURE 2.1 Trading is the tip of the iceberg.

putting in the necessary time or effort to get ahead of the curve. Everybody wants a free lunch. As a result, impatient people trade without conviction, change strategies repeatedly and get whipsawed about, often losing more money than they would with a little more staying power.

Trading is a constant learning process. It is important to equip yourself for the task with a philosophy that has powerful underlying principles, which only you can define. You should also understand the limitations and advantages of the strategies you use and stick to your trading plans after you have made them as much as humanly possible. Easier said than done, of course, and there are so many distractions along the way. Trading magazines are filled with ads for holy grail systems that would have had 20 percent+ compounded returns for the past 10 years. What is often overlooked is that it would be nearly impossible for most human beings to use the same investment strategy for a decade throughout the system's hills and valleys. Do you have that kind of patience and discipline? Most people want to see that a system is an ironclad method of making dreamy profits, but they forget or ignore that the market's behavior is often largely unpredictable and can change on a dime. Also, who would give away a holy grail system for free anyway? The truth is that few have the patience to stick to any system or trading plan, whether excellent or mediocre.

This is why it is of paramount importance for you to develop your own market philosophies and trading plans from scratch. Developing a trading plan is like planning a long trip; if you check maps beforehand and make yourself aware of possible sightseeing destinations and hotels along the way, you'll be much better prepared than you would by just driving off without a second thought. Only if you believe in the ideas underlying your plan will you be able to withstand the inevitable losing trades that you will have to endure as part of your strategy. Even if you use the guidelines in this book to develop your trading plans, they will ultimately have to be your own. The temptation to change plans in the middle of a trade or in the middle of implementing a strategy can be almost overpowering sometimes, even if you strongly believe in your reasons for holding. You should thus be able to articulate your reasons for employing a strategy in a few short sentences; this will allow you to sleep at night.

Trading with Trend Following Techniques Is Contrary to Natural Instincts

Only you can decide if incorporating trend following methods into a trading plan is right for you. However, you should be aware that trading with trend following techniques is contrary to natural human instincts. Although the term "trend following" may seem to imply that a trend follower is following the crowd, managing your open position P&L with a trend following trading strategy is a contrarian thing to do, for several reasons.

1. Trading an idea with a trend following trading plan may require you to risk substantial portions of your open profits in the pursuit of larger profits.[6]
   - This requires tremendous courage and patience.
   - This may involve seeing a substantial profit accumulated over months disappear entirely or even turn into a loss.
   - Most traders prefer instead to book limited profits when they have them, as they are afraid of losing these newfound profits.

2. Trading an idea with a trend following trading plan often requires you to liquidate your position if your open loss on that position reaches a certain point.[7] Using such a strategy repeatedly may also mean that you encounter strings of limited losses in the pursuit of overall profitability.
   - Many traders prefer to hold on to losing positions in the hope that they will rebound in their favor.
   - Some traders even add to losing positions, which may work for a while—until it does not, and a massive loss occurs.
   - It is not easy to continue trading with the same style after a string of losses. You must believe strongly in your trading style to stick with it through bad periods.

3. Trading an idea with a trend following trading plan means that you have accepted that you cannot really predict the future.
   - Although you may spend a lot of time trying to uncover profit opportunities, there are no certainties. You can still be wrong no matter how much homework you've done. It is good to stay humble, because the market respects no one.
   - Rather than wasting time and emotional energy fighting the tape, instead plan as many aspects of your trading strategy in advance as you can and let the tape tell you what to do. Treat trading as a serious business.

4. Trading an idea with a trend following trading plan means that you are disciplined about how much capital you allocate to individual positions.[8]
   - Most traders do not spend a lot of time thinking about how much of a stock they will buy, or they may simply choose their position size on a whim. They thus run the risk of overtrading or undertrading, by investing erratic amounts of capital in different opportunities.

- Trend followers know that in the long run, the position sizing methods they use are crucial. A sound position sizing methodology can protect capital while allowing it a reasonable amount of room to grow. A poor position sizing methodology can destroy capital rapidly.

It should be clear from this very basic list of what trading with a trend following trading strategy entails that not many traders would be able to trade like this consistently.

Whipsaws

If you enter *and* exit the markets by chasing trends, there is a possibility that you will encounter a sustained choppy period in the markets that erodes your capital dramatically because of whipsaws, like those illustrated in Figure 2.2. Of course, the number of whipsaws you encounter will be partially dependent on your method of timing entries and exits in a market. Let's say that your strategy consists of buying new 20-day highs and then selling new 20-day lows in a particular stock. It is conceivable that you could run into a sustained period where as soon as the market makes a new 20-day high (where you buy), it immediately re-

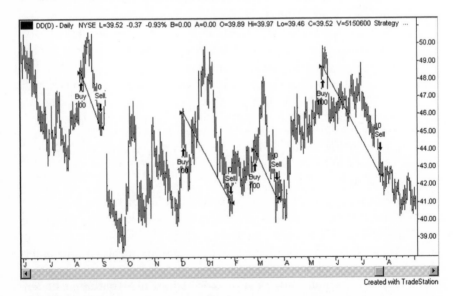

FIGURE 2.2 Whipsaws encountered when using a trend following strategy can lead to large losses. (*Source:* © TradeStation® 1991–2006. All rights reserved.)

verses and falls to a new 20-day low (where you sell), and then reverses and rises to a new 20-day high (where you buy again), and then immediately reverses and falls to a new 20-day low (where you sell again), and so on. No rule says that this process could not continue forever, and thus it should be clear from this example that use of a pure trend following strategy (i.e., one in which both entries and exits are based on trend following) could lead to your capital base being dramatically reduced or even wiped out.

The potential for reward exists to compensate risk takers, but a reward can never be truly guaranteed. Even if you buy and hold a mutual fund, you run the risk of encountering a dramatic drawdown. However, simply holding the fund forever means you have no say in cutting off your losses and may be exposed to a large open loss in your investment, even if the fund is diversified. I find exposing *all* of my investment capital to such a risk in this manner without personal control of the investment process unacceptable.

However, the risk of a large decline in your capital also exists if you trade with technical strategies, although you'll have more control over the investment process than buying and holding a fund. Many completely mechanical trend following strategies have less than half of their trades as profitable trades. Winning percentages can be in the range of 30 to 40 percent in fact,[9] making losing percentages in the range of 60 to 70 percent. This means that for some of these strategies, two out of every three trades is a loser. Furthermore, they have a reasonably high probability of encountering long strings of losses with percentages of losing trades like these. The probability P of enduring N losing trades in a row, given *completely independent* trades subject to *fixed* probabilities of losing, is:[10]

$$P = L^N$$

L in this formula represents your percentage of losing trades. Table 2.1 gives an indication of some of the probabilities of encountering N losing trades in a row (if the probability of a trade being a losing trade is fixed). Note that for a losing percentage of 70 percent (in this very simplified example), the probability of having 10 losses in a row are 2.82 percent, that is, about 1 in 35. This is without even examining the chances of, for example, five losses in a row broken by a single win that is in turn followed by another five losses. This particular case might not be much different in practice from having eight or nine losses in a row. Clearly, if you are going to make trades with trend following strategies (or any strategy, in fact), you should be aware that you will eventually encounter sustained drawdown periods.

TABLE 2.1 Probabilities of having N losses in a row, given a fixed losing percentage. Even with what might appear to be a losing percentage that's not so bad, long strings of losses can be encountered.

Losing Percentage	Number of Losses in a Row (N)									
	N=1	N=2	N=3	N=4	N=5	N=6	N=7	N=8	N=9	N=10
30%	30.00%	9.00%	2.70%	0.81%	0.24%	0.07%	0.02%	0.01%	0.00%	0.00%
40%	40.00%	16.00%	6.40%	2.56%	1.02%	0.41%	0.16%	0.07%	0.03%	0.01%
50%	50.00%	25.00%	12.50%	6.25%	3.13%	1.56%	0.78%	0.39%	0.20%	0.10%
60%	60.00%	36.00%	21.60%	12.96%	7.78%	4.67%	2.80%	1.68%	1.01%	0.60%
70%	70.00%	49.00%	34.30%	24.01%	16.81%	11.76%	8.24%	5.76%	4.04%	2.82%

A fallacy that sometimes arises when people observe long strings of losses taking place is that many losses in a row portend an imminent winner.[11] In truth, the past results of your trading are completely unrelated to whether your next trade will be a winner. You may even hypothetically encounter 30 losses in a row, although the odds for this may be similar to your winning the lottery. There's no need to obsess about these ultrarare occurrences, however. Focus instead on trading good ideas and sticking patiently to your plans. You may also want to note to yourself that if your capital base drops, for example, by 50 percent from what you have initially funded an account with, that you will liquidate all positions and either stop trading for a while or let someone else manage your money.

RISK–REWARD PROFILES OF VARIOUS TYPES OF TRADING STRATEGIES

This section discusses the risk–reward profiles of various long-only equity trading strategies used for single trades, including trend following strategies. In the following list I give risk–reward profiles from four different long-only strategies. Some of these have loose similarities to some simple options trading strategies. Note that by stop price and target price in the list I am referring to *initial* stop prices and target prices when a position is initiated, and by "fixed time limit" I mean that the position is immediately liquidated at market when the time limit expires. Note also that actual risk and reward may be different in reality depending on slippage and other trading costs.

1. Fixed time limit trade with no other exit rules.

    Maximum risk per share: entry price.

    Maximum reward per share: unlimited.

2. Fixed time limit trade with a fixed stop price, or alternatively, unknown time limit trade with a trailing stop.

    Maximum risk per share: entry price – stop price.

    Maximum reward per share: unlimited.

3. Fixed time limit trade with a fixed target price, or alternatively, unknown time limit trade with a trailing target price.

    Maximum risk per share: entry price.

    Maximum reward per share: target price – entry price.

4. Fixed time limit trade with both a fixed stop price and a fixed target price.

   Maximum risk per share: entry price – stop price.

   Maximum reward per share: target price – entry price.

Strategy #1 is a trading strategy in which you hold a stock for a limited time period and liquidate the stock at the end of that period, ignoring its price action in between. This strategy has a maximum risk per share of your entry price and an unlimited maximum reward per share. Since these risk–reward characteristics remain true regardless of your holding period, they also apply to a *buy and hold* trading strategy.

Strategy #2 (the first version) is a strategy in which you enter a market for a fixed time period and exit that market either if your fixed stop price is hit or if the period expires. Similar to being long a call option, your maximum risk per share is theoretically limited with this strategy (to your entry price minus your stop price in this case), while your maximum reward per share is unlimited. A *trend following* trading strategy (the second version of Strategy #2) in which you use a trailing stop, with an unknown holding period for the position, has a similar risk–reward profile.

Strategy #3 (the first version) is a strategy in which you enter a market for a fixed time period and exit that market either if your target price is hit or if the period expires. Similar to being short a put option, your maximum risk per share is limited with this strategy (to your entry price), while your maximum reward per share is limited to your target price minus your entry price. A *trend fading* trading strategy (the second version of Strategy #3) in which you use a trailing target price, with an unknown holding period for the position, has a similar risk–reward profile. A trailing target price is the opposite of a trailing stop.

Strategy #4 is a strategy in which you enter a market for a fixed time period and exit that market either if your target price is hit, if your stop price is hit, or if the period expires. Similar to being long a call option at one strike price and short another call option at a higher strike price (a strategy known as a bullish call spread[12]), both your maximum risk per share and your maximum reward per share are limited with this strategy. Your maximum risk per share is limited to your entry price minus your stop price, while your maximum reward per share is limited to your target price minus your entry price.

Another possible strategy that I have not listed is to *monitor* both a trailing stop price and a trailing target price on the same trade. However, only exit at the trailing stop price if the trailing stop price is *greater than* your entry price. If the trailing stop price is less than your entry price, you would ignore it. Conversely, you would exit at the trailing target price only if the trailing target price is *less than* your entry price. If the trailing target price is *greater than* your entry price, you would ignore it. For example, you may choose to exit a stock if it makes a new 40-day low that is *above your entry price* OR if it makes a new 40-day high that is *below your entry price*. This strategy would have a similar risk-reward profile to Strategy #1, with a maximum risk per share of your entry price, and an unlimited maximum reward per share.

Human nature seems to prefer an *undisciplined* version of Strategy #2. Many investors do not plan their trades thoroughly in advance. When they enter the market and are faced with its raw uncertainty, they become strongly gripped with an urge to lock in open gains that they are *afraid* will disappear, while remaining content to hold onto open losses that they *hope* will reverse themselves. This can be a lethal tendency, as Jesse Livermore suggests in *Reminiscences of a Stock Operator*:

> *[The successful trader] has to reverse what you might call his natural impulses. Instead of hoping he must fear; instead of fearing he must hope.*[13]

Livermore describes the philosophy of a trend follower very accurately. However, even trend fading or more complex trading strategies can be used if you believe that you have an edge and employ proper trade planning discipline to capitalize on that edge. Problems arise when your trading lacks discipline.

COPING WITH THE REALITIES OF A TREND FOLLOWING TRADING STRATEGY

This section presents my take on coping with some of the difficulties that trend following traders have to deal with on a regular basis, along with some of my own notes from putting on trend following trades. The best way to get a good feel for the psychology of top traders and how they handle market situations is to read as much as you can about their methods and opinions, and use the information to improve your own trading. Several master trend followers are elegantly profiled by Covel in Chapter 2 of his book *Trend Following*, entitled Great Trend Followers.[14] In Lois Peltz's excellent work, *The New Investment Superstars*, she offers a profile of John Henry,[15] one of the most famous and most successful trend followers of all time. Many trend following CTAs also have their own Web sites, where you can find more information. Furthermore, the Institutional Advisory Services Group's Web site, www.iasg.com, contains a large database of managed futures funds, their performance, and their *own* descriptions of what they do.

Coping with Slippage and the Difficulty of Chasing Prices

Chasing prices on entries or exits is tough to do. Depending on the amount of stock you are moving relative to the volume in a stock, chasing prices may sometimes lead to some costly situations. Take courage in Livermore's words that "stocks are never too high for you to begin buying or low to begin selling."[16] Of course, the larger the size you wish to move, the more expertise you will likely need to move it. I do not go into great detail about trading strategies for large order sizes in this book, but you may use any combination of market, limit, and stop orders to accomplish whatever you need to accomplish. You may even choose to spread your orders over several days if you need to trade really large size. I believe that the engine of your profitability must not lie primarily in your method of trading your ideas, but rather in your ideas themselves. If you trade based on excellent insights, the hope is that any slippage you encounter will be dwarfed by the extent of your profitability. You may also trade on time frames where slippage has less of an impact. For example, if you try to buy and then sell 10,000 shares of a stock that trades 200,000 shares a day within three hours on the same day, you will be dramatically more affected by slippage than if you enter the stock that day and exit three months later. I find it simpler to trade on time frames for example, on the order of months where slippage due to chasing prices is rarely a significant issue. Alternatively, you may try to use technical timing methods in either the entry or the exit phase of a trade with which you will not necessarily always be chasing the market when you trade. I discuss some of these methods later in this book.

Coping with Dramatic Open Profit Swings

Watching a small profit grow into a large profit because you had the patience to hold your position can be great. However, watching a large profit dramatically melt because you are sticking with the same discipline can be mind numbingly difficult. This is *far* easier than seeing your original investment capital dwindle because of an open loss, however! Imagine seeing a 15 percent open profit obtained in one month evaporate into a 6 percent open profit after another two months before you lock it in. Or imagine seeing an even larger open profit evaporate into nothingness! These types of trading situations can be tough to endure, but your hope in trading with a trend following style is that your patience with open profits will allow you to beat the vast majority of more fickle market participants over the long run. Volatility in open profits is a fact of life with a trend following trading strategy. If you choose this style of trading, take comfort in the fact that many have experienced what you are experiencing. For example, Livermore states that:

> *I have been short one hundred thousand shares and I have seen a big rally coming. I have figured—and figured correctly—that such a rally as I felt was inevitable, and even wholesome, would make a difference of one million dollars in my paper profits. And I nevertheless have stood pat and seen half my paper profit wiped out, without once considering the advisability of covering my shorts to put them out again on the rally. I knew that if I did, I might lose my position and with it the certainty of a big killing.*[17]

Coping with Whipsaws, Drawdowns, and Flat Periods

The often unpredictable nature of the markets means that whipsaws, drawdowns, and flat periods will be an inevitable feature of your trading no matter what style of trading you use. Trend following strategies are no exception to this fact. The quest for the holy grail has hurt many market accounts, and the beginner's assumption that a holy grail exists is fundamentally flawed because markets are dynamic, not static. The market is less like a math problem with one correct answer and more like a modern art painting with a different meaning to everyone. Concentrate on trading with plans that protect your capital while giving it adequate room to grow in an open-ended fashion. From there, it is on to research. Stick to trading strategies that are in line with your beliefs about the markets, and study the characteristics of the strategies you intend to use as thoroughly as possible. Once you have decided on a trading strategy that agrees with your philosophy, however, you must move on to the very important step of uncovering insightful ideas to trade on.

Deciding what to Pay Attention to

I talk a great deal about position sizing and exit timing in this book, and touch lightly on instrument selection and entry timing for the simple fact that there are so many books about these topics, and so many different ways that people arrive at investment ideas. However, in the Bibliography and Recommended Reading sections I give a list of books, newspapers, and Web sites that can help you to develop your own ideas in these areas. Of particular note on the subject of trade timing is the annually published

Stock Trader's Almanac by Yale Hirsch and Jeffrey A. Hirsch, which gives a wealth of information about seasonal tendencies and other fascinating market facts.[18] A great compilation of some of the almanac's ideas is given in *The Almanac Investor: Profit from Market History and Seasonal Trends.*[19] The newspaper *Investor's Business Daily* is also an excellent source for identifying interesting companies and industries. I list additional books in my recommended reading list that can give you further insight into the minds of top traders, the nuances of crowd behavior and other topics.

It is important that you read voraciously and listen intently to the anecdotes of those around you. This does not necessarily mean scanning every piece of market commentary or newspaper article. Rather it means paying attention to the headlines each day for clues about public sentiment. It means listening to the stories you hear around you about how people might feel about the economy or their investments. The picture you get of the investment climate in this manner may not necessarily be quantifiable, but it nevertheless may be able to point you toward some investing ideas. The Internet can be a powerful tool in your studies, because of its property of linking pages to each other in a web. While following up on one idea, you may encounter another thread that gives you an even better perspective. There is also no reason to confine your research exclusively to readings about domestic companies, industries, and markets. In addition to domestic opportunities, there are worldwide investment opportunities in both emerging and established markets, and there are a large number of exchange-traded funds (ETFs) and other funds for those who wish to to take advantage of these opportunities.

If you observe public sentiment overwhelmingly leaning one way, try to make it a point to read some contrarian articles about other investment opportunities, to broaden your perspective. If you are in a clear bull market, read bearish commentary as well as bullish. As prices rise, the bears will have increasingly well thought out theories as to why they should fall. As prices fall, the bulls will have increasingly well thought out theories about why they should bounce. All in all, the U.S. stock markets have paid optimists very well through all sorts of bad news over the past decades, a fact to keep in mind when you hear the words of doomsayers. No matter what your trading style, good listening skills can always help to clue you in to some new investment factors that you had not considered.

Alternatively, you may choose to focus on a specific niche and read very little beyond that niche; there are numerous ways to manage your time. Nicholas Darvas,[20] the famous author of two books on his trend following trading method, actually did a substantial amount of trading while traveling around the world. He received daily telegrams of prices and read a weekly copy of *Barron's* while on the road.[21] In order to trade like this, you must first define an investment niche that you want to focus on and your approach for trading that niche. This will still require you to research the price movements and/or fundamentals of stocks in your niche, however, which means you will still be quite busy.

The criteria that drive you to select a market idea may not always be quantifiable, but as much as possible you should note the ideas that lead you to a decision, so that you can refer to them in retrospect and learn from your successes or mistakes. If you can structure a conditional *instrument selection and entry timing list* that you refer to when deciding whether to invest in or rotate into in a particular stock or industry, this is certainly great. However, your reason for investing might be as simple as seeing that a new chain of health food stores seems to be spreading everywhere you look. Only you can know the conditions that an investment must meet to make you comfortable holding it through market volatility. Insight drives the process.

Coping with Missed Opportunities or Failure to Follow Your Rules

Psychological pain in trading can come in many forms. There is the pain of missing a massive profit opportunity that you didn't think of, which is far secondary to the pain of not acting, or acting poorly on a profit opportunity that you did think of. There is the pain of losing money within the parameters of a strategy, but to me this is far worse than the pain of losing money due to lack of a strategy or a failure to follow your own strategy. To undisciplined traders there is occasionally the relief of making money back after a drawdown induced by trading without a strategy or breaking their own rules. Trading like this can lead to a lot of second guessing and is thus psychologically dangerous. Although you may get away with breaking your rules a few times, eventually statistics catch up and the market may deal you a blow that you have not planned for and are not psychologically prepared for.

Place all your creativity and any second-guessing of past experiences into the plans you use to trade the markets—before you enter them. Once you are exposed to market forces you are exposed to the unpredictable, and I prefer to have disciplined rules in place to help me cope. Imagine yourself as a dispassionate outsider given strict instructions by a friend on how to trade your friend's portfolio when he is away. Follow the instructions as best you can and make adjustments to your strategy afterward if necessary. Avoid adjusting your plan of action in the middle of a trade, and note any doubts that come to mind in a trading diary.

Keeping a Trading Diary

I suggest that you keep a *good* trading diary. Write your opinions about how current events relate to market conditions in this diary. Write the thoughts that pass through your head before, during, and after you have made a trade. Write about the emotions that grip you in various phases of the investment process. Were you afraid of giving back an open profit? How disappointed were you to see a profit turn into a loss? Were you gripped with a sudden urge to jump on the latest darling stock of the day, contrary to your original plan? Were you annoyed about a fill you received? Write about instances when you failed to follow your rules. Did you fail to get out when a stop loss was triggered? Try to analyze your mistakes and come up with solutions for fixing them. Try to analyze your successes and come up with ideas about new possible avenues of success.

A trading diary helps you to remember what you did and thought in the heat of battle. It alerts the unconscious mind to the fact that you want to improve your trading. It sharpens your awareness of your trading by helping you to remember the multiple clues that you considered before you entered a trade. Looking back at a chart alone will not give you this information. Looking back at your trades alone will not give you this information. A trading diary helps you to identify issues that are hurting your performance; it helps you to diagnose yourself, because trading is a very intense process.

Here follow two sample entries from my own trading diary, which show that you do not need to write a book to write a diary entry. Just be honest with yourself. The first entry indicates some apprehension about my portfolio's performance, and a time when I considered altering my predefined rules. The second entry indicates some concern about the amount of volatility I am experiencing in the account. By making a record of my concerns, I essentially cautioned myself to stick to the rules. I quote verbatim from my entries (including spelling errors due to quick typing).

5/27/05 update

Today I started to feel nervous about the downside risk of the portfolio, which I'd previously calculated to be about 17% of base capital. I have had a runup of about 5% so far, but yesterday the portfolio stalled, moving up less percentagewise than the nasdaq, followed today by a larger percentage drop than the nasdaq.

My intention up to this point has been to sell stop the portfolio at a loss of $17,000. Now I am thinking of possibly making this a trailing stop loss based on the $5,000 peak, or reducing position commitments. The 17% stopamt represents about 3% of my actual capital, so my trepidation is clearly irrational, especially considering the upside potential.

7/29/05 update

Yesterday for a brief period of time I was up over 15% since inception of the account, due to a strong rally in [stock omitted] following earnings news. However, the stock gave back most of the gains, and my account cloes flat on the day, up about 12.5%. Today it is down about another 2.5%, a tremendous swing in a very short period of time. I note that the QQQQs are down 0.7% only. Tremendous volatility has entered the account, but I intend to stick to the system until stopped out by the market.

Keeping a Research Notebook

A trading diary helps you to identify weaknesses and strengths in your execution of trading plans. A research notebook (or research notes) helps you to aggregate clues about potentially profitable market strategies and your studies of them. In a research notebook, you simply write down your brainstorms and any subsequent research of them. Perhaps you think you have observed a seasonal tendency in a certain industry, or a serial correlation between two stocks. You then write down, without being frivolous, what you think you have seen. There is no need to make entries every day; instead make them only when you have something to report. Perhaps you have a hunch that a flurry of activity in the bond and currency markets will lead to a stock market rally, or perhaps you feel that a certain stock that has been ignored by institutional investors would be a good candidate for application of a fully mechanical trend following strategy. Write down your evidence for what you believe, and then try to find both corroborating and contrary evidence. Note that you will never have the luxury of 100 percent certainty. You don't need all the pieces of information, just enough to make an educated guess about the future direction of the market, which you then trade with discipline. Research will ultimately drive your results, and so you must focus the bulk of your time on research, while developing in yourself the discipline you will need to capitalize on the opportunities you have identified in your research.

Your follow-up research on your market insights may consist of back testing of historical data, or qualitative studies of what you consider to be similar situations in the past. Try to note your insights as much as possible, without going over the top. Look for simple but powerful relationships. Are there high momentum areas where you may be able to make decent money with a technical trading strategy? Are *multiple* financial instruments moving in unison in the same direction? Keeping a research notebook and trading diary reinforces in your mind the importance that you place on these two pillars of speculation (i.e., research and trading) and will help you to come to conclusions that you may not otherwise have seen if had not taken notes. Of course, you should also review your notations periodically. Take inspiration in your toil from the tremendous accomplishments of the astronomer Johannes Kepler, who in the seventeenth century pored over thousands of pages of data on planetary orbits, noting his insights, and unlocked the mysteries of planetary motion as a result. All research scientists take notes; if you are serious about making money in the markets, you will quickly realize that you can't be an exception to that rule.

CHAPTER 3

Equity Trend Following in Action

FAMOUS EQUITY TREND FOLLOWERS

Charles Dow, Trend Following Theorist

Charles Dow, a brilliant technical analyst who lived around the beginning of the twentieth century, has made tremendous contributions to the world of equity technical analysis. The fact that the Dow Jones Industrial Average bears his name is testament to this fact. What may be less commonly known is that the technical analysis theory that bears his name, known as Dow Theory, is a trend following theory. My mention of Dow Theory will be brief and based on the writings of Robert D. Edwards and John Magee in their landmark book *Technical Analysis of Stock Trends*.[1] Dow Theory has been transcribed, interpreted, and/or refined over many years by authors such as William Hamilton, Robert Rhea, and E. George Schaefer to make it easier to use practically.[2]

Edwards and Magee state that "one of the best of all reasons for a student of market technics [sic] to start with the Dow theory is because that theory stresses the *general market trend*."[3] Not all of the tenets of Dow Theory are rigorously defined, however, which leaves room for interpretation. According to Edwards and Magee, the basic tenets of Dow Theory are:

- "The Averages Discount Everything (except 'Acts of God')."[4]
- The market has primary, secondary, and minor trends.[5]

- "Primary up trends are usually (but not invariably) divisible into three phases." The same goes for primary down trends.[6]
- "The Two Averages Must Confirm"—These averages were the Dow Industrials and Rails at the time of their writing.[7]
- "Volume goes with the trend."[8]
- "'Lines' may substitute for secondaries," referring to secondary trends.[9]
- "Only Closing Prices Used."[10]
- "A Trend Should Be Assumed to Continue in Effect Until Such Time as Its Reversal Has Been Definitely Signaled."[11]

Dow Theory is clearly a trend following theory, because it defines trends of certain types. According to Edwards and Magee, the long-term investor's "aim is to buy stocks as early as possible in a Bull Market—just as soon as he can be sure that one has started—and then hold them until (and only until) it has become evident that it has ended and a Bear Market has started."[12] This is a literal definition of trend following. Dow Theory cannot tell you individual stocks to buy, but Edwards and Magee note that "most stocks tend to go with the [primary market] trend."[13] Implicit in Dow Theory is the belief that stocks in general move with the action of the broader market—not step for step—but in a general enough sense that the action of the averages is a reasonable proxy for the action of individual stocks (see box).

Dow Theory thus assumes that it is only worth owning stocks *during confirmed bull markets* in the major indices, and that one should be out of stocks otherwise.

Dow Theory thus satisfies the criteria of being in the market only when it feels an edge is present! It defines certain windows, albeit not strictly, during which holding stocks is likely to be profitable. One might imagine applying the theory by doing intensive research about specific stocks during bear markets when you are on the sidelines, and then buying and holding those stocks during bull markets, which is detailed in Figure 3.1.

Dow Theory includes some rather broad definitions of market action, such as the existence of primary, secondary, and minor trends.[14] These trends are initiated with breakouts or breakdowns that occur in the presence of other confirming criteria. Furthermore, the existence of a trend can generally be recognized only after it is already in place. According to Edwards and Magee, primary trends are "extensive up or down move-

Price

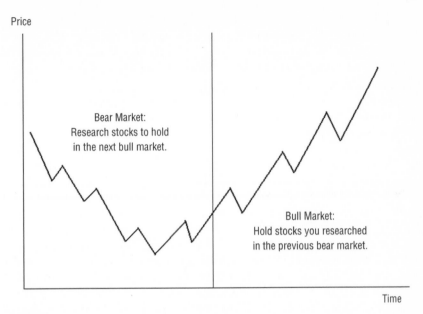

Bear Market:
Research stocks to hold
in the next bull market.

Bull Market:
Hold stocks you researched
in the previous bear market.

Time

FIGURE 3.1 A possible method of applying Dow Theory to trading individual stocks.

ments which usually last for a year or more and result in general appreciation or depreciation in value of more than 20%."[15] This is a rather vague definition, because it is easy to imagine a prolonged market period where the Dow is considerably more volatile or less volatile. This definition is not a very solid basis on which to trade because it is based on percentage movement of the Dow. Dow Theory's definitions of secondary and minor trends are not much better, and sometimes differences of opinion occur as to when various trends begin.[16]

The Edwards and Magee definitions of Dow bull and bear markets also consist of descriptions that are often more qualitative than quantitative (see box).

> Although this may make the definitions difficult to use for purely mechanical trading, the definitions are very useful for understanding similarities in investor psychology during bull and bear market phases.

For example, Edwards and Magee mention that during the third phase of a bull market, "All the financial news is good; price advances are spectacular and frequently 'make the front page' of the daily newspapers; new issues are brought out in increasing numbers."[17] Doesn't this have a familiar ring to it? Any student of market psychology would do well to read more about Dow's fascinating theory, which has laid the foundation for much of modern technical analysis.

One of the most interesting tenets of Dow Theory is the so-called Principle of Confirmation, which requires that, for a bull or bear market to be confirmed, both the Dow Jones Industrial Average, and the Rails (now known as the Dow Jones Transportation Average) must confirm each other's price action—simultaneously.[18] Thus, it uses a technical filter rule in an attempt to objectively define bull and bear markets. Examples of more rigorously defined market filter rules are given later in this book.

To Edwards' and Magee's great credit (their book is undoubtedly a classic) they go into some rather detailed examples of Dow Theory in practice in Chapter 4 of their book. What stands out in their analysis is that there can be quite a bit of subjectivity in interpretation of the theory. The latest (eighth) edition of their book, however, shows that trading the Dow based on the exhibited interpretations of Dow Theory would have been highly profitable during the twentieth century, with a starting investment of $100 on July 12, 1897, growing to $362,212.97 by September 23, 1999 (excluding the effects of dividends and taxes).[19] Dow Theory achieved this hypothetical result while spending considerably less time in the market than a buy-and-hold strategy, and without catching market tops or bottoms.

Richard Russell, a leading modern proponent of Dow Theory, has written:

> *The Dow Theory (actually it is a set of observations) has basically to do with buying great values and selling those values when they become overpriced. Value is the operative word in Dow Theory. All other Dow Theory considerations are secondary to the value thesis. Therefore, price action, support lines, resistance, confirmations, divergence—all are of much less importance than value considerations, although critics of the Theory seem totally unaware of that fact.[20]*

I take from my readings about the theory that a good speculator must be well versed in both the application of technical/price analysis to trading *and* how broader market psychology can drive or affect prices. Understanding of market psychology can help you to interpret whether it is an optimum time to invest in perceived bargains in the marketplace. Understanding of technical analysis, on the other hand, can enable you to time your actual trades based on objective criteria, removing emotions from the trading process.

Jesse Livermore, Trend Following Speculator[21]

An adequate homage to Jesse Livermore is impossible even in the space of an entire book. The insights of this magnificent speculator, as set down in the timeless classic *Reminiscences of a Stock Operator*, have stood and will continue to stand the test of time. *Reminiscences* is generally considered to be a thinly disguised biography of Jesse Livermore. For example, the book is dedicated to "Jesse Lauriston Livermore,"[22] and uses the pseudonym Larry Livingstone for its protagonist.[23] As an equity trader, I do not view *Reminiscences* as a book that is meant to be sifted through for clues of the exact technical details of Livermore's trading (such as the magnitudes of price fluctuations in individual stocks). The structure of the markets and the U.S. economy have vastly changed since then. All of the nuances of market behavior that Livermore profited from cannot possibly still exist today. As the structure of the markets evolves, the level of public participation waxes and wanes, and different strategies fall in and out of favor, thus constantly creating new forms of opportunity while dulling the effectiveness of other forms.

Although Livermore apparently met a tragic end following the loss of one of *several* fortunes that he had made and subsequently lost in his lifetime (the mark of quite a few successful entrepreneurs), he mentions a silver lining in *Reminiscences*. In Chapter XIV, he mentions his comeback from the loss of a fortune:

> *After I paid off my debts in full I put a pretty fair amount into annuities. . . . after I married I put some money in trust for my wife. And after the boy came I put some money in trust for him. By doing what I did my wife and child are safe from me . . . I have fixed it up so that no matter what I want or my wife wants, that trust holds.*[24]

So whether or not Livermore passed away "broke," he made sure that he took the time to take care of his family—an excellent example for traders and nontraders alike.

Reminiscences is a moving story of Livermore's education as a pure trader. He began his trading as a young boy, when he traded in unscrupulous establishments known as "bucket shops"[25] that were essentially gambling parlors. Livermore, an excellent reader of tape fluctuations, became known as "the boy plunger"[26] for his trading acumen. However, as he outgrew the bucket shops and started to trade sizeable positions (often with dramatic leverage), he gradually began to understand that:

> *. . . the big money was not in the individual fluctuations but in the main movements—that is, not in reading the tape but in sizing up the entire market and its trend.*[27]

Chapter V of *Reminiscences* is absolutely essential to the education of any trader, most especially one who intends to use trend following techniques in equities. While the entire book is filled with valuable lessons, this chapter is especially important because Livermore recounts his moments of trading *enlightenment* in it. Livermore recaps the story of one Old Man Partridge, a customer in the brokerage house he frequented who never gave out tips about individual stocks. Rather, when individuals would ask the old man for advice on various positions and market situations, his singular answer was to tell them the broader market's trend, as in, "You know, it is a bull market!"[28] or "Well, this is a bull market, you know!"[29]

Livermore realized from listening to Old Man Partridge that the discipline of holding positions until the trend of the broader market had clearly reversed was crucial for successful speculation. This profound truth echoes the tenets of Dow Theory, and to put it in practice requires a tremendous amount of self control. Livermore describes Old Man Partridge as not only having "the courage of his convictions but the intelligent patience to sit tight."[30] He also states:

> It was never my thinking that made money for me. It was always my sitting. Got that? My sitting tight! . . . Men who can be both right and sit tight are uncommon. I found it one of the hardest things to learn. But it is only after a stock operator has firmly grasped this that he can make big money. It is literally true that millions come easier to a trader after he knows how to trade than hundreds did in the days of his ignorance.[31]

Livermore's trading dramatically improved when he effectively abandoned his focus on intraday noise and began to concentrate on aligning his individual stock positions with the broader market's trend. In his words:

> Nobody can catch all the fluctuations. In a bull market your game is to buy and hold until you believe the bull market is near its end. To do this you must study general conditions and not tips or factors affecting individual stocks. Then get out of all your stocks; get out for keeps![32]

Much of Livermore's trading after his enlightenment is described in Chapter V in the book through the prism of the broader market's condition at the time. Paying attention to the state of the broader market is absolutely crucial in the equity markets, as even the best analysis about a company's fundamentals may be of little use in a bear market where volumes are low due to investor disillusionment with underwater stock positions. Livermore had his own particular methods of defining trends in a particular stock market group.[33] (Elsewhere in this book I describe some of my own.)

Nicholas Darvas, Trend Following Investor

Nicholas Darvas was a professional dancer who made a $2 million fortune in the 1950s (a lot of money back then) largely from scratch. Much of Darvas's fortune was made trading by telegram while he toured the world as a professional dancer. His phenomenal books *How I Made $2 Million in the Stock Market*[34] and *Wall Street: The Other Las Vegas*[35] detail as specifically as possible the trend following investment method that he used. Darvas would scan *Barron's* once weekly to identify a short list of stocks to watch and potentially buy, based on technical criteria.[36] He excluded stocks from his short list that were not near their historical peaks,[37] and also checked other fundamental and technical aspects of the stocks he had chosen to aid his decision to buy. Since he was often traveling, he also requested that his broker send him a daily telegram describing the high, low, close, and volume of stocks on his watchlist.[38]

Darvas concentrated his investments in a small number of stocks, scaled into positions over time (sometimes using leverage) and used periodically adjusted trailing stops to limit his losses while allowing open-ended upside potential. Although he gives a lot of detail in his books, his stock selection method is not strictly quantifiable and is based on a combination of fundamental and technical based decision making that he calls his "techno-fundamentalist theory."[39] As Darvas advanced as a trader he also began to request the price of the Dow Jones Industrial Average on his daily telegram.[40] In this manner, he was able to view the action of his stocks in the context of broader market action.

Darvas used a unique trailing stop method that consisted of the following:

1. He would make his first purchase in a chosen stock as soon as it made a new all-time high, placing a very close stop on his position. In his case, this initial stop was generally a few fractions of a dollar below the new all-time high.

2. If not stopped out, he would wait for the stock to make a new high since his entry that held as a high for at least three full days afterwards; this high defined the top of an imaginary "box," which is somewhat like the top of a temporary, horizontal price channel.

3. After the box top had been defined, he would wait for the stock to make a new low (following the previous box top) that held as a low

for at least three full days afterwards. This low defined the bottom of the "box."

4. Once the bottom of the box had been established, he would raise his previous fixed stop to just below the bottom of the newly defined box.

5. He would then repeat this process as many times as possible, that is, waiting for a new box top and then a subsequent box bottom to be established, until he was stopped out of the stock.

6. He sometimes made additional purchases at strategic points during this process. He does not strictly define these points, and neither does he strictly define the number of purchases he scaled into a position with.

Darvas's use of close stops when entering a position meant that if the stock did not immediately carry through and define a higher box top and subsequent box bottom, he would be quickly stopped out for a small loss. This was a smart method of entering very high momentum stocks, which got him out quickly if he was wrong and kept him in for a long time if he was right. Note that with his technical trading method a stock might hypothetically rally straight up and then fall straight back down through the stop level, making a tremendous inverted-V without setting any short-term box lows along the way that would make you raise your initial stop level. Darvas found it just fine for the purposes of making a fortune, however.

A simplified version of Darvas's trade timing methods can be used to either enter or exit positions, which I mention later in this book. Figure 3.2 illustrates a sample Darvas-like trade. Darvas's boxes are shown, with their tops circled and the bottoms surrounded by squares.

Darvas would clearly have held his winning positions indefinitely if they had simply continued to advance to the moon without indicating that he should stop himself out. In other words, he resembled a buy and hold investor while uptrends in his positions were taking place, but he sat on the sidelines when they were not. Note also that he placed stop orders with his broker as soon as he entered a position, so that he wouldn't have to worry as he was traveling around the world. Although this may be feasible for some small investors, you may also wish to be automatically alerted when a stop point has been reached—and then go into the market to trade. This requires more discipline than simply leaving an order with your broker, of course. Another fact to note is that Darvas's hold times on losing positions were dramatically lower than his hold times on winning positions, a hoped for characteristic of sound trend following strategies; he literally spent more time experiencing open profits than open losses, which must have provided a powerful psychological boost.

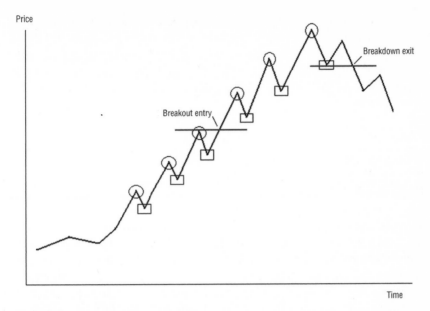

FIGURE 3.2 Illustration of a sample Darvas-like trade, with box tops circled and box bottoms highlighted by squares.

To summarize, Darvas was:

- Very selective in the stocks and times he picked to trade. He did not trade constantly, but only when his take on market conditions indicated that it was favorable to do so. As commissions were generally much larger during the time he mentions in his book than today, his relatively infrequent trading was a prudent practice.
- An investor who used considerable discretion to pick stocks that he believed in, but who then entered and exited his positions using a mechanical trend following methodology that limited his risk while leaving his potential profits open ended.
- An investor whose portfolio was often highly concentrated rather than diversified, allowing him to reap large benefits from being right.
- An investor without strictly defined position sizing criteria, but who still sized his positions so that his risk was within acceptable parameters. He would make an initial purchase with a close stop and would then add to his position in several steps if a cushion of profits developed. Although Livermore also advocated scaling into positions, this choice is largely subjective.

Darvas provides a shining example for individual equity investors because he bucked conventional wisdom by using both technical and fundamental information in his decision making. Although he was a Wall Street outsider, his meticulous discipline and patience enabled him to develop an inspirational system that enabled him to extract a great deal of money from the markets.

A SECULAR TREND TRADING EXAMPLE

Every time you trade, there is a cost. Not just the commissions and slippage, but there are also capital gains taxes and missed dividends to worry about if you are going in and out of the market too quickly. I believe that the best trends to trade in equities are trends that last for long time periods on the order of years, and these can't always be predicted with technical analysis or back testing. Above all, you must strive to accurately gauge investor sentiment, search constantly for bargains around you and muster the courage to act on your convictions. In this chapter I talk about the thought process that I went through to invest in and profit from the boom in commodities stocks over the past few years, in my personal accounts. I relay my experience as an example of secular trend following in equities. I discuss purely technical trend following tools in Part II of this book. By sizing my positions properly, and holding onto several winning positions for long time periods (through high volatility in my personal account), I have been able to make good profits.

This section is not meant to be a recommendation to enter or exit any particular investment, so I do not mention particular stocks by name. During the time period discussed in this section, I also invested only a fraction of my assets in this area of the markets. I also held investments in other stocks as well, some of which I lost money in. However, the one investment theme that I stuck with and kept returning to were commodities stocks, simply because their potential seemed so high and I was making money in them. As of this writing, I also still own many of the stocks that I refer to in this section.

During the bull market run up of the late 1990s, as bullishness in the media became increasingly common, I began to wonder how long the rally would last. Euphoria was everywhere. Internet stock IPOs were trading at multiples of their offering prices on opening day. Analyst comments on television often caused massive amounts of volume to sweep into stocks in seconds, moving them all over the map. Although my only market experience up to that point had been bull market experience, I began to read bearish commentary to counter-balance the euphoria I was seeing every day. Some of the sites I looked at included:

www.financialsense.com.
An investment-related site run by the brilliant Jim Puplava, providing well-thought-out commentary about ideas not seen in the mainstream news.

www.gold-eagle.com.
A site featuring the commentary of electronic newsletter writers that are generally bullish on gold, silver, and other precious metals.

www.zealllc.com.
A site featuring great ideas about contrarian investing and the art of speculation itself.

www.fiendbear.com.
A site providing links to other generally bearish Web sites and commentary.

On these and other sites I read the views of analysts or newsletter writers that were often commodities bulls or stock market bears, and their commentary added a new dimension to my worldview. They lamented how the valuations of gold and gold stocks were historically at rock bottom. They lamented how stock market valuations were historically astronomical. Their commentary grew more and more sophisticated, but the equity bull market continued to rise while commodities continued to flounder. I dabbled in personal investments here and there, more or less experimenting with the market during this time, but I did not have a major angle on things yet. Among my investments, I also briefly held the shares of a gold and silver mining company in 1999 due to my interest, but sold for a loss, as the shares drifted down soon after my purchase. In 2000 I reentered the same stock, and still own some of my shares today. I was just beginning to probe at this time for a bull market in commodities stocks.

In the spring of 2000, the NASDAQ crashed, as shown in Figure 3.3, and the public's sentiment changed from euphoria to despair. To illustrate how wild it was, a friend of mine had made a great deal of profit trading personal money and was thinking of opening a hedge fund due to his success. He quickly had to abandon his idea as prices melted. I realized that the bears I had been reading, who had been wrong on prices for so long, were finally correct.

Fortunately, I also had a great deal of my personal money in cash at the time of the crash, and thus had money available to invest. It seemed

FIGURE 3.3 A very familiar chart—the NASDAQ Composite index. Note its price action in the year 2000. (*Source:* © TradeStation® 1991–2006. All rights reserved.)

logical that the views of the bears were likely to hold sway for a while, because as the saying goes, "Even a broken clock is right twice a day." The broader market's season had temporarily changed from summer to winter, and I had already read a great deal about precious metals and commodities stocks during the tech stock run-up. I had read:

- How commodities were at multiyear lows.
- How gold had been in a bear market for nearly 20 years.
- How commodities generally did well when the stock market did poorly.

Valuations seemed so low that I figured I would almost be a fool not to invest in something gold or commodities related. So in late 2000 I invested in the shares of a South African gold mining company, some of whose shares I still own. This company is a gold mining giant in a country that's a giant producer of gold. The stock had been pummeled and was trading around multiyear lows. The gold mining industry was relatively tiny at the time in terms of market cap, and I was aware that even a small amount of institutional interest could take industry stocks to unprecedented heights. Finally, the company was not a major hedger of its forward production of gold, compared to some other major companies at the time. This meant that it was well positioned to participate in the upside of a gold rally. So I bought some stock, sizing my position and keeping a mental stop in mind to get out if I was wrong. The stock soon moved into the money, and I foolishly scaled out of some of my position during its rise. I realized, though, that this was a mistake based on the long-term outlook for gold, so I hung onto the remainder of my position. The month after I had bought this stock I then bought some shares of an New York Stock Exchange (NYSE) traded closed end fund that mainly invests in South African gold mining companies.

I figured that at the very least, the bull market in gold had years to run, since its bear market had dragged on for so long. Conversely, the bull market in stocks had already run for about two decades. The ongoing bear market in Japan provided me with a reminder of what can happen to a formerly hot bull market, namely extended periods of sideways and downwards movement with no end in sight. So by buying precious metals stocks at that time, I essentially saw myself as buying the stock market around 1982 or so. My horizon was for years. Gold was around $270 and some of the bulls in gold had predictions north of $500 even back then.

As I had learned from the recent bull market in stocks, P/Es wouldn't matter much when a bull market was underway in earnest. The Amazon dot-coms and Yahoo!s of the world had already proved that to me. Furthermore, if gold itself actually began to rise, I had read arguments that gold stocks could potentially behave like perpetual call options on gold itself. Gold mining companies had a certain cost of extracting the metal from the ground, say $230 an ounce or so. In a simplistic illustration, if gold was at $280 an ounce and a company was making $50 an ounce gross profit off it, with gold at $330 an ounce their gross profit might approximately double (assuming no complicated hedging procedures and ignoring other factors). Did this mean that the stock's price would have to double to keep its P/E the same? Not necessarily, but it was a possibility that seemed tantalizing nonetheless. Of course, there might be a possibility of new producers coming online to take advantage of the higher prices, but the industry had become very consolidated over the bear market, and the Bre-X Mining scandal and central bank sales had further dampened the mood. It seemed like a low-risk play to me, even though prices were depressed. Feelings in the contrarian camp ran strong around gold's trough. The following quote, from Adam Hamilton's April 27, 2001, article called "The Great Commodities Bull of the 00's," illustrates this perfectly:

> *From where is the next mega-bull going to emerge and stampede to undreamed of heights in the coming decade? We believe there is a very high probability that the answer is COMMODITIES. . . .*

Commodities are hated and loathed right now by conventional investors. Commodities are out of favor. Commodities are not sexy. Commodities are not lusted after at the moment. Capital has abandoned commodities. It is enough to warm the contrarian heart![41]

The bull market in gold stocks began to strengthen, and silver also happened to be drifting up. I noticed that there were very few pure silver plays around, so I bought a Canadian silver stock in 2002 and a U.S. silver stock in 2003. I saw it as a simple supply/demand issue. There weren't a lot of silver company shares around, and if the bull market was about to heat up even further, they would have to move up. Gold and silver had skyrocketed together about two decades ago, and some electronic newsletter writers seemed to think that the commodities supply/demand equation in silver was even better than in gold. I made some sales in both of these stocks after my initial purchases but continued to carry core positions.

The bull market in gold and silver stocks progressed further, and then stalled. Due to the long-term nature of my views and the fact that I was well in-the-money on several positions, I continued to hold my core positions. Figure 3.4 shows the price action of the AMEX Gold Bugs Index over the past few years.

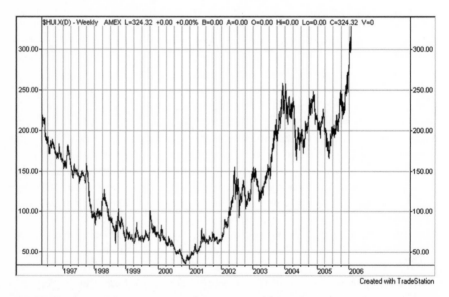

FIGURE 3.4 The reversal from bear market to bull market in gold stocks, as represented by the AMEX Gold Bugs Index (symbol: HUI). Contrast the NASDAQ Composite's action after its 2000 peak to the action of the AMEX Gold Bugs Index around the same time. (*Source:* © TradeStation® 1991–2006. All rights reserved.)

I still read the wise commentary of Jim Puplava, creator of the Web site www.financialsense.com. Jim Puplava had succinctly reasoned why a major bull market in commodities was underway,[42] so I began to consider buying other types of commodities stocks to diversify while participating in the move. In 2002 and 2003, the Commodities Research Bureau (CRB) Index, which is heavily weighted toward energy, had rallied strongly. Multiple commodities now had upward momentum. A secular bull market was clearly underway. I invested in four separate oil and gas stocks in March and April 2004, some of which I reduced my positions in due to a drop soon after my initial purchases. I also entered a palladium stock around the same time, selling a little afterward but also holding onto a core position (which performed relatively poorly afterward). A year later in 2005, I added to my energy stocks position, buying the stocks of three other energy related companies. Figure 3.5 is a chart of the AMEX Oil and Gas Index.

As of this writing the CRB Index continues to hold, and I continue to hold many investments in commodity related stocks. Gold has more than doubled from its 1999 low, recently reaching a two decade high over $650 an ounce (as of May 2006).

FIGURE 3.5 The AMEX Oil and Gas Index (symbol: XOI) breaks out of congestion into a clear bull market, adding fuel to the commodities stocks boom. (*Source:* © TradeStation® 1991–2006. All rights reserved.)

I learned the following lessons about trading equity trends from my experience:

- The longer term the opportunity you identify, the better. If your horizon is on the order of years, you can afford to move into an opportunity cautiously, and wait for some confirmation of the move. Trading with a long-term horizon reduces commission and slippage costs compared to frequent trading, and you also receive the benefits of any dividends on stocks you hold. There is also a cushion of profits if you are right, which can dramatically embolden your trading and your willingness to absorb volatility. With a long-term investment horizon, even if you make the mistake of selling part of a winning position on its way up, you can always afford to reenter the market. This was proved over and over again in the recent equities bull market.
- You have to be prepared for significant volatility in the open profits in your account. The only way to endure this is to believe in why you own what you own. I waited through a sideways market in precious metals stocks for nearly two years, during which time the AMEX Gold Bugs Index (symbol: HUI) was stuck between 163.81 and 258.6. However, my time horizon for the move was longer, so I held. The HUI Index is now above 320. I hold commodities stocks on the belief that the commodities bull will last at least half as long as the two decade bull market in stocks. This opinion means that I had to sit through a rapid drawdown in my account when the XOI Index (AMEX Oil and Gas Index) cratered 10 percent in a matter of days in October 2005. As oil and gas stocks began their recovery, I bought shares of an energy ETF on an intermediate-term technical basis, effectively adding to my commodities stocks position.
- I also learned not to take on any level of risk that I was uncomfortable with. My advice is to size all your positions appropriately according to the risk you are willing to take. If you can't realistically handle a theoretical loss that you might be exposed to, use a smaller position size if you haven't entered the market yet, or consider reducing an existing position if you have.

As the bull market in commodities continues to play itself out, I plan to reevaluate the situation periodically. Eventually, if we come to the level of euphoria that we saw in the latter part of the tech bull market, my hope is to recognize the situation based on my previous experience and begin placing technical stops. Alternatively, if the bull market suddenly and dramatically reverses itself before then and sentiment changes, I certainly plan not to allow the open profits I have accumulated to turn negative before liquidating.

This has been my experience with long-term trend following. It requires a constant lookout for long-term profit opportunities around you and a great deal of comfort with your reasons for picking positions. To broaden my perspectives, I read the opinions of electronic newsletter writers and pay some attention to the progress of previously battered markets such as Japan and Brazil, the latter of which I invested in 2005 via an ETF. I keep on the lookout for extended bear markets that may be close to turning, or market situations where prospects seem likely to be positive for an extended period of time, because to me these situations can be traded with more room for error than a difficult-to-capture statistical anomaly in the S&P 500. In this way, I am comfortable with what I buy and feel a degree of safety when I encounter drawdowns because of my longer-term horizon. My experience is not exactly quantifiable, but it shows you the thought process, mistakes, and so on that I made in trading a long-term secular trend. I hope that you will be able to learn from this section the thought processes necessary to embark on your own journey.

Based on my trading experiences and philosophies, I developed methods of my own to analyze and/or trade equity trends, which I shortly present. I have developed or adapted these methods to enable me to participate in the upside of the broader market in a disciplined manner while limiting my risk. I am currently investing only a fraction of my money based on some of these purely technical methods and recommend once again that you do your own due diligence.

PART II

Trend Trading Tactics

CHAPTER 4

Three-Dimensional Technical Analysis

BASIC TREND FOLLOWING INDICATORS: TWO-DIMENSIONAL TECHNICAL ANALYSIS

I have developed technical trend trading methods to enable me to enter stocks on a short-term basis whose fundamentals I am not as convinced of as in my previous commodities stocks example. Tech stocks in general are one such group. Whereas I see the commodities bull market as being in its early stages, the dramatic run-up and subsequent crash of tech stocks in the 1990s indicated to me that although the sector might still have tremendous price appreciation potential, I should exercise caution when trading it. So I continue to hold commodities stocks, but have developed my own technical methods to analyze and trade tech and other stocks that generally move with the broader market. To do this I first defined an objective method of identifying a stock market trend for myself. When the market enters what I have defined as an objective uptrend, I take this as a signal that I can buy stocks or ETFs that I believe will be outstanding performers for the trend's duration. When the market signals an objective downtrend, I take this as a signal to exit any stocks I am holding on this short-term trend following basis. Trading with a similar method means that your success will lie largely in your stock picking prowess, and it can also be very volatile, but it is an example of how you can time the market short-term.

The Power of Simplicity

I do not use very complex indicators when trading, because I believe that technical indicators that are too complex can be distractions from the trading process. According to Jesse Livermore:

> *I should say that a chart helps those who can read it, or rather who can assimilate what they read. The average chart reader, however, is apt to become obsessed with the notion that the dips and peaks and primary and secondary movements are all there is to stock specula- tion. If he pushes his confidence to its logical limit he is likely to go broke.*[1]

In the heat of battle, you do not want to spend a great deal of time checking whether the rate of change (ROC) of stock ABCD is above such and such value while its relative strength indicator (RSI) is above another value and its average directional movement index (ADX) is above a third value. As an individual trader, you need simple trading rules—so simple that they are idiot-proof and can be written on the back of an envelope. Simplicity is a powerful thing. A simple method of trad- ing a logical insight is easier to understand and thus easier to stick with. It requires less maintenance work than a more complex method. Fur- thermore, if you initially practice simple technical trading methods, you will quickly find out whether you have the ability to stick with a more complex method. A trend following strategy may not be the world's best method for managing an existing position, but it is a very good one that is definitely worth learning about. Let's examine some trend following indicators now.

Donchian Channels (or Bands)

Donchian channels (also known as Donchian bands or price channels) are one of the simplest trend following technical indicators. If you plot the se- ries of N-period highs and N-period lows on a stock chart (connecting the dots within each respective series), you get an envelope that surrounds price, known as a high-low envelope or Donchian channel. Richard Donchian was a revolutionary commodity futures trader who came up with many powerful concepts that are taken for granted in trend following today.[2] A Donchian channel consists of an upper and a lower Donchian band, with the upper band consisting of the series of N-period highs and the lower band consisting of the series of N-period lows. Figure 4.1 shows a sample Donchian channel.

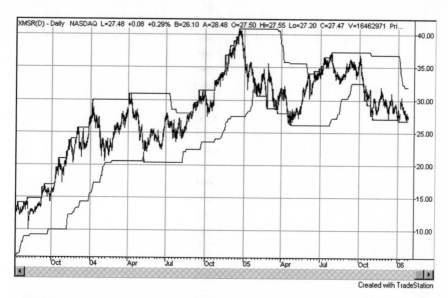

FIGURE 4.1 A 63-day Donchian channel around XM Satellite Radio (symbol: XMSR). (*Source:* © TradeStation® 1991–2006. All rights reserved.)

To construct an N-day Donchian channel, the following method should be used:[3]

- Upper Donchian band value for the current period is the highest high of the *past* N periods (not including the current period).
- Lower Donchian band value for the current period is the lowest low of the *past* N periods (not including the current period).

Please note that although you may construct Donchian channels that include prices from the current period, doing so will lead to difficulties in determining when prices break through the bands. Here is why. Imagine that a stock's highest high over the past 30 days *including* today is $50 when the market opens at $49. The stock then immediately rockets up from $49 through $50, reaching a high of $50.35. This high of $50.35 is also a new high for the past 30 days including today, since it is higher than $50. Thus, if your upper Donchian band is calculated by including today's high, then your upper band value will start off the day at a value of $50, but *shift intraday* to a value of $50.35. Clearly, if you include prices from the current period in your calculation of the bands, there is no way that price will be able to break out beyond the bands, as they will simply adjust if any new intraday highs or lows happen to be new highs for the period that you are watching. Therefore, it makes more sense to use the prices of the *past* N periods, *excluding the current period*, when calculating the value of a Donchian band.

An alternative method of constructing Donchian bands is to use opening or closing data only. This is useful if you are unable to watch prices closely intraday. For example, using opening prices allows you only to make a trade soon after you observe what the opening price of a particular day is. You may still experience some slippage, though, since prices often move rapidly around the open. Therefore, this method is probably better used on a time horizon where such slippage is likely to have minimal impact on your returns. Donchian bands based on closing prices only may be constructed as follows:

- Upper Donchian band: The highest close of the past N periods (not including the current period).
- Lower Donchian band: The lowest close of the past N periods (not including the current period).

Note that this rather simple refinement means that you will need less data to calculate the values of the bands. Rather than following the highs and lows for each day, you will use closing prices exclusively. This means that prices may sometimes break through your Donchian bands *intraday*. However, since you will be using opening or closing prices only, you would not trade based on those intraday breaches, but rather only on what the respective opening or closing value ends up being! Using opening or closing prices exclusively in your calculations can also allow you to trade instruments for which prices are published once daily, such as mutual funds. You essentially observe prices at fixed time intervals, and use the prices you observe to calculate your bands. If you use intraday highs and lows in your calculations, you are likely to pick prices that were likely barely touched during the day, and also occurred at irregular time intervals from one another.

You can trade with Donchian bands constructed using intraday highs and lows by:

- Buying when price makes an intraday breakout (by one tick) above the upper Donchian band.
- Selling when price makes an intraday breakdown (by one tick) below the lower Donchian band.
- If you are already long because of a previous buy signal, you ignore subsequent buy signals. Conversely if you are already flat because of a previous sell signal, you ignore subsequent sell signals.

I illustrate this process in Figure 4.2.

S(D) - Daily NYSE L=23.33 -0.37 -1.56% B=0.00 A=0.00 O=23.57 Hi=23.57 Lo=23.24 C=23.33 V=1777700 Price Channel (...

FIGURE 4.2 Donchian buy and sell signals on a sample stock chart with properly drawn Donchian bands. (*Source:* © TradeStation® 1991–2006. All rights reserved.)

If your bands are constructed from opening prices only, you may instead

- Buy immediately after today's open if today's open exceeds the upper Donchian band constructed from the openings of the last N days.
- Sell immediately after today's open if today's open is below the lower Donchian band constructed from the openings of the last N days.

If your bands are constructed from closing prices only, you may instead

- Buy immediately on tomorrow's close (or alternatively tomorrow's open) if today's close exceeds the upper Donchian band constructed from the closes of the *previous* N days.
- Sell immediately on tomorrow's close (or alternatively tomorrow's open) if today's close is below the lower Donchian band constructed from the closes of the previous N days.

Of course these guidelines are very simplistic, and would have to be refined further to realistically trade. However, Donchian channels are a basic technical building block that can be incorporated into a wide variety of trading rules. Even though Donchian bands are easy to calculate, it is clear that application of them in trading involves details that can easily become complex. This is why I prefer to stick with simple indicators in my trading.

No rule says you have to chase prices on both sides of a trade by buying new N-day highs and selling new N-day lows all the time. What if you do not wish to chase prices when entering a stock? Perhaps your research has uncovered what you think to be a profitable opportunity that you are ready to act on. However, you don't trust yourself to time your exit perfectly, because you know that there is no way that you will be able to know the top or bottom of the move you expect. In this case, you may set a fixed stop that holds until price *either* makes a new N-day low *or* until your fixed stop is triggered, as shown in Figure 4.3. In other words you would:

- Buy based on your own proprietary criteria, arrived at through research.
- Sell either when (whichever comes first):

    Price makes an intraday breakdown (by one tick) below the lower Donchian band.

    OR price makes an intraday breakdown (by one tick) below a fixed stop-loss level.

Clearly in the Figure 4.3 scenario, you are allowing your profits significant room to run, while limiting your losses to fixed amounts.

George Lane's Stochastic and Larry Williams's %R

The Stochastic and a Different Way to Use It   The stochastic is an ingenious price strength indicator developed by George Lane that tells you where a stock is relative to the range of its N-day high and low. For example, if a stock had a range of 10 to 20 over N days, but is currently at 15, the %K value of the N-day stochastic would tell you that the stock is halfway between 10 and 20. If the stock happens to be at 17.50, the %K value would tell you it is $^3/_4$ of the way to the high of 20. If the stock is at 12.50, %K would tell you it is $^1/_4$ of the way to the high of 20, and so on. The %K value is often accompanied by a %D value, which is a moving average of the information given by the %K indicator.[4]

The %K value is usually calculated:[5]

%K = 100 × [Today's Last Price – Lowest Price of the Past N Days (including Today)] / [Highest Price of the Past N Days (including Today) – Lowest Price of the Past N Days (including today)]

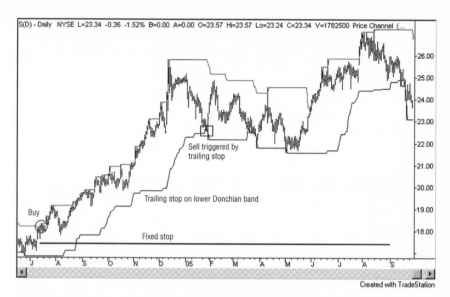

FIGURE 4.3 Buy and sell signals on a sample stock chart with a fixed stop-loss level and lower Donchian band only. (*Source:* © TradeStation® 1991–2006. All rights reserved.)

Note that the stochastic will never exceed a value of 100 with this definition. If price makes a new N-day high on a particular day, it simply expands the range that the stochastic is calculated over, and the stochastic temporarily hits 100 when the new high is made. The %D moving average of the stochastic complicates things unnecessarily in my view, so I exclude it in my mention of the stochastic going forward. In other words: My mention of a stochastic going forward will refer only to its %K value.

The stochastic is often used to signal overbought levels above 80, where it is close to the top of its N-day range, and oversold levels below 20, where it is close to the bottom of its N-day range. The concepts of overbought and oversold are questionable to a trend following trader, however, as trend following traders try to profit from continuations rather than reversals of trends. Thus, a trend following trader can use the stochastic indicator in a manner similar to Donchian bands, for example, buying on the next day's close when %K closes over the 80 level (on its way from the 20 level) and selling on the next day's close when %K crosses below the 20 level (on its way from the 80 level). I illustrate this process in Figure 4.4.

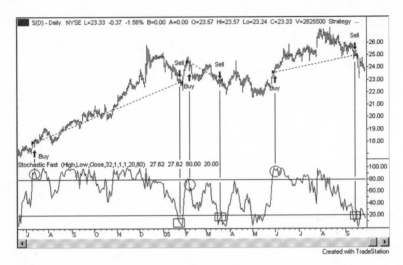

FIGURE 4.4 Using the stochastic as a trend following indicator. (*Source:* © TradeStation® 1991–2006. All rights reserved.)

Using a Periodic Snapshot of the Stochastic to Trade In order to use stochastics to time actual trades, we once again have to be careful about how and when we read it. For example, in the preceding calculation, the stochastic's value will change intraday, and may sometimes bob up and down around a trigger level such as 80 that you wish to use for a trade. You can avoid ambiguity in this instance by defining a *snapshot* time at which you will follow the instructions of the indicator. For example, you may decide to make trades based on what the stochastic's value is at the opening each day or noon each day. The latter method will of course be more difficult to study for long periods into the past (i.e., finding extensive records of stock price at noon each day might be difficult). You may also check the value of the stochastic after the market's close on each day to see if it signals you to trade, and then if it does, you could trade, for example, on the next day's open or the next day's close.

Using Prices Separated by Fixed Time Intervals to Calculate the Stochastic You may also define a stochastic that does not change intraday by using opening prices only or closing prices only to calculate it, as follows:

$$\%K = 100 \times [\text{Today's Open} - \text{Lowest Open of the Past N Days (including Today)}] / [\text{Highest Open of the Past N Days (including Today)} - \text{Lowest Open of the Past N Days (including Today)}]$$

You may also exclude today's prices from certain areas of the stochastic calculation, which would allow you to use it if it breaks through a level intraday. Here is one such example:

$$\%K = 100 \times [\text{ Last Price} - \text{Lowest Price of the Past N Days}$$
$$(excluding \text{ Today})] / [\text{ Highest Price of the Past N Days}$$
$$(excluding \text{ Today}) - \text{Lowest Price of the Past N Days}$$
$$(excluding \text{ Today})]$$

This particular method will sometimes yield negative %K values or %K values that exceed 100, albeit temporarily. Thus, any band value from 0 to 100 may be used as a trigger level for an intraday trade.

Sometimes using this method, however, you may be unsure if the stochastic broke above a certain trigger level for a trade since only its last price will be shown (i.e., it may break above a trigger level and fall back intraday). To see if it did indeed pass through a certain price, you may substitute either the current day's high or the current day's low in place of Last Price in the preceding equation. This will yield the high and low values of the stochastic for that day, respectively. Note using this method that a breakout above the 100 band is the same as the stock making a new N-day high, that is, breaking out above an upper N-day Donchian band. In other words, the stochastic is closely related to Donchian bands.

Larry Williams's %R   Larry Williams's %R[6] is an alternative method of determining where a stock is trading within its N-day range. To calculate %R:

$$\%R = 100 \times [\text{ Highest Price of the Past N Days (including Today)}$$
$$- \text{Today's Last Price}] \div [\text{Highest Price of the Past N Days}$$
$$(\text{including Today}) - \text{Lowest Price of the Past N Days}$$
$$(\text{including Today})]$$

This is very similar to the stochastic calculation except that rather than subtracting "Today's Last Price" from the "Lowest Price of the Past N Days (including Today)" in this equation's numerator, we instead subtract "Highest Price of the Past N Days (including Today)" from "Today's Last Price." This yields similar information to the stochastic on a reversed scale. That is, if a stock is trading around the low end of the range, it will have a %K value close to 0 but a %R value close to 100, and vice versa. Thus, the scale for %R is usually vertically flipped so that 0 is high and 100 is low. Analogous to %K, the 20 and 80 bands in Williams's %R may also be used as trade triggers in a trend following strategy.

Other Trend Following Indicators

Bollinger Bands   The famous technical analyst John Bollinger developed what have become known as Bollinger bands. We may construct Bollinger bands for trading purposes as follows (excluding today's prices from our calculations).

- Upper Bollinger band: The moving average of the past N periods (not including the current period) PLUS twice the standard deviation of the past N closing prices (not including the closing price of the current period).
- Lower Bollinger band: The moving average of the past N periods (not including the current period) MINUS twice the standard deviation of the past N closing prices (not including the closing price of the current period).

The distance between Bollinger bands expands and contracts based on the standard deviation of prices over the period being used. Although Bollinger bands may be used to time trades in a similar manner to Donchian bands (i.e., buying breakouts and selling breakdowns), some issues may arise if doing this. For example, let's say that you use the trading rules:

1. Buy when price makes an intraday breakout (by one tick) above the upper Bollinger band.
2. Hold position and sell when price makes an intraday breakdown (by one tick) below the lower Bollinger band.
3. Repeat.

Although this method may make sense in some cases, Bollinger bands sometimes exhibit a characteristic that Donchian bands do not. Namely, a lower Donchian band will never drop unless price breaks below it first, as shown in Figure 4.5, and an upper Donchian band will never rise unless price breaks above it first. The lower *Bollinger* band, on the other hand, may sometimes drop even when price has not broken down through it first, as shown in Figure 4.6.

This means that if you want to use the lower Bollinger band as a trailing stop level, you may sometimes find yourself in the unusual situation in which your stop is lowered further as the stock drops toward it. Therefore, you can't use Bollinger bands as trailing stops without the use of an additional fixed stop; otherwise your perceived risk might actually increase in the middle of a trade! Thus, you may decide that if price breaks

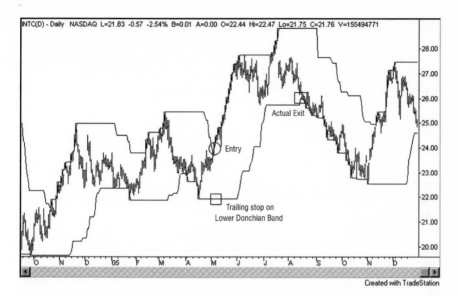

FIGURE 4.5 Lower Donchian bands cannot drop before price falls through them. (*Source:* © TradeStation® 1991–2006. All rights reserved.)

FIGURE 4.6 Lower Bollinger bands can drop *before* price falls through them. (*Source:* © TradeStation® 1991–2006. All rights reserved.)

down through *either* a fixed stop level *or* the lower Bollinger band first, then you will exit.

Technical Curves   Next, let's discuss the various curves that some traders use for trend following purposes. The most common example is the simple moving average, which is just an average of a stock's closing prices over the past N days. Once again, to calculate today's N-day moving average for trading purposes, you can exclude today's prices from the average and take the average of the closing prices of the previous N days. Alternatively, you may use an N-day moving average of *opening* prices only, which will stay at a fixed value intraday.

If you use a single line or a curve to time your trades, and decide that you want to be long above the line and flat below the line, you can easily run into a situation where you are whipsawed in and out of the market quite frequently. With moving averages it is just too simplistic to say that one should buy when price rises above the moving average and then sell when price falls below the moving average—as this may happen multiple times within the same trading session! Even if you use a snapshot of price to trade, for example trading based only on whether price closes above or below a moving average, you may easily find yourself getting whipsawed several periods in a row. For this reason, additional buy and sell rules must be imposed on a simple moving average so that it can be used for trend following without a lunatic number of whipsaws. One such method may be to create simple percentage bands around a moving average, for example at 1.02 and 0.98 times the average, respectively. These bands would then be used to trade in a manner similar to Donchian bands. Bollinger bands are a more complex variation of this simple method; the latter leads to less volatility in the shape of the bands. The possibilities for creating bands around a simple moving average are limited only by the imagination. Just about anything can be done, but keep in mind that as your eyes light up about how great these indicators might be, the market will keep on just being itself. The market does not know that technical indicators exist, so you may just be complicating things unnecessarily by using more sophisticated indicators.

Trend followers past and present have also sometimes used double moving averages (with different calculation periods) to time their entries into or out of a stock. The idea is that if the moving average with the shorter period (also known as the "faster" moving average) crosses above the moving average with the longer period (the "slower" moving average), a buy signal is generated. If the fast moving average falls below the slow moving average, a sell signal would conversely be generated. The use of a slow moving average in place of price itself helps to prevent excessive whipsawing. Of course, following two price averages is more complicated than following a single one, increasing the chances for confusion. In my opinion, the only advantage of using more complex indicators might be to prevent others from mimicking or anticipating what you are doing. However, if you trade small size, this should not be a concern.

Several other types of channels or curves, such as Keltner channels and exponential moving averages, may also be constructed from a price series. The one feature that any such innovative bands will share is being more complex than Donchian bands, whose values require no involved mathematics to calculate. For example, moving averages require a summation of the past N-days prices, while Donchian bands simply require you to pick the highest or the lowest price.

Bollinger bands require the calculation of both the moving average *and* the standard deviation of price over a certain period. You alone can decide the level of complexity of the indicators that you wish to use. However, the market does what it does, and these indicators are only tools, not holy grails, so the simpler the ones you trade with, the better, in my opinion.

Trend Following Patterns

Peak and Trough Patterns Nicholas Darvas's somewhat complicated method of identifying box tops and box bottoms can be broken down into what I call N-day peak patterns and N-day trough patterns, with the N specifying the number of days that defines the pattern. Here's how they would work in practice.

> Peak patterns and trough patterns are simple methods of objectively defining local highs and local lows in a stock, without the need to specify the tops or bottoms of individual box like channels as Darvas did.

First, specify the number of days, N, that your pattern will be defined by. An N-day peak pattern occurs if:

- At least N *full* days pass *after* the day on which a high price (the "peak") is made, during which the peak is not exceeded (although it may be equaled).
- AND if at least N *full* days have passed *before* the day on which the peak *occurs*, during which prices do not exceed the peak.
- So in general, *at least* $(2N + 1)$ full days must pass for an N-day peak (or trough) pattern to be definable as such.

In other words, for a 5-day peak pattern, at least $[(5 \times 2) + 1] = 11$ full days must pass for it to be definable. The peak in this case would occur on the middle day, day 6. No prices on days 1–5, and days 7–11 can exceed the high price on the peak day (day 6); otherwise the pattern is not valid. Furthermore, since this particular pattern requires 11 days to define it, only on day 12 (i.e., the sixth day after the day on which the peak occurs) would the pattern be considered defined. Note also that this definition means that prices on days 1–5 and days 7–11 may *equal* the peak price without exceeding it, although you may of course define a pattern, such that this is not the case. On any day starting from day 12 onward (e.g., day 12, day 14, day 25, etc.), a breakout above the peak price would be considered an objectively defined "breakout." If you buy this breakout, you will then be buying the stock as price makes a "higher high." The peak pattern may thus be used as a trend following entry timing method, as shown in Figure 4.7.

At least N full days must have passed *before* the peak day, in which prices did not exceed the peak, to satisfy one requirement of defining a peak pattern. However, in practice price may have failed to exceed the peak for more than this number of days. For example, with a 3-day peak pattern, 50 full days might have passed before the day on which the peak occurs on which all prices were lower than the peak. After the day on which the peak occurs, only three subsequent full days must pass with lower prices than the peak for the pattern to be established.

FIGURE 4.7 A series of 5-day peak patterns (five full days after the peak must pass before they are identifiable). (*Source:* © TradeStation® 1991–2006. All rights reserved.)

The trough pattern is the exact opposite of the peak pattern, as shown in Figure 4.8. Thus, the simplest 5-day trough pattern would analogously require 11 days to define. The lowest price in the pattern ("the trough") occurs on the middle day, day 6. No prices on days 1–5 and 7–11 can be lower than the trough price, otherwise the pattern is not valid. The pattern is thus only definable from day 12 (i.e., the sixth day after the day on which the peak occurs) forward.

Once a peak or trough pattern is defined, an objective and easily observable peak or trough will exist on a stock chart. This is much different from drawing a trendline based on eyeballing peaks or troughs on a chart, which is largely subject to the whims of the artist. You can use peak and trough patterns to time buys or sells, alone or in combination with other technical trading methods. For example, you might choose to:

1. Buy when price breaks out above an 8-day peak.
2. Count the number of days from the peak day to your entry day, for example, 14 days.
3. Sell your position if price makes a new 14-day low.

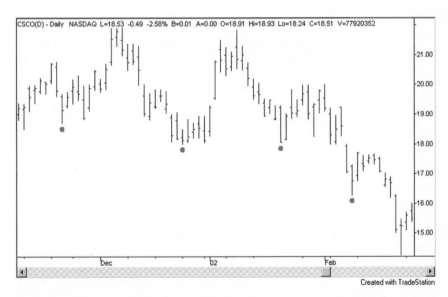

FIGURE 4.8 A series of 5-day trough patterns (five full days after the trough must pass before they are identifiable). (*Source:* © TradeStation® 1991–2006. All rights reserved.)

This method would combine a peak pattern breakout entry and a Donchian band breakdown exit. You may alternatively mix the periods of peak and trough patterns, for example:

1. Buy when price breaks out above an 8-day peak.

2. Count the number of days from the peak day to your entry day, for example, 14 days. If price breaks below the lowest price during that period (i.e., the 14-day period before your entry day), sell your position.

3. Otherwise, sell your position if price (after your entry) breaks down below a 4-day trough, ignoring all price action on days before your entry date when defining your trough.

4. This means that you must wait at least 8 full days after your entry day for price to establish a 4-day trough. Once the 4-day trough has been established, set your stop just below this level, and sell if price breaks below the level. If it does not, wait for a higher trough to be established, and raise your stop to this level, and so on.

Clearly, to apply technical analysis in real life, you need to be very precise about the criteria that must be satisfied in order for you to make trades.

MEASURING THE HERD EFFECT: THREE-DIMENSIONAL TECHNICAL ANALYSIS

Imagine a filing cabinet filled with folders containing stock price charts. You open the cabinet and pick up the chart of a stock that you are interested in. Its price looks mostly random, but seems to be slightly drifting up. Your analysis of this two-dimensional piece of paper tells you something about the public's perception of that stock, but not much. You then replace the chart and begin to look at other charts in the cabinet—perhaps stocks in the same industry, perhaps stocks in different industries. In so doing, you begin to notice similar upward drifting movement across multiple stocks; this is information that you could not possibly have gleaned from looking at one chart alone, and it tells you something about the group behavior and psychology of the investing public in general. Does the public like stocks? Do they like specific industries? Are investors making money? The answers to these questions will be hinted at in water cooler anecdotes, the tone of media headlines, and so on.

By analyzing the price action of multiple stocks simultaneously, you will have moved your technical analysis beyond simple two-dimensional analysis and into a third dimension (see box).

In three-dimensional technical analysis you focus not just on how *price* behaves over *time* in a single stock, but on similar information in *multiple stocks simultaneously.*

Now I am sure you realize that stock market averages like the Dow Jones Industrial Average neatly distill the prices of multiple stocks into a single, objective average. But how do you apply the price action of a market average to the trading of individual stocks? Simple eyeballing of charts is not objective enough to accomplish this. To apply your three-dimensional technical analysis to actual trading, you will have to remove all subjectivity from it, which I discuss shortly.

Three-dimensional technical analysis is often used by sophisticated participants in other markets such as the bond and derivatives markets. The "yield curve" is one such example. A yield curve is a curve that displays the yields of bonds of different maturities simultaneously. A bond's yield is directly related to its market price, coupon payment schedule, prevailing interest rates, and assumptions about future interest rates. For example, for Treasury debt instruments expiring in $1/4$, $1/2$, 1, 2, 5, 10 and 30 years, the yield curve may show yields of 3.8 percent, 4.1 percent, 4.4 percent, 4.6 percent, 4.8 percent, 4.9 percent and 5.0 percent, respectively. These different yield values can be linked together with an imaginary line to form a curve, which would be "upward sloping" in this case since at each consecutive point on the curve, the yield is higher. Yield curves of different shapes have different names, like "flat," "inverted," "humped," and so on, and analysts interpret the shapes differently.

In derivatives markets, where instruments have limited lives, three-dimensional technical analysis is also used by sophisticated participants. For example, crude oil is a single product, but futures contracts can be traded on it for delivery at different times in the future. The prices of futures contracts that expire at varying times in the future include assumptions about the costs of carrying the underlying instrument and other factors. For example, for crude oil futures contracts expiring in 1, 3, 5, 7, and 9 months, we might find prices of $60, $61, $62, $63, and $64 in the market. The futures markets even have terms for the shape of these forward curves. If a forward curve slopes upwards, so that prices for later expiring contracts are higher than prices for closer expiring contracts, the market is said to be in "contango." If the curve slopes downwards, so that prices for closer expiring contracts are higher than prices for further expiring contracts, the market is said to be in "backwardation."

Both bonds and derivatives have finite lifetimes and this dramatically differentiates them from equities, which have unlimited lifetimes. Note, however, that both yield curves and forward curves display information based on the *current* market values of multiple freely trading instruments simultaneously. In the normal stock market, there's no directly analogous time curve for individual stocks. However, the equity market has its own method of analyzing the price behavior of multiple stocks, in the form of market indices, which display an average of the prices of multiple stocks simultaneously. Market averages give an educational view of the group behavior of multiple stocks, but it is necessarily a biased view, depending on the choice of stocks in an average, the weightings of certain stocks, the rebalancing methods used, and so on. Most people watch the major averages mainly as a barometer of business conditions, spending little time on objective interpretation of the price action of the averages for their personal investing.

However, the pioneer of market averages, Charles Dow (and his successors), worked on developing methods to *interpret* the three-dimensional information given by the averages for use in trading. As Dow's methods were not quantified in exact detail, there is still room for differences of interpretation, which may make objective application of his methods to trading difficult. In an attempt to solve these issues, I have worked on methods defining exactly how to time trades based on the technical analysis of large numbers of stocks simultaneously, some of which I present in this chapter. As with any form of technical analysis, your application of these methods will have to be part science and part art.

WHY MIGHT ANALYZING MULTIPLE STOCKS SIMULTANEOUSLY BE MORE USEFUL THAN ANALYZING SINGLE STOCKS?

Over and over again throughout history, the public imagination becomes gripped with fads, like tulips,[7] Beanie Babies, or Internet stocks, which sometimes turn into buying panics. A hysterical buying frenzy occurs, sending prices through the roof, and creating temporary feelings of public euphoria. Charles Mackay's excellent book, *Extraordinary Popular Delusions and the Madness of Crowds*, gives many examples of this phenomenon. Although these buying frenzies often end in sorrow for those late to the party, they can be very profitable for those able to get in reasonably early and leave before the fun ends. Trend following is a method that can allow you to participate in some of the upside of these buying frenzies and avoid some of the downside of the subsequent selling frenzies (although it cannot save you from whipsaws along the way). To try to minimize whipsaws, you should focus your research on situations that you think have the potential to develop into major, sustained buying frenzies. Some of the main questions I consider when choosing markets to trade are:

- What industries (or country stock markets) are most likely to grip the public imagination next, possibly leading to buying frenzies or "runaway bull markets"?
- What industries are likely to continue being darlings of the public, causing them to outperform the broader market during its rallies?

Runaway moves do not happen overnight, so you have to develop longer-term views on the industries you study. To better understand how a move may turn into a runaway move, and you have to study how the public behaves in the different stages of bull and bear markets, so that you can alert yourself to clues that one may be underway or imminent. Books like Mackay's can help you in this pursuit. In other words, you have to compare or contrast public sentiment, the valuations you see in the marketplace, and so on with technical price action, which is an art rather than a science.[8]

In the depths of a bear market, negativity is rampant, volumes are low, and bullishness is ridiculed. For example, *BusinessWeek*'s cover headline on August 13, 1979, in the midst of a terrible bear market, was "The Death of Equities." Negativity abounded about the stock market around that time although fundamental valuations were low, but a new bull market was about to begin in a few years. Conversely, in the late 1990s, euphoria about the stock market could not be contained. Everyone was talking about the market, but tech stocks especially had grabbed the public's imagination. The public imagination can take stocks to unprecedented heights, and so you have to constantly strive to be aware of themes that the public might latch onto. In short, take notice of extreme public negativity or elation, and of clearly bullish price action that is considered suspect by many experts for a plethora of well-thought-out reasons (a situation called "climbing the wall of worry").

Since the end of public *negativity* toward an industry cannot be timed, I believe it is better to observe such bear market situations mostly from the sidelines until you see the beginnings of strong, sustained price action following a multiyear or even a multidecade period of low, choppy, or sideways prices and extreme disbelief or negativity. Using trend following trading strategies to enter a market at this point allows you to make each trade with the knowledge of what your maximum downside will be. You can also watch for signs that industries that have trudged along reasonably quietly have suddenly gripped the public imagination, and try to get on board those.

I do not mean by these statements that every bear market rally in a shunned industry should be bought. Timing the end of a bear market is extremely difficult, as anyone who owned gold stocks during most of the 1990s can attest to. Long-only trend following during a bear market can also lead a trader into massive and repeated whipsaws. Insight alone can guide you in your selections, because any advice I can give in this regard might be useless tomorrow. I have spent a lot of personal time trying to gain insights about herd behavior, because groupthink about multiple stocks in an industry or market has a higher potential of developing into runaway bull market situations that grip the public imagination than groupthink about a single stock.

Although an individual stock may be a darling, the public mind is much more likely to latch onto a class of stocks, or the prospects of an entire country, because more public money can be invested in these areas. The more people who are making or losing money in an area, the more people who will be talking about that area to others, feeding the effect. Thus, I believe in the use of technical analysis to objectively analyze the behavior of multiple stocks rather than single stocks. Three-dimensional technical analysis can be used to:

- Objectively monitor if the price action of certain industries is confirming your thesis about how they should behave.
- Define the beginnings or ends of trends in particular areas of the market with *objective* criteria.
- Time your trading in individual stocks based on industry or broad market price behavior rather than single stock action, thus attempting to trade in line with the public consensus.

BINARY TREND IDENTIFICATION METHODS FOR EQUITY INDICES

Objectively Defining Market Uptrends and Downtrends

One of the underlying themes of Dow Theory is that the motion of multiple stocks in the same direction (i.e., the averages) is a much more reliable indicator of the potential for individual stocks to continue in the same direction than the price series of the individual stocks themselves. Dow Theory advocates identification of the consensus trend, and then holding/trading in the same direction as the trend, allowing your portfolio to be buoyed by the rising tide of market sentiment. Since Dow Theory uses information beyond the price series of an individual stock to define when to hold stocks, it seems to be in direct opposition to the semistrong version of the efficient market hypothesis. It is clear, however, that sometimes individual industry trends (such as Internet stocks or energy stocks recently) can far outperform the market over the short term. So if a practitioner is continually able to identify the industries or asset classes most likely to outperform the market over the short term, he should theoretically be able to outperform the market over the long term.

In other words, repeated short-term portfolio concentration in industries or asset classes that one considers likely to outperform has the *potential* to outperform the market over the long term. As all major market or industry price trends must begin with the aggregate motion of multiple stocks, we need methods of objectively classifying the aggregate directional motions of stocks. There is no way of knowing if the next trend in an industry will be the big one; this is where your research comes in, but there are methods of identifying trends objectively. Dow Theory uses a partially subjective and somewhat complex method for identifying market trends. I introduce here some much simpler ways to identify these trends, all of which involve adapting standard trend following indicators to this use.

The first method that we can use is to adapt Donchian bands for use as a market trend indicator. To do this, using a 32-day Donchian period as an example, we *objectively define* market trends as follows. I use the NASDAQ Composite index as an example:

- Donchian market uptrend: Any period in which the NASDAQ Composite has more recently made a new 32-day high than a new 32-day low.
- Donchian market downtrend: Any period in which the NASDAQ Composite has more recently made a new 32-day low than a new 32-day high.

If the market is in an uptrend according to this definition, I say that the market is in a "32-day Donchian uptrend," or "Donchian uptrend" for short. If the market is in a downtrend according to this definition, I say that the market is in a "Donchian downtrend." Of course this also means that:

- A market uptrend *begins* (and the previous market downtrend ends) when the NASDAQ Composite makes the *first* new 32-day high following a previous 32-day low.
- A market downtrend *begins* (and the previous market uptrend ends) when the NASDAQ Composite makes the *first* new 32-day low following a previous 32-day high.

This forces the market to always exist in one of only two possible states: a market uptrend or a market downtrend. For balance, I show an example of this in Figure 4.9 that identifies trends relatively well, and another example in Figure 4.10 that identifies trends poorly. No other market states are possible under this definition. Now, of course market trends don't just switch abruptly from picture-perfect uptrends to picture-perfect downtrends, but at least this is an *objective* definition of market trends that we can work with going forward.

In my studies in this area I found that 32-day Donchian bands on the NASDAQ Composite seem to catch trending periods better than on the S&P 500. This may be because of the NASDAQ stock market's focus on (and the public's fascination with) technology, which may produce cleaner trends. It is also likely a characteristic of the particular time frame used. (See the box.)

The fact that this method might work well on a limited number of indices and time frames may be a result of *curve-fitting*. You should be aware of the dangers of curve-fitting when choosing to use a completely systematic trading method in which all aspects of your trading are automated, and you have no discretion in the process.

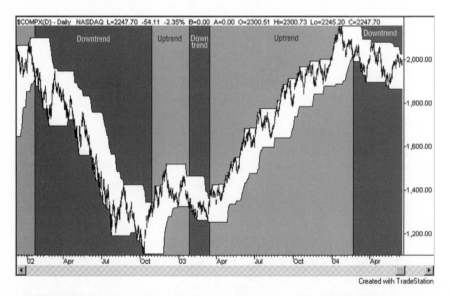

FIGURE 4.9 Objective identification of trending periods in the NASDAQ Composite index using 32-day Donchian bands, during a period where this method works relatively well. (*Source:* © TradeStation® 1991–2006. All rights reserved.)

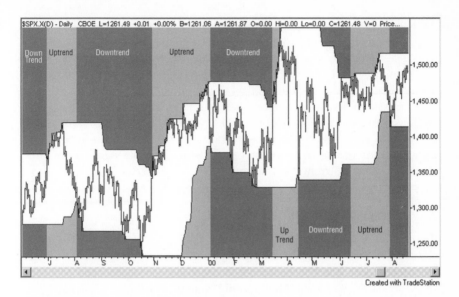

FIGURE 4.10 Objective identification of trending periods in the S&P 500 index using 32-day Donchian bands, during a period where this method does not work well. (*Source:* © TradeStation®1991–2006. All rights reserved.)

Although you may study how well a Donchian trend identification method identifies trends in different time frames, the fact that you may pick one that works perfectly today does not mean that it will work perfectly tomorrow; you may have just made a lucky guess. However, no matter how many time frames you study, at some point you will have to make a decision to commit your capital, because you will never find a perfect zero risk/tremendous reward opportunity. The underlying reason I might use a trend identification method like this on tech stocks is because I believe that the long-term upward drift of the market is likely to continue and that tech stocks will continue to excite the public imagination for the foreseeable future. This method would thus provide some guidelines for honing the timing of my trades.

Other bands such as Bollinger bands can be used for binary trend identification on the market in an analogous manner.

Fixed levels on a stochastic can also be used to objectively define market uptrends and downtrends, because the stochastic indicator is closely related to Donchian bands. I call these "stochastic uptrends" and "stochastic downtrends," respectively. Stochastic market trends can be defined as follows:

- Stochastic market uptrend: Any period in which the market's %K value has broken above 80 more recently than it has fallen below 20.

- Stochastic market downtrend: Any period in which the market's %K value has fallen below 20 more recently than it has broken above 80.

Remember that the stochastic simply tells you where a stock is trading in relation to the extremes of its N-day range. It is not rocket science, albeit the fancy name. Both stochastics and Donchian bands adjust spontaneously to the volatility of the market, something that tracking simple percentage advances or declines in the market is unable to accomplish. Donchian bands also tell you objectively which market highs or lows will signal a change of trend if surpassed.

A Double Trend Identification Filter

If you want to try to mimic Dow Theory more closely, you may choose to use a double trend identification filter to identify trends on both the Dow Industrials and the Dow Transports separately. For example, using a Donchian trend identification method you may say:

- If the Dow Industrials are in an uptrend (as defined by 63-day Donchian bands) AND the Dow Transports are also in an uptrend (as defined by 63-day Donchian bands), then a bull market is in effect.
- If the Dow Industrials are in a downtrend (as defined by 63-day Donchian bands) AND the Dow Transports are also in a downtrend (as defined by 63-day Donchian bands), then a bear market is in effect.
- In times when the trends of the Dow Industrials and the Dow Transports do not confirm each other, consider the previously existing bull market or bear market (as defined by the last joint confirmation of both indices) to be in effect.

This is a double filter that would identify a bull market for different periods than a single filter on the Dow Industrials would.

PILOT SIGNALS

Let's now explore how to apply an objective definition of a broad market trend to the trading of individual stocks. Both Dow and Livermore observed herd behavior in the markets, which pulled individual stocks along in the direction of the broader market. It has been said that a large portion of an individual stock's motion may be attributed to the market's action, and only a fraction to the stock itself. The existence of the herd effect thus paves the way for trading a stock using *price* signals EXTERNAL to the stock, which can have the following advantages.

- Timing your trades in a stock based on *fluid* prices (external to the stock) allows you to rapidly respond to changes in market conditions rather than waiting, for example, for new fundamental data to be released.
- Basing your actions in a stock on price signals external to that stock can reduce the amount of slippage that you'd encounter in the stock compared to using a trend following trading strategy on that stock's price series alone.
- Basing your actions in a stock on a *less choppy* external price signal can also reduce the whipsaws you would encounter by technically trading that stock based on its own prices!
- Basing your actions in a stock on an external, broader market price signal can provide stronger mental justification for holding a position. That is, your belief in the stock may be complemented by other stocks in the industry moving in your preferred direction. This means that multiple stocks in the industry are being bought and thus that the move has broad based momentum.

Going back to our definition of a Donchian market trend, let's give an example of how we would use this in actual trading. Let's say you know that an individual semiconductor stock, call it ABCD, generally tends to drift in the same direction as the NASDAQ Composite. However, ABCD is much more choppy than the NASDAQ Composite, so if you were to use a 32-day Donchian, long-only trend following strategy on ABCD alone (i.e., being long during ABCD uptrends and flat during ABCD downtrends), you would likely get whipsawed quite a bit.

The alternative is to time your trades in ABCD entirely based on the NASDAQ Composite's price action. I call this using the NASDAQ Composite as a "pilot signal," because it brings to mind a pilot flying through dense fog by relying on an external radio beacon to guide him. Since both the NASDAQ Composite and ABCD generally move in the same direction, it is reasonable to expect that over long periods of time in which the NASDAQ Composite drifts up, ABCD should also drift up. You will likely have to deal with more volatility in the ABCD position than you would if you held the NASDAQ Composite alone, however (and you will also be more exposed to sudden gap downs following negative news releases). For example, perhaps the NASDAQ Composite might move up 10 percent after the beginning of a Donchian uptrend before settling back to up 5 percent, at which point it goes into a Donchian downtrend. ABCD, on the other hand, might run up 30 percent before settling at a 20 percent gain during the same period. If you believe that ABCD will perform better than the NASDAQ during your holding period (and you are comfortable with the additional volatility), you buy.

So continuing with my example, you might then:

1. Buy ABCD if *the NASDAQ Composite* enters a 32-day Donchian uptrend.
2. Sell ABCD if *the NASDAQ Composite* enters a 32-day Donchian downtrend.
3. Optionally repeat the process.

I show an example of this with KLA-Tencor Corporation stock (symbol: KLAC) in Figure 4.11. In the figure, the NASDAQ Composite and its Donchian bands are in the upper price chart, while KLAC (without Donchian bands) is in the lower price chart.

Conversely, in Figure 4.12, I show an example of trading KLAC with its own Donchian bands. KLAC is shown in both the upper and the lower chart. In this particular case, you can see that technically trading KLAC with its own price signal adds an extra whipsaw trade during the period of the chart.

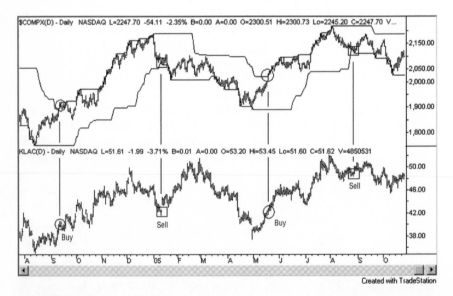

Created with TradeStation

FIGURE 4.11 Trading KLAC using 32-day Donchian bands on the NASDAQ Composite as a pilot signal. (*Source:* © TradeStation® 1991–2006. All rights reserved.)

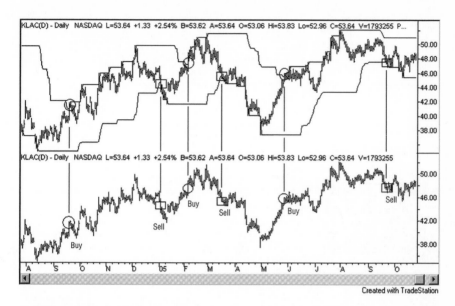

FIGURE 4.12 Trading KLAC using its own 32-day Donchian bands. (*Source:* © TradeStation® 1991–2006. All rights reserved.)

Alternatively, you could time your trades in KLAC using the NASDAQ Composite's stochastic, and for example:

1. Buy KLAC if the NASDAQ Composite's 32-day stochastic rises above 80 (after more recently rising above 20 rather than 80).
2. Sell KLAC if the NASDAQ Composite's 32-day stochastic falls below 20 (after more recently falling below 80 rather than 20).
3. Optionally repeat the process.

Figure 4.13 shows an example of doing this with the NASDAQ Composite's 32-day stochastic. The NASDAQ Composite's price chart is shown at the top of the picture, and its stochastic is shown at the bottom. KLAC's price chart is shown in the middle of the picture.

The NASDAQ Composite is a diversified average of thousands of stocks, reflecting the varied opinions and market intelligence of millions of investors worldwide. Therefore, its volatility is not as high as the volatilities of many of the individual stocks in it. Thus, you can use its price action as a pilot signal to try to profit from the extra *upside* volatility in an individual stock without getting whipsawed by the stock's characteristic choppiness. Of course you are also exposed to the possibility that the

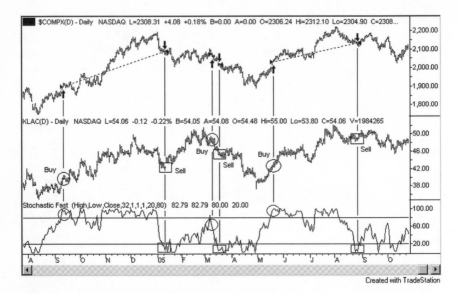

FIGURE 4.13 Trading KLAC using a 32-day stochastic on the NASDAQ Composite as a pilot signal. (*Source:* © TradeStation® 1991–2006. All rights reserved.)

close relationship between a stock you are trading and a broad market index you are using for a pilot signal may unexpectedly and dramatically unravel. Therefore, to trade this properly, you may want to add additional constraints such as fixed stops, which I get into later. The bottom line is that in many circumstances it is possible to trade a stock using an external index's price action as a guide.

Continuing with my example, stock ABCD will not be 100 percent correlated to the NASDAQ Composite, so it is conceivable that when a buy or sell signal is received based on the broader market entering an uptrend, that ABCD may be temporarily moving in the opposite direction, reducing entry slippage! Thus, using this method would prevent you from always chasing prices in ABCD, which increases your slippage. By trading ABCD with a pilot signal, some days you might buy ABCD while it is rising and other days you might buy ABCD while it is falling. Slippage can dramatically eat into your returns if you trade with a trend following strategy, and using a pilot signal has the potential to reduce it. The flip side is that the stock you are trading may enter a period where it does not respond very well to the pilot signal, so there are always tradeoffs.

You may also use a pilot signal to time *only* your exits from individual stock positions entered during a market uptrend. This allows you to enter a stock with any method you like during a market uptrend, and gives you the possibility of experiencing less whipsaws once in the position and reduced slippage when you exit. As an example, you might use the following filters and trading instructions:

1. Filter condition: It is acceptable to be long ABCD if the NASDAQ Composite is in a 32-day Donchian uptrend. Do NOT be long ABCD if the NASDAQ Composite enters or remains in a 32-day Donchian downtrend.

2. Go long ABCD if it makes a new 24-day high *while* the NASDAQ Composite is in a 32-day Donchian uptrend.

3. Set a fixed stop in ABCD at its 24-day low at your instant of entry. This stop does not move during the lifetime of your trade. Liquidate your ABCD position if your fixed stop is triggered.

4. If your fixed stop is triggered and you liquidate your position while the NASDAQ Composite is in a 32-day Donchian uptrend, reenter ABCD *only* if it makes a new 24-day high. Set a fixed stop again exactly as in 3, and repeat the process.

5. Liquidate any existing ABCD position if the NASDAQ Composite enters or remains in a 32-day Donchian downtrend.

If you want to trade a portfolio of multiple stocks, this method might also give you the advantage of not being fully invested during each whipsaw that the market happens to have. Wait for the market to enter an uptrend before buying, which you consider as a green light to own stocks, but still wait for each individual stock that you want to buy to show strength by making a new 24-day high. By waiting for each individual stock to make a new 24-day high before you enter it, you stagger your entry into investments across the portfolio, and thus should be fully invested only if a really strong market trend comes along that pulls each stock on your watchlist to a new 24-day high. Once in the markets, simply wait until your fixed stop in the stock is triggered, or until the market's trend switches from up to down, and then exit.

These are all variations on a theme. If trading with the use of a pilot signal, you can literally say to yourself, "I'm long stock ABCD because the market (and hopefully also stock ABCD) is in an objectively defined uptrend. Thus, multiple stocks besides stock ABCD are also trending up." Knowing that you're trading in agreement with an objectively defined market trend can be reassuring at times.

STOCHASTIC AVERAGING

It can be useful to use a broad market index's price as a pilot signal for trading individual stocks. But what if you want to trade stocks that aren't closely correlated to the broader market? What if there are a handful of stocks that tend to confirm one another's price action strongly, and you would be comfortable buying one of these stocks if there is a consensus in the price action of all of the stocks in this group? Stochastic averaging allows you to objectively track the behavior of smaller waves in the gigantic stock market sea.

The stochastic is a normalized function, because the stochastic of *any* stock can take on values only between 0 and 100. The %K value simply tells you where a stock is trading relative to the extremes of its N-day range. Thus, the information it provides about individual stock trends is directly comparable on the same scale whether you are dealing with a $3 stock, a $30 stock, or a $300 stock.

> Since the trend information contained in a stochastic is expressed on the same scale for all stocks, the stochastics of each stock in a basket of stocks can be averaged together to give you an objective picture of the trending state of that basket of stocks. I call this process *stochastic averaging*.

Stochastic averaging can be used to study the trend action of smaller groups of stocks than are usually contained in indices. Some broad market indices are weighted by market cap, some by price, and some by equal dollar weighting. Indices are also often periodically rebalanced by the index creators since index components change, and stock prices drift over time, dragging index weightings away from their original starting values. For example, if you invest equal amounts of money in two stocks today (i.e., 50 percent in each), but a year from now one stock has doubled while the other has halved, you will be 80 percent weighted in the stock that has doubled and 20 percent weighted in the stock that has halved. Indices may be periodically rebalanced to reduce the effects of weighting discrepancies like this. In addition to the selection process for index components, armies of analysts are required to take care of complexities such as updating certain index multipliers to adjust for stock splits, determining changes in an index's composition, and other issues. Indices are complex to maintain, and cannot capture certain nuances of market behavior. Due to stock price drift between rebalancing dates, all stocks will end up having different weights from their weights on the previous rebalancing date, so a broad market index may not necessarily give the most accurate picture of the average trending state of a group because the index may weight certain stocks more heavily than others.

A stochastic average, on the other hand, requires no rebalancing. It continually provides an objective average of the *trending* state of each individual component that is being averaged. By trending state, I mean the position of a stock relative to the extremes of its N-day range. Let's take a look at an example of this technical analysis technique with three different coal industry stocks, Arch Coal Inc. (symbol: ACI), Foundation Coal Holdings Inc. (symbol: FCL) and Massey Energy Company (symbol: MEE). In Figure 4.14, I show a price chart of Arch Coal Inc. superimposed with its stochastic (they share the same scale). Arch Coal Inc. trends up during most of the period shown, and as a result, its stochastic stays above 20 the entire time.

In Figure 4.15, I show a price chart of Foundation Coal Holdings Inc. superimposed with its 40-day stochastic. The general upward drift in this stock is interrupted by several significant drawbacks.

In Figure 4.16, I show a price chart of Massey Energy Company superimposed with its 40-day stochastic. This stock spends the most time of the three below the 20 level on the stochastic, and actually falls slightly over the period shown.

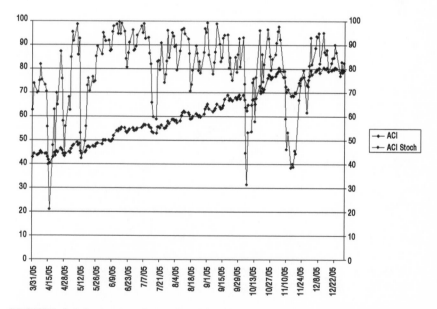

FIGURE 4.14 A price chart of Arch Coal Inc. (symbol: ACI) superimposed with its 40-day stochastic. (*Source:* Stock price data from Yahoo! Finance.)

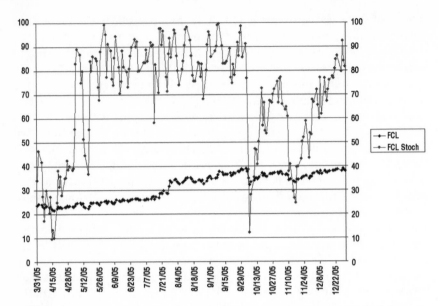

FIGURE 4.15 A price chart of Foundation Coal Holdings Inc. (symbol: FCL) superimposed with its 40-day stochastic. (*Source:* Stock price data from Yahoo! Finance.)

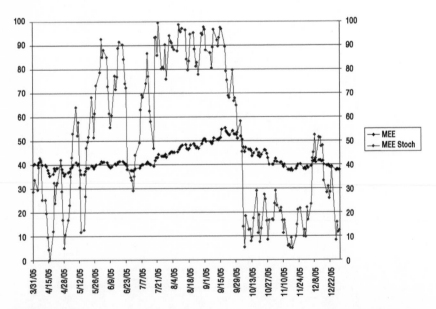

FIGURE 4.16 A price chart of Massey Energy Company (symbol: MEE) superimposed with its 40-day stochastic. (*Source:* Stock price data from Yahoo! Finance.)

It's clear that, even within an industry, there can be major differences in the price behavior of individual stocks. To get a consensus view of the trending behavior of these different stocks, there is no need to set up and maintain a three-stock index. You simply average the stochastics of the three stocks, as in Figure 4.17.

To average the stochastics of a group of stocks together, you simply average the stochastic (i.e., %K) values of the three stocks on each day to get an average value for that day. For example, if on a particular date, ACI's stochastic closed at 25, FCL's stochastic closed at 50, and MEE's stochastic closed at 75, the closing value of the stochastic average for that day would be (25 + 50 + 75) / 3 = 50. Note in Figure 4.17 the day on which the stochastic average of the three stocks rises above 80 for the first time, and the day on which it falls below 20 after this. If you were to buy *any* of the three stocks in the average on the day after the stochastic average rises above 80 for the first time, and then liquidate your position on the day after the stochastic average subsequently falls below 20, you would be able to catch a decent portion of the trends in all three stocks. In the case shown in Figure 4.17, you would also be able to avoid times in the market when the stocks do not exhibit a consensus in their price action.

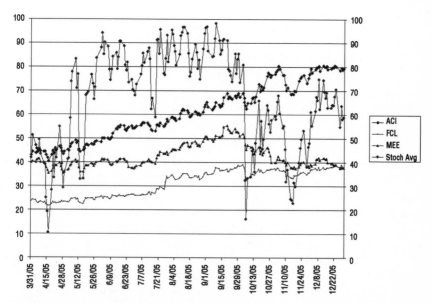

FIGURE 4.17 A 40-day *stochastic average* of Arch Coal Inc. (symbol: ACI), Foundation Coal Holdings Inc. (symbol: FCL), and Massey Energy Company (symbol: MEE). (*Source:* Stock price data from Yahoo! Finance.)

You, the trader, now have the power to choose the components of a basket of stocks whose aggregate trend state you wish to monitor, rather than exclusively watching the popular indices or having to create an entire index of your own from scratch. You may also alter the weightings of the individual components you use in a stochastic average. For example, you may average the stochastic of an energy stock like Chevron Corporation (symbol: CVX), the stochastic of the AMEX Oil and Gas Index (XOI), and the stochastic of the S&P 500 index, but weight the S&P 500 index twice as much as CVX and the XOI Index, respectively. Or you may weight the NASDAQ 100 Trust Shares (symbol: QQQQ) stochastic twice as much as you weight that of the NASDAQ 100 index component Altera Corporation (symbol: ALTR) in an average of the two. Stochastic averaging thus allows you to directly control the weight that you wish to give to an individual stock's stochastic versus those of other stocks. Individual stocks are usually quite volatile compared to the major averages, so using a stochastic average as a pilot signal to time trades in an individual stock rather than its individual price can enable you to reduce the number of whipsaws you endure, while still allowing the market's price action to objectively influence your trading decisions. Using a stochastic average *as a pilot signal* to trade an individual stock would be a similar process to using the stochastic of a broad market index as a pilot signal to do this. For example, you might:

1. Buy stock ABCD if the 40-day stochastic average (of stock ABCD and three other industry stocks) rises above 80 (after having most recently risen above 20 rather than 80).
2. Sell stock ABCD if the 40-day stochastic average (of stock ABCD and three other industry stocks) falls below 20 (after having most recently fallen below 80 rather than 20).

Alternatively, of course, you may use the stochastic average simply to time your exit (e.g., after a fundamentals based entry) or to indicate the objective trending state of the stocks in a basket you are monitoring. Although you may of course use a stochastic average as a pilot signal to trade a basket containing *any* combination of stocks, as it gives you aggregate trend information for the entire basket, it might be more useful to use it for intraindustry rather than interindustry trades. I say this because stocks within the same industry should be more likely to exhibit a consensus in their price action. Thus, if you want to trade a very mixed basket of stocks, it might be simpler to use a broader market index as a pilot signal.

You should of course do your own research to see which concepts you are most comfortable with. All I can do as a writer is to bring this fascinating concept to your attention as a reader. If you don't have very sophisticated charting software, you can chart your stochastic averages in Microsoft Excel. This involves first manually downloading the price data of the individual stocks in your intended average into Microsoft Excel. After this, you then calculate individual stock stochastics from this data, average the stochastics together, and then analyze them.

Of course you might also choose to use other stochastic average threshold levels for trades than 80 and 20, based on the frequency of trading that you are comfortable with and/or the volatility of the stochastic average itself. The closer together your threshold levels are, the higher the frequency with which your trading signals should occur. For example, instead of threshold levels for trades at 80 and 20, you may choose symmetrical levels at 75 and 25, 70 and 30, and so on. Using these alternative threshold levels, you might:

1. Buy a stock if the stochastic average rises above 75 (after having most recently risen above 25 rather than 75).
2. Sell a stock if the stochastic average falls below 25 (after having most recently fallen below 75 rather than 25).

Or you may choose to shift your trade initiation and trade exit thresholds in a particular direction, for example:

1. Buy a stock if the stochastic average rises above 90 (after having most recently risen above 30 rather than 90).
2. Sell a stock if the stochastic average falls below 30 (after having most recently fallen below 90 rather than 30).

Note that this latter method confines both your buys and sells in the stock to the 30–90 range of the stochastic, which is more squarely in uptrend territory than the 20–80 range.

If a stock has a split, and all prices in its price series are correspondingly adjusted, this should not alter its stochastic values, because the positions of all prices relative to their N-day extremes will keep the same proportions. For example, imagine a stock with a 40-day range between 20 and 30 that closes at 28, and then splits 2:1 after the close. Its split adjusted closing price for that day would be 14, and its split adjusted 40-day range would be between 10 and 15. The stochastic for that day will be the same both before and after split adjustment, namely $100 \times (28-20)/(30-20) = 100 \times (14-10)/(15-10) = 80$.

Since not all industry groups have their own indices, stochastic averaging can be handy for the trend analysis of minibaskets of stocks.

Although you may also construct an artificial index of real stocks on your own, it may be difficult to maintain, as you would have to periodically deal with the same issues as the creators of large benchmark indices do. To simplify some of these issues, Jesse Livermore in his book *How to Trade in Stocks* details how he would watch the sum of the prices of two of the leading stocks in an industry that he was focusing on.[9] More specifically, he would create a price weighted index based on only two stocks! In his words:

> *[T]here is danger in being caught in a false movement by depending on only one stock. The movement of the two stocks combined gives reasonable assurance.*[10]

To accomplish this in the modern world, you can simply go to a site like Yahoo! Finance, rank the stocks in an industry by market cap, and pick the two highest market cap stocks. You then add their price series together on a daily basis, and track the price behavior of the sum, for example defining Donchian uptrends and downtrends based on it. If any events such as splits occur during your trading of a position using the sum as a pilot signal, you may have to adjust the sum using a multiplier, and so on. I discuss this in more detail later. Note that although you will not be able to tell what the intraday highs and lows of the sum are, you can at least approximately tell where the sum opened (by adding the opening prices of both stocks) and where the sum closed (by adding the closing prices of both stocks). These two daily price points will enable you to create a daily Japanese candlestick for the price sum that has a body without shadows (i.e., open and closed prices but no high and low prices). Charting these truncated candlesticks allows you to have a better idea of the intraday volatility of the price sum than you would if you used opening prices exclusively or closing prices exclusively. If you don't want to bother with artificial index construction in this manner, you may of course simply average the stochastics of these two stocks.

AVERAGING OTHER TYPES OF NORMALIZED FUNCTIONS

There is a wide set of other normalized functions that you can average across multiple stocks to provide an objective picture of aggregate trend behavior. For example, what if you want an objective picture of the average percentage extension of multiple stocks above their respective N-day moving averages? Then you could define a function like the following "ratio oscillator" to provide this information. Ratio oscillator: The ratio of today's last price to the moving average of the past N closing prices (excluding today's price).

This definition makes a ratio oscillator similar to a momentum indicator, except that it shows what fraction of the moving average the current price in a stock represents. For example, a 200-day ratio oscillator value of 1.5 would mean that the current price is 150 percent of a stock's 200-day moving average (i.e., 50 percent higher than it). Since prices cross up and down over a moving average over time, the ratio oscillator of any stock will oscillate up and down around 1, because a price *equal* to the N-day moving average represents a ratio oscillator value of 1. The ratio format normalizes the function so that different stocks can be compared on the same scale.

This particular form of oscillator enables averaging of the ratio oscillator functions of multiple stocks simultaneously, to get an *average picture of the extension* of multiple stocks above their respective moving averages. For example, if the 40-day ratio oscillator values of stocks ABC, DEF, GHI, and JKL are 1.2, 1.3, 1.1, and 1.4, respectively, we know that the *average* of the four ratio oscillators is $(1.2 + 1.3 + 1.1 + 1.4) / 4 = 1.25$. This indicates that the average extension of all four stocks above their respective 40-day moving averages is 25 percent. Alternatively, if the 40-day ratio oscillator values of stocks ABC, DEF, GHI, and JKL are 1.1, 0.9, 1.1, and 0.9, respectively, we know that the *average* of the four ratio oscillators is $(1.1 + 0.9 + 1.1 + 0.9) / 4 = 1.00$. This function is lower bounded by 0 with an unlimited upper bound, similar to price itself. This makes it different from a stochastic, which is lower bounded by 0 with an upper bound of 100. Both a ratio oscillator and a stochastic do *distort* the underlying price functions, however, so you should be aware of their limitations and behavior if you choose to use them.

Because the ratio oscillator is calculated by excluding today's price from the moving average calculation, intraday changes in today's price will not affect the value of the moving average that is used to calculate the ratio average, which reduces confusion. A possible drawback of averaging ratio oscillators is that a more volatile stock should affect the ratio oscillator average more than a less volatile stock. In any case, a ratio oscillator average provides an easy to construct alternative to a stock index.

ARE CANNED TREND FOLLOWING STRATEGIES USEFUL IN EQUITIES?

The possibility of using a completely automated trend following strategy (i.e., a canned strategy or a "black box" strategy) in trading is very alluring.

However, using such a strategy requires lots of caution in real world application, especially in a single asset class like stocks. Remember that although futures trend followers are often diversified across multiple asset classes like currencies and commodities, many of them still experience considerable portfolio volatility. Imagine how much more this must be the case in a portfolio containing a single asset class like stocks, in which so many portfolio components are strongly correlated to one another. Clearly, repeated whipsaws and sustained drawdowns are very possible if you use a canned trend following strategy in stocks. Like any other profit seeking strategy, a canned trend following strategy's effectiveness can also be reduced over time if competition increases. In the words of Ed Seykota:

> *The profitability of trend following systems seems to move in cycles. Periods during which trend following systems are highly successful will lead to their increased popularity. As the number of system users increases, and the markets shift from trending to directionless action, these systems become unprofitable, and undercapitalized and inexperienced traders will get shaken out. Longevity is the key to success.*[11]

Seykota also wisely points out that:

> *Systems trading is ultimately discretionary. The manager still has to decide how much risk to accept, which markets to play, and how aggressively to increase and decrease the trading base as a function of equity change. These decisions are quite important—often more important than trade timing.*[12]

Before you attempt to use such a canned strategy *in any asset class*, you need to make sure that you conduct feasibility studies whose results you are comfortable with. You also need to make sure that you believe strongly in your *reasons* for using the strategy.

I personally like to think on my feet about new opportunities for market profit, which may include thinking about both completely and partially technical strategies. In order for you to trade with peace of mind, you need to make sure that you can clearly articulate your reasons for following a particular course of action, and that you are not just trading based on the fact that some back tested results from a black box look great on paper. Imagine yourself down money in a canned strategy you intend to use before you begin using it. What information would you research or repeat to yourself to allay your worries? What factors haven't you considered yet? Research this information before you trade to protect your peace of mind and help you prepare for unexpected situations.

The returns of some of the leading futures trend followers in the 1970s were absolutely phenomenal—but completely mechanical trend following at the time was not a widely used strategy with a lot of institutional money behind it, and computing power was not as widely available as it is today. There is much more competition now, and heavy competition from a lot of profit seeking participants nudges markets toward efficiency. CTAs often trade stock index futures, so there is already some trend following money moving the major indices about. This may make it difficult for you to make great returns with similar strategies on the same indices. By seeing if trend following strategies are applicable to areas where they are less likely to be used, you may have a better chance of finding exploitable profit opportunities.

Once you have identified your target instrument or instruments for a canned strategy, it is wise to back-test your strategy to obtain a general picture of how it would have performed in the past, and also to yield some baseline statistics that you can use to estimate the probability of strings of losses of various length or drawdowns of various magnitudes, and so on. In this context, back testing is a feasibility study tool that adds another piece of information to your decision about whether to implement a particular strategy. If you are anticipating a major change in the way the markets trade, however, poor back test results for a strategy you intend to use will simply confirm the fact that that strategy failed to work in the past. Although this provides no information about your anticipated future, it may still be good information to be aware of.

CHAPTER 5

Structuring a Trend Trade

IMPORTANT DIFFERENCES BETWEEN EQUITY TRADING AND FUTURES TRADING

Instrument Lifetimes and the Fate of Invested Cash

Futures traders have made trend following famous as a strategy, but the portfolio structuring techniques they generally use in the futures markets cannot be used in the equity markets. In fact, some aspects of equity portfolio management may be more complicated than their futures portfolio management counterparts.

A stock investor actually buys an asset with the money he invests. That money is physically transferred to the individual who sells him the asset, and disappears from his available capital. He only subsequently recovers money from his investment if he liquidates the stock he holds. In the futures market, however, nothing is invested in when a futures contract is "bought." A futures contract is basically an agreement to deliver some good in exchange for a cash payment at a later date. The buyer agrees to make a future cash payment to the seller (the value of which is determined in the futures marketplace), and in exchange he receives a quantity of the underlying commodity at an agreed upon time in the future. However, to make this agreement, no money actually needs to be exchanged between the buyer and the seller. In fact, the agreement would not even have to be officially recorded if the counterparties trusted each other's words sufficiently. This is like agreeing with a friend that you'll pay him $10,000 in exchange for his car next week after you get your pay-check. Since the underlying commodity does not change hands when fu-tures contracts are "traded" in the marketplace, no money is being tied up in the goods underlying the contracts. The only purpose, then, that the money in futures accounts serves is as a good faith deposit to ensure that payment in full will be exchanged for the specified goods when the con-tract expires. In *Getting Started in Futures*, Todd Lofton summarizes this concept succinctly:

> *A futures position confers no rights of ownership to the underly-ing asset. The owner of a futures position does not gain any in-come or benefits from the asset. A futures contract is really just a pair of promises: one to deliver the underlying commodity and an-other to receive and pay for it. Futures margin is a good faith de-posit. The balance of the value of the futures contract is not borrowed, so no loan interest is paid by the holder of a margined futures position.*[1]

In other words, a futures account often contains cash (or acceptable substitutes for it), which serves as a good faith deposit to the exchange against the market value represented by the futures contract positions. The exchange has to ensure market integrity by making sure that market participants keep up their ends of the deals they enter into. A futures ac-count may also contain positions in futures contracts, which represent promises to deliver or buy goods in the future. As long as the broker and exchange you are trading with are comfortable that you have sufficient cash (or acceptable substitutes) in your account that you will be able to cover the promises represented by the futures contracts in your account, you are allowed to hold these contracts and to enter into other contracts freely. If your broker deems that you have insufficient cash to cover your obligations, you may either have to provide the extra cash immediately, or some of your futures contract positions may be liquidated until you *do* have sufficient cash covering the obligations you have entered into. In a stock account, on the other hand, when you invest in a stock, the stock certificates are yours, and the cash you have invested vanishes from your account permanently. This vanished cash cannot be used for any other purposes, as it is literally, physically gone. This means that *you can use only remaining available cash* to invest in new positions. This fact means that the portfolio structuring techniques you must use will be very differ-ent from the money management techniques a futures investor might use. Equities tie up cash, and are perpetual, while futures do not tie up cash, and have limited lifetimes.

A futures trader is never really invested in anything, so he can size his positions by deciding to risk a fraction of the total cash sitting in his account. Not so with an equity investor. For example, let's say that an equity investor *with a cash account* invests 10 percent of his portfolio in 10 different stocks respectively (for a 100 percent total). He then proceeds to lose 20 percent on one of the positions, that is, 2 percent on the overall portfolio, with all the other positions unchanged. This leaves him with 98 percent of his original capital, 90 percent of which is tied up in stock positions and 8 percent of which is in cash. Let's say that the trader's rules then require him to invest 10 percent of his overall portfolio value in the next position, which would now represent 9.8 percent of his *original* capital. Even in this simple example, it is clear that he can invest only a maximum of 8 percent of his original capital in the next position because *this is all that's available in cash.* Clearly, it is prudent for this equity trader to adapt a money management method better suited to the specifics and minutiae of equity investing.

Correlations among Positions

A diversified equity portfolio with multiple positions is a very different animal from a diversified futures portfolio with multiple positions, because of the high degree to which many stocks are correlated to the market, and thus to one another. A managed futures portfolio is often composed of futures positions in a wide variety of asset classes, including equity indices, interest rate products, currencies, and physical commodities.[2] A long-only equity portfolio, on the other hand, holds positions in the single asset class of equities, and thus has vastly different behavior.

The idea behind diversifying trend following futures portfolios across weakly correlated asset classes is that some of the individual position losses and gains should tend to offset one another through time, reducing overall portfolio volatility. An equity portfolio, on the other hand, is much more likely to have losses and gains clustered together in time, because so many stocks are affected by the broader market. To see an example of this, simply look at the net asset value charts of several different domestic equity funds, and then contrast this with the performance charts of managed futures funds on a site like www.iasg.com, the Web site of the Institutional Advisory Services Group. Clearly, a diversified futures trend follower's portfolio's equity curve should behave very differently from an equity portfolio's equity curve (partially because of the weaker correlations among managed futures portfolio instruments). This is especially the case if the equity portfolio is concentrated in a particular industry instead of being diversified across industries. Equity investors must be aware of these facts if considering the use of a canned trend following strategy that is confined only to equities.

Since I do not currently have sophisticated correlation monitoring and risk management software, in long-only equity investing *I often trade with the ultraconservative assumption that all positions in my equity portfolio are essentially part of one very large equity trade.*

In other words, I assume that my entire portfolio has a very real likelihood of having all positions stopped out *simultaneously* for a loss after dropping in unison. Of course this is seldom a completely accurate assumption, but it is a *safe* one when one is estimating total portfolio risk in an all stock portfolio. It is much safer to *overestimate* the correlations between positions when one is calculating risk than to underestimate them, because correlations can increase without warning (especially in times of market stress), but are capped at 100 percent. Think of the herdlike behavior that occurred in various market crises like the 1987 and 1997 October drops as examples of this fact.

Even the major averages, which are diversified to the point of containing tens or even hundreds of individual positions, behave somewhat like single stocks. By buying the NASDAQ 100 Trust Shares (i.e., the QQQQs), you are essentially holding a portfolio position of 100 separate stocks. For simplicity's sake, assume equal weightings and 100 percent correlations among all the positions in the QQQQs portfolio for a moment. In this tremendously simple case, if you risked 10 percent of your capital on a QQQQs trade, this would mean a respective risk of 0.1 percent (i.e., 1/10 of 1%) on each stock in the portfolio. Although you'd be risking very little on each individual position, your overall portfolio risk would still be a considerable 10 percent of your capital. I thus prefer to think of my risk more in portfolio terms than in single stock terms.

Position Size Constraints

A major difference between futures contracts and equity shares is that futures contracts have standardized position sizes, like 1,000 barrels of crude oil, while equities trade in single shares. Since the minimum trading increment on the major U.S. equity exchanges is currently one cent, this means that the minimum value fluctuation you can encounter on a one-share position is one cent as well. Exchange traded futures contracts, on the other hand, often have minimum value fluctuations on the order of $10 or so, which is three orders of magnitude larger than equities. The large standardized sizes of futures contracts may sometimes entail risks that small investors are not willing to take.

For example, imagine that you were required to buy stocks in lots of 1,000 shares each (with no smaller position units allowed). This inflexibility might make you unable to afford certain stocks altogether (e.g., one lot of a $90 stock would represent a $90,000 investment), or unable to achieve small position sizes such as 150 shares, which may be better suited to the risks you actually want to take. There is a tradeoff to this relative position sizing flexibility of equities, though—a general lack of exposure to other asset classes. Exchange traded funds like the streetTRACKS Gold Shares (symbol: GLD) and the iShares Lehman 20+-year Treasury Bond Fund (symbol: TLT) provide some hope that investors will be able to gain increased exposure to other asset classes in the future, with the added benefit of better position sizing flexibility.

Back Testing Differences

Anyone who wants to back-test a trading strategy on equities must first pick which equities they are going to trade from the universe of stocks. The universe of commodities, currencies, and financial instruments that underlie futures contracts contains a limited number of real goods (like coffee) or financial instruments (like Treasury bonds) that are likely to exist for quite a while. This means that an individual running tests on historical price data in futures often has a relatively stable universe of instruments from which he can choose those to run his tests on. The universe of equities, on the other hand, is constantly changing. Companies become public, go out of business, merge with others, and acquire others as business conditions evolve. Thus, back testing of equities can be much more complicated than back testing of futures. Although you might be able to solve this problem in part by picking stocks only from the historical components of major indices or newspaper/magazine lists, you should realize that this characteristic of the equity markets can make fully rigorous back testing very expensive. Back testing can help you get your bearings, but a considerable amount of discretion will always rest with you as an investor. This fact requires you to be forward looking, which is positive in my view.

There are numerous ways to participate in market moves. As managed futures fund manager Robert Rotella says:

> *The acceptance or rejection of any trading method is really a function of a person's philosophy, because no trading method can be proven to work in the future. . . . Our beliefs and emotions about ourself [sic] and the world ultimately determine what we want, how we approach, and what methods we use in trading.*[3]

As long as your risk management methods are sound, it is your correct read on future conditions and your perseverance in staying with profitable moves in your favor that will make the big difference in your profits. It is crucial, however, that you understand how to logically structure your portfolio to give yourself the flexibility that you will need to trade multiple opportunities simultaneously.

ENTRIES AND REENTRIES

All trade entries and reentries are discretionary in some sense, since you choose the technical or fundamental factors that you will employ to get into the market. Earlier I discussed technical methods of entering the market like band breakouts, %K or %R breakouts, N-day peak and trough patterns, and other methods such as moving average crossovers. Keep in mind that if you both enter and exit the same market with a technical trend following method, your slippage may be quite large. However, since I define trend following more generally as a method of managing your open position P&L, you are not limited exclusively to chasing markets to get in. You can use fundamental or other discretionary criteria to enter as well.

However, because of the nature of the markets, you will sometimes be forced out of positions due to choppiness or other reasons when you still believe that conditions are favorable for you to make money. In other words, following your trading plan may cause you to be forced out of the market during a period when you still believe that you have an edge. In addition to making plans for exiting the market, which control your actions when in the market, you should also define the conditions (if any) under which you will reenter a stock if you get stopped out of it.[4]

Consider the example of using a market pilot signal (e.g., going long or staying long during a 32-day Donchian market uptrend) with a fixed percentage stop. What happens if your percentage stop is triggered and you exit the stock while the market still indicates that it is in an uptrend state (i.e., the market has not made a new 32-day low since making its last new 32-day high). How would you reenter the stock if the market remains in an uptrend? Here are several possibilities:

- Reenter the stock if it makes a new 32-day high *of its own*.
- Reenter the stock if it breaks up through your original entry level.
- Wait two full trading days and reenter the stock if the market makes a new 32-day high after your two-day wait has elapsed.

I mention reentry possibilities to emphasize that you should continue to play the markets when you believe that the odds are strongly in your favor. If you time your exits technically, you will sometimes be stopped out or forced to cut your position size, but you should take any loss as a point against you in a game like tennis or basketball. Losing one or two points does not mean the game is over by a long shot, and you must continue to press your advantage in order to win overall.

EXITS

Conditional Exit Lists

Stops are an absolutely necessary part of trading, inseparable from entries. Just as it is irresponsible to enter any business venture without a reasonably precise estimate of your risk and exit plan, it is also irresponsible to enter any stock without a reasonably precise risk estimate and exit plan. What a boon the market gives you, in that you can exit any stock position freely during market hours without any catch. Most business executives cannot exit their deals so easily! Of course, even if you plan well, there is certainly always a chance of catastrophes occurring and your losing more than your worst-case estimate. However, preplanning should be an indispensable feature of all your trade campaigns, and thus planning (and following) your stops is a necessary component of any trade that you do. A trade is a two-step process. Never think of a trade as simply an entry, because this is as illogical as imagining a coin with only one side or a magnet with only one pole. Instead, remember that each trade always consists of both an entry and an exit. A preplanned method of exiting the market is thus an integral companion to any entry method.

The majority of the public thinks of entries and exits as separate trades from each other rather than as two components of the same campaign. Your exit method should be preplanned and this plan should go into effect as soon as you enter the market; all you are responsible for once you have put on a position is sticking to your exit plan. Since no one can predict the future, and since I recommend preplanning your exit method, it stands to reason that you will not be able to exit consistently at tops no matter how hard you try. It is also folly to try to catch bottoms consistently; you should instead concentrate your time on identifying favorable *conditions* for making money. Some traders have their entire trade process—including entering and exiting the market—handled by computers, but as an individual investor you will need to have the discipline to stick to your plans on your own. Even computer software that trades for you can be overridden, so discipline is absolutely essential to trading. Break the bad habit of looking at a chart and daydreaming about selling the top of a move after buying at the lowest price. Instead, realistically imagine where you might have exited after various types of entries (good and bad) if you used preplanned rules.

Stops are commonly considered to be a kind of safety feature for protecting capital when in the market, like the eject lever in a jet pilot's cockpit. This is the wrong way to think about them. In fact, the term "stop," short for "stop loss," unfairly singles out losing trades in my opinion. Since the term is in such widespread use, I use it, but keep in mind that a stop refers to an exit of the market that you do *in a particular condition*, usually when your open losses reach a certain value. If your open losses do not reach that value, there are of course numerous other ways in which you can exit the market.

Think of a trade as going to see a movie in a theater with two exits, for example. You can see the movie only by first entering the theater, sitting inside for a while, and then eventually coming out through one of the two exits. No matter what happens on that screen, it is an unquestionable fact that you will have to exit the theater eventually. Is it worth obsessing over the names of the exits, for example whether you call one the "left exit" or another the "green exit"? Of course the answer is no. An exit is an exit, and you will eventually have to take one to leave the theater. It is of course prudent to plan in advance that if a fire breaks out close to one exit, you will take the other one, and vice versa. Similarly in the markets, you should plan in advance which exits you will take under different conditions, and so stops are not exclusively a safety feature; they are an integral part of the two-step process of extracting money out of the markets. In a nutshell:

- Your goal as a trader is to *extract* money from the market.
- You can extract money from the market only by first entering and later exiting the market.
- Thus, the mechanism for extracting money necessarily includes *both* your entry trade and your exit trade. Your entry and exit trade are two sides of the same coin, so you should strive to never enter without knowing how you will exit.
- To extract as much net money as possible out of the markets, it is logical to limit your open losses on individual trades while allowing your profits room to grow indefinitely. This entire process must be preplanned as much as possible; in my experience, emotion can cloud judgment if it is not.
- The method you use to extract money from the markets will produce net profits over the long run only if you have an edge in your trading.

All your possible exits from the market can be written as a series of *if-then* statements, as in *if* Event A happens *then* I will do Action Z. *These if-then statements should cover how you will exit under all possible price scenarios in a stock after you have entered the stock, so I call them "conditional exits."*

Here is a sample money extraction strategy containing several conditional exit statements:

1. I go long the stock.
2. If the stock drops *$1 or more below my entry price* at any time, then I will exit immediately (even if this occurs due to a gap down).
3. If the stock closes *above my entry price for four consecutive days*, then I will exit on the next open.
4. If the stock closes *less than $1 below my entry price for two consecutive days*, then I will exit on the next open.
5. If I still own the stock after 20 days, then I will exit on the next open.

You can see in the this strategy that all scenarios of what the stock could possibly do are covered in the if-then statements (2 to 5). These if-then statements are conditional exit statements, and there are infinite possibilities for constructing them. Statement #2 is what would traditionally be termed a "stop," because it specifies that you will cut off open losses if they reach or exceed $1 per share.

Now for some definitions: The difference between your entry price and your stop price in a stock is the *maximum* amount *of that stock's price* that you are willing to risk on a trade (see box).

> I call this maximum amount your "dollar risk," and denote it by the letter R. If you divide your dollar risk R by your entry price P into the stock, you get the maximum percentage of the stock's price that you are willing to risk on a trade, which I call the stock's dollar risk to price ratio, or "R:P ratio."

For example, if you want to enter a stock at $30 and place a stop at $25, then your dollar risk would be $30 − $25 = $5 and your R:P ratio would be ($30 − $25) / $30 = 16.67 percent. *Alternatively, you can arrive at the same R:P ratio by subtracting the ratio of your stop price to your entry price from 1, that is, [1 − (stop price/entry price)].*

In the preceding example this method would yield (1 − $25/$30) = 16.67 percent, the same R:P ratio. Note that I use a sign convention to keep the R:P ratio percentage number positive; in other words, you should be aware that the 16.67 percent I refer to in this example is a loss of 16.67 percent. However, you can of course switch the sign if you are more comfortable with this. I use the term "R:P ratio" a lot more going forward.

Conditional exit statements are simply tools; no exit method is intrinsically powerful. However, a conditional exit list objectively states in writing your strategy to extract profit from the market based on a perceived edge that you have arrived at through studying the markets. In simple cases, you may choose to leave fixed stops with your broker to satisfy the requirements of your conditional exit list. However, if your conditional exit statements are very complicated, this may not be feasible. Also, if you are moving large amounts of a stock relative to the liquidity of that stock, it may be prudent to execute your stops manually so that you can observe and control their market impact more directly. Let's examine some stop placement methods now.

Percentage Stops

Percentage stop levels are simple to calculate, but not always appropriate to use in practice. When using a percentage stop, you risk a certain fixed percentage (let's call it "Q") of the stock's value at entry, so that your dollar risk is (Q × entry price). Clearly, your R:P ratio will then be the fixed percentage Q that you risked, since (dollar risk) / (entry price) yields Q.

The price level of your percentage stop will be simply (100% – Q%) × (entry price). For example, let's say you decide to trade a $50 stock with an 8 percent stop. Your stop level will then be (100% – 8%) × $50 = (92%) × $50 = $46.

One problem with percentage stops is that using the same fixed percentage to set stops in all stocks may give you tremendous room in liquid, low volatility stocks but give too little room in others based on the size of minimum fluctuations and regular spreads in a stock. For example, a 10 percent stop may be useful in a $30 stock, where it allows $3 of price movement. However, in a $2 stock the same stop would allow only 20 cents of movement. If the latter stock has a minimum price variation of 1 cent, but is so illiquid that spreads are often 10 cents or more, a fixed percentage stop may not be the best tool, as you may be stopped out within a matter of hours simply due to illiquidity when you had intended to hold on the order of months. In such a case, a volatility based stop might be more appropriate.

Dealing with Slippage and Gaps with a Percentage Stop   In the course of your trading, you will find that although you may want to buy or sell a stock at a certain price, market forces (such as gaps due to overnight news) can easily move it well away from that price, often forcing you to chase prices if you want to make a trade. In situations like these you may sometimes have to adjust your stops from the levels you had originally theorized to compensate for the slippage you have had to endure. By simply calculating your stop based on your eventual long entry price, you can determine where to place your updated stops without much trouble, and thus worry less about gaps in prices.

When using a percentage stop, it is relatively easy to adjust for slippage. For example, let's say that you want to use a 9 percent stop in a stock. You ideally want to enter the stock at $98 (with a stop at $89.18), but end up having to pay $99 instead. Simply adjust your stop level to $(100\% - 9\%) \times (\$99) = \$90.09$, and your R:P ratio will remain unchanged at 9 percent. In another example, let's say you're forced to enter at $52 instead of $50 due to a gap. Your 8 percent stop level will then simply be $(92\%) \times \$52 = \$47.84$.

Sometimes, of course, you will have to deal with halted markets, fast markets, or very illiquid markets. I suggest that you think through what you will do in each of these scenarios, and try to make some basic plans. For example, if liquidity in a market suddenly dries up to a quarter of its original value, you may write into your trading plan that you will split up your order into four pieces and sell it over two days rather than all at once.

Fixed Floor Stops

I have already discussed Donchian band exits, in which you exit a long position if price makes a new N-day low. This is a form of trailing stop, but as it is relatively easy for the street to calculate N-day highs and lows, there is of course a possibility of other traders using the same stop levels. As a small trader, you should rarely be concerned, however. Even if you don't trade with a Donchian trend following strategy, you may still use the price difference between Donchian bands as a dollar risk amount, to calculate the level at which you will set a fixed floor stop. A fixed floor stop is a stop that remains fixed for the life of a trade. Fixed floor stops can be incorporated into a conditional exit list by using the following if-then statement. *Fixed floor stop: If price drops one cent or more below the fixed floor stop level at any time during a trade, then exit the stock immediately.*

Of course, the alternative to this scenario occurring is that price *does not* drop below the fixed floor stop level. Additional conditional exit statements are of course required to cover alternative scenarios.

A *pilot signal* is one such alternative method of exiting the market that is similar (but not identical) to the use of a trailing stop. In a slightly different example, perhaps you've observed that the leading stock in an industry, for example, Intel Corporation (symbol: INTC), tends to lead other stocks in the industry in general directional movement with a lead time of two days. You decide to try to extract money from the market based on this inefficiency, by trading a lagging stock in the industry such as KLA-Tencor Corporation (symbol: KLAC). When you study INTC's price action in a vacuum, you observe pure randomness, with no predictable behavior, and the same goes for when you study KLAC individually. Yet after studying both stocks together, you see that one clearly leads the other. How could you profit from this purely hypothetical scenario?

Well, since INTC leads other industry stocks, you ideally would like to buy KLAC after INTC moves up a certain amount, for example, by making a new 32-day high. To protect yourself, you would set a fixed floor stop that enables you to limit your risk, as follows:

Money Extraction Strategy

1. Go long KLAC as soon as INTC makes a new 32-day high.
2. If KLAC drops to less than 90 percent of your entry price, then exit KLAC immediately.
3. If INTC makes a new 32-day low, then exit KLAC immediately.

Note that you are literally using INTC's price action to determine some of your trading actions in KLAC. That is, you are using INTC as a pilot signal to time your trades in KLAC. Of course, you set a stop level in KLAC in case things don't work out the way you would like, so that your conditional exit statements cover all scenarios. You should also decide what you will do if either INTC or KLAC is halted during your trade. Losses are strictly limited with the preceding percentage stop method, while gains could theoretically move up indefinitely as long as INTC avoids making a new 32-day low. With this strategy you attempt to exploit the opportunity and give yourself some room to profit from the unexpected. You may also define your dollar risk with an alternative method when using a pilot signal, for example using the 32-day Donchian bandwidth or the 32-day standard deviation of closing prices as your dollar risk in the stock you are trading. The possibilities are endless.

Regarding Stochastics and Fixed Floor Stops

Since stochastics are calculated based on the same N-day range that defines an N-day Donchian channel, you may set stops based on the extreme prices of this range as well. For example, if you buy a stock the day after its 40-day stochastic crosses above 80 on a closing basis, you can set a fixed stop at that stock's 40-day low and a trailing stop that is triggered if the stochastic closes below 20. However, since the stochastic will signal an exit if the stochastic closes below 20, you will most likely be stopped out before your fixed stop has been triggered. Therefore, you may try to set your stop a bit closer to the real world price implied by the exit level that you want to use on the stochastic. For example, let's say you enter a position in a stock while its 40-day stochastic is at 60. You plan to exit the stock either if its stochastic closes below 25 or if your fixed floor stop is triggered in the stock, whichever comes first. You may then set a fixed floor stop at your time of entry that is given by this value:

Fixed stop = 40-day low + (25/100) × (40-day high – 40 day low)

This fixed stop price corresponds to the price the stochastic would have to drop to immediately after you have entered the stock for the stochastic to have a value of 25. For example, let's say that the stock is currently at $76, with a 40-day high of $80 and a 40-day low of $70. This corresponds to a stochastic of 100 × (76 – 70)/(80 – 70) = 60, by definition. If you enter at $76, and want to immediately set a fixed stop at a price equivalent to a stochastic of 25, you would calculate:

Fixed stop = $70 + (25/100) × ($80 – $70) = $72.5

Checking in reverse, if the stock's price immediately gapped down to $72.5 after you have entered at $76, the stochastic's value would change to 100 × ($72.5 – $70)/($80 – $70) = 25.

Trailing Stops

The Continuous Trailing Stop   In one form of trailing stop, you simply stop yourself out of a position if price backs off by a fixed amount from its most extreme move in your favor. To monitor prices this closely without watching them constantly requires the assistance of a computer—either yours or your broker's. You should check with your brokerage to see if they allow you to place trailing stops like this with them. I know of at least one broker that currently allows you to place both fixed dollar trailing stops and fixed percentage trailing stops, allowing you to use very basic trend following exits without constantly monitoring the markets.

The Ratchet Stop   Another very simple type of trend following exit is to use is what I call a ratchet stop. You determine the dollar risk you are willing to use on a position, enter the market using proprietary criteria, and set a fixed stop level at your entry price minus your dollar risk. You then *add* this dollar risk to your entry price, and note that price, which I call the first ratchet level. Add the same dollar risk to this new price and mark the second ratchet level, and so on. This is a simplified form of a trailing stop that does not require you to track every tick in a stock.

Here is how you would use a ratchet stop in practice, calling your entry price E and your dollar risk R:

1. If price breaks below your initial stop level (E − R) or any subsequent stop levels, then exit the stock.
2. If price breaks above the first ratchet level (E + R), then raise your stop level to your original entry point.
3. If price breaks above the second ratchet level (E + 2R), then raise your stop level to the first ratchet level.
4. If price breaks above the third ratchet level (E + 3R), raise your stop level to the second ratchet level.
5. And so on, until you are stopped out of the stock.

One property of using a ratchet stop is that *only you will know* where your various stop levels and ratchet levels have been placed. If you use a technical exit method like a stock making a new N-day low to exit, this is more likely to be also used by others. Furthermore, you can set ratchet levels so that your profits on trades will fall approximately into multiples of the amount that you originally risked on the trade, also

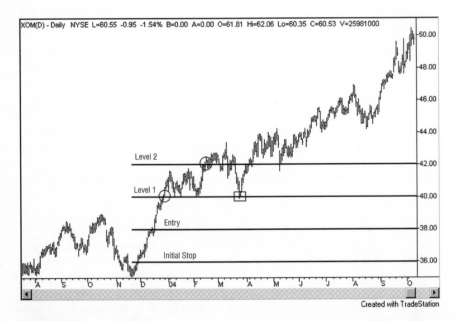

FIGURE 5.1 Placement of ratchet levels on a stock chart of ExxonMobil (XOM). (*Source:* © TradeStation® 1991–2006. All rights reserved.)

known as R-multiples. Figure 5.1, is an example of setting ratchet levels on a stock chart.

In this figure, when price breaks through ratchet Level 1 (circled), you raise your stop to your entry price. When price breaks through ratchet Level 2 (also circled), you raise your stop to ratchet Level 1. Thus, when price subsequently falls back below ratchet Level 1 (highlighted with a square), you exit the stock immediately.

Of course there is no reason for your ratchet levels to be separated exactly by your dollar risk. The important thing is that you stick with the plan you have chosen. Your ratchet levels may also be separated by multiples or fractions of your dollar risk. For example, imagine that you enter a trade at entry price E and with dollar risk R, specifying exit rules as follows:

1. If price breaks below your initial stop level (E – R) or any subsequent stop level, then exit the stock.
2. If price breaks above E + 2R, then raise your stop level to E + R.
3. If price breaks above E + 4R, then raise your stop level to E + 3R.
4. If price breaks above E + 6R, then raise your stop level to E + 5R.
5. And so on, until you are stopped out of the stock.

This method allows the stock room to move up in steps of 2R, and then pulls the stop level in so that it is 1R lower than the target level hit. Obviously, you can see that the methods shown are essentially cases of "six in one hand, half a dozen in the other." What are really crucial are the insights that lead you to apply these methods in your trading, not the methods in and of themselves.

An alternative trailing stop is to exit a stock if an N-day trough is breached after your entry. For example, after entering the stock on the long side, you first set an initial fixed stop. You then wait for an N-day trough to be established (that is above your fixed stop level), and then raise your stop to this level. For simplicity, you would consider your entry day to be the first possible day that can be part of the N-day trough pattern, meaning that the first day that the N-day trough will be definable after you have entered is the (2N+1)th day. In this manner you do not need to watch every tick of the stock as it moves, and you may thus leave a stop with your broker if you wish.

Triggers

Price Triggers   Earlier, I defined a trend following strategy as one in which your losses are strictly limited while your profits, under certain circumstances, would be allowed to grow indefinitely. A price trigger is a price level that, when crossed in a particular direction, causes you to reevaluate holding your position in a stock based on objective information other than the stock's price. In real life, you may choose to check something like whether a stock's 10-day average volume stays above certain threshold levels after price *closes below* a trigger level *from above.* For example, if you bought a breakout in a stock that typically traded 100,000 shares a day but happens to trade 2,000,000 shares on the day of the breakout, you could check the daily volume each day after price drops below a trigger level (after previously closing at or above it), to ensure that the public is still excited about the stock. For example:

1. Go long stock ABCD at $50.

2. If ABCD ever closes below $48, then exit ABCD immediately.

3. If ABCD closes *below* $52 after closing *at or above it* on the previous day, then check that day's volume and the volume of all subsequent days. If any of these days' volumes are less than 500,000 shares, then exit ABCD immediately on the next open; otherwise continue to hold.

4. If ABCD closes below $54 after closing at or above it on the previous day, then check that day's volume and the volume of all subsequent days. If any of these days' volumes are less than 1,000,000 shares, then exit ABCD immediately on the next open; otherwise continue to hold.

5. If ABCD closes below $56 after closing at or above it on the previous day, then check that day's volume and the volume of all subsequent days. If any of these days' volumes are less than 2,000,000 shares, then exit ABCD immediately on the next open; otherwise continue to hold.

6. And so on, doubling the daily volume threshold that has to be exceeded to keep your position after price drops below each higher trigger level (they are all separated by $2 increments).

Here is a strategy that incorporates a volume based exit and a target price:

1. Go long stock ABCD at $50.

2. If ABCD ever closes below $48, then exit the stock immediately on the next open.

3. If ABCD's volume for any full day is less than 500,000 shares (based on your check of the day's volume after the close), then exit ABCD immediately on the next open.

4. If ABCD closes above $60, then exit ABCD on the next open.

Time Triggers and Fundamental Triggers   Time triggers are simply dates on which you check some objective criteria (which may be fundamental or otherwise) to determine whether to continue to hold a position. Fundamental triggers constitute objective fundamental information (such as a stock moving through a P/E ratio threshold) that causes you to make a trade in a stock. Based on this definition, the probability of your continuing to hold past a time trigger date should be greater than 0 percent. However, if you preplan your exit for a fixed date, then the time trigger would be known as *a time stop*. In a time stop, you simply liquidate a position after a certain number of days if you have not exited by some other means already.

Let's look at an example of a time trigger, in which you check fundamental company data at certain intervals. Imagine that a company has just publicly announced first quarter earnings of five cents a share, and unveils a product that you think will do very well. The stock's price has not done much yet, but you are sure that it will cause a surge in earnings, hopefully driving up the stock price as well. You can add a time trigger based on earnings performance to your conditional exit strategy, as follows:

1. Go long stock ABCD at $50.
2. If ABCD drops below $48 at any time, then exit the stock immediately, otherwise stay in.
3. If ABCD's second quarter earnings are *less than* 10 cents per share, then exit immediately, otherwise stay in.
4. If ABCD's third quarter earnings are less than 15 cents per share, then exit immediately, otherwise stay in.
5. If ABCD's fourth quarter earnings are less than 20 cents per share, then exit immediately, otherwise stay in.
6. Repeat the process indefinitely, increasing the earnings hurdle by 5 cents for each subsequent quarter, while maintaining the fixed stop at $48 as a backup exit mechanism.

You can also use other fundamental metrics to define conditional exits for a position. For example, perhaps you buy a stock with a P/E of 5, which you think makes it fundamentally undervalued. You decide in advance that you will sell the stock if its P/E reaches 15. You enter stock ABCD and set a fixed percentage stop of 10 percent to limit your losses on the downside, as follows:

1. Go long stock ABCD, which currently has a P/E of 5, at $40.
2. If ABCD drops below $36 (meaning that your dollar risk is $4), exit the stock immediately, otherwise stay in.
3. If ABCD's P/E rises above 15, exit the stock immediately.

Note that this conditional exit list allows price the possibility of moving up indefinitely, while limiting your downside with a fixed stop. For example, ABCD's P/E ratio may remain constant at 5 if its price increases but its earnings increase proportionally. Conversely its P/E ratio may rapidly increase if its earnings fall and its price remains the same.

You may also choose to go long (with a fixed stop) until a certain time period expires, after which you use both a trailing stop and a fixed stop. For example, if your research has led you to believe that a secular bull market has commenced in the semiconductor industry that will last for approximately 7 to 10 years, you may use a strategy like the following one on ABCD, a hypothetical stock in the industry:

1. Go long ABCD at $40.

2. If ABCD drops through your fixed stop of $35, exit the stock immediately, otherwise hold the stock.

3. If five calendar years from your initial entry date have passed and you still hold the stock, then either exit ABCD if it makes a new 126-day low, or exit ABCD at $35 (whichever comes first).

4. If you exit ABCD after five calendar years from your entry date have passed, do not reenter the stock.

5. If you are stopped out of ABCD at $35 before five calendar years since your first entry date have passed, reenter ABCD if it breaks out above $40, and repeat this process from step 2.

In this particular method, you resign yourself to holding ABCD for as many as five years if your fixed stop has not been triggered. If your fixed stop *is* triggered before the five years have passed, you have a plan of reentry, because you believe from your research that the bull market in semiconductor stocks should still be in effect at that time.

You may of course base your conditional exits on numerous other combinations of fundamental ratios, pilot signals, time triggers, price triggers, and so on. By setting up a conditional exit plan you are essentially placing the stock in the movie theater I mentioned earlier. Once in the theater, the stock has to exit through one of its doors. Thus your job is to define what price or other behavior will prompt you to exit through a particular door, so that you can exit the stock without emotion when you see this behavior occurring.

Price–Time Exit Curves   A final possibility for exiting a position is what I call a price–time exit curve. You simply create a series of price levels that a stock *must be above* on certain dates (separated by fixed time intervals or otherwise) in order for you to exit. For example, let's say you enter a stock at $50 on the first trading day of the year, setting an initial fixed stop at $48. You might then say to yourself:

1. If price *does not* close above $52 on February 1, then I'll exit my position.
2. If price *does not* close above $54 on March 1, then I'll exit my position.
3. If price *does not* close above $56 on April 1, then I'll exit my position.
4. And so on.

You can see with this method that you will not always be chasing prices when exiting a stock, because you will be exiting based on *whether* the price is above certain levels *on certain dates*, and leaving price to float freely in the meantime. Note that I have made the price–time exit curve in this example upward sloping, because it makes little sense to lower your stop over time. Thus, if you use hand drawn price channels to trade, for example, you may use the bottom line of an upward sloping channel as your price–time exit curve. If you buy above a moving average or hand drawn trend line (which you view as support), and want to use it to exit, you can use values on the moving average or trend line for your price–time exit curve (in conjunction with a separate fixed stop).

Alternatively, for example, if you are trading a stock based on an external pilot signal, you might choose to have a flat price–time exit curve, and do the following:

1. Enter the position at $50 based on an external pilot signal's indication to buy.
2. If price does not close above $50 on February 1 or March 1, or April 1, or May 1, and so on, exit your position on the next day's open.
3. If the pilot signal indicates an exit, exit your position.

Note that this leaves your downside risk open ended in between the dates on which you check price, so caution must be exercised if you are using such a method.

What If You Have an Existing Position with No Exit Plan?

If you have an existing position (or positions) with no exit plan, there is an easy solution: Make one and stick to it. After that, avoid entering another position again without having your conditional exit list written out in advance. You must come to think of a trade as a *round turn* that includes both the entry and the exit. Pledge to stop thinking about trades as the majority of the public does—as a one-way gravy train to riches—because if you do this your bias about what you think the market should do will cloud your judgment. You need to protect your confidence when trading, and the only way you can do this is if you are able to look yourself in the mirror after each trade and say, "I did the right thing because I followed my plan." If you have no plan, you can't follow one. If you do have a plan that seems to have performed poorly after you have used it, then you can work on fixing it.

We saw a classic example of the dangers of trading with no exit plan in the 2000 tech bubble crash. For many years tech had seemed to go up nearly without interruption, so a buy and hold strategy seemed to be working terrifically. It was not uncommon to see stocks doubling in less than a year. All of a sudden, and in a few short months, euphoria turned to depression, and billions of dollars in market value unceremoniously evaporated. Stocks commenced a relatively steady drift down, and previously happy investors were left wondering, "How long should I hold before I get my money back?" The losses continued to mount until some investors were wiped out, while others lost the bulk of their bull market profits. Where did some of these investors make a mistake? They allowed themselves to be wiped out without even attempting to take control of the situation; many did not even scramble to set up a plan B in the midst of the chaos. If someone during this time had been truly a long-term investor, and holding through the drop in prices was within the parameters of his plan, that's one thing. But you never want to be forced into being a long-term investor in a position that you intended to be a short-term trade. Never go into battle without a strategy. If you follow a strategy and lose, so be it—but better to have a strategy to follow than to have none at all.

Chances are that if you have positions with no exit plan, the positions you have held the longest may be some of your worst performers. It is tempting to want your money back, and to fantasize about the days when your account size was at its peak. But the market is reality based: The current price is the *only* price! It is as if yesterday never existed. So don't complain about how your portfolio ran from $100,000 to $200,000, and then dropped back to $150,000 ("I lost $50,000!"). Act as if the portfolio never hit $200,000, but instead went directly from $100,000 to $150,000. In the stock market, since you tie up money in a position, it is tempting to believe that the position will eventually be worth more if you just hold a little longer. It is tempting to feel that a loss only becomes real when you lock it in. This is dangerous; open losses are just as real as if you had locked them in already. In the futures markets, each day's change in the value of your account is literally added to or subtracted from your account in electronic cash, constantly driving this point home. Thus, the only question that should matter to you in a position is, "What do I do now?" Although you may be talented enough to find profitable insights in the market, also be humble enough to realize that you cannot consistently anticipate its semirandom fluctuations. This is why planning your trades in advance (e.g., with a conditional exit list) is absolutely essential for your long-term trading survival. If you have doubts about how to act, simply look up the applicable line in your conditional exit list, like looking up the word "exit" in the dictionary, and act accordingly.

Once you are in a position, especially if the losses are heavy, it becomes extremely tempting to hold and wait for a rebound in your favor. This is human nature. But the market could not care less about what's going on with your position (remember that other people have positions, too; you're not the only one in the world suffering). There are no cosmic forces aligned against you; there is only a price number that relates directly and immediately to your net worth. No matter what the losses you may have sustained, make sure you set up an exit plan if you don't have one; otherwise your default exit plan most likely is:

1. I am long a stock (likely with a large loss).
2. If the stock rallies back above my entry price, I will exit immediately.
3. If the stock does not rally back above my entry price, I will hold indefinitely.

This exit plan literally means that you are risking the entire price of the stock while limiting your upside gains; it is trend fading, not trend following. Furthermore, there is a possibility that you may tie up capital in this losing position for an indefinite amount of time (although you may decide, for example, to exit at a new 40-day high to get out of the stock on some form of a rally). Is limiting your open gains while leaving your open losses open-ended a wise use of capital? What if the company goes bankrupt and you lose everything? Definitely don't throw good money after bad by adding to your position simply because it is down. Let's take a look at an example of such a loser averaging strategy:

1. Buy 1,000 shares of ABCD at $50.
2. Buy 1,000 shares of ABCD at $49.
3. Buy 1,000 shares of ABCD at $48.
4. If ABCD falls below $45, exit immediately, otherwise stay in.

5. If ABCD rises above $60, exit immediately, otherwise stay in.

6. If one calendar year passes after your entry date, exit on the opening of the next trading day.

This combines a loser averaging strategy with both a target price and a time stop. What are your worst case losses from this strategy? If price drops directly to $47, you will own 3,000 shares of ABCD and have an open position loss of $6,000. If it then drops further, and sets off your $45 stop, your total loss will be $12,000. The most you can make with this strategy is $33,000, but you would have to experience a drawdown of anywhere from $3,000 to $12,000 *first* to accumulate the necessary 3,000-share position required to achieve this maximum gain. This is a very risky method of trading that I do not recommend. How successful do you think CEOs are who continually throw more money at the losing segments of their businesses? I prefer holding winning positions much more than waiting for losing positions to bounce back.

Let's return to my discussion about how to treat open positions for which you have no existing exit plan. Simply treat any such positions as if you had entered them anew on the very same day that you create an exit plan for them. You may wish to set a fixed stop level from the current price, and use a trend following exit strategy like a ratchet stop. Write your plan down and then execute it. Maybe after you have done this you immediately get stopped out on the low tick of a move and the stock proceeds to rocket right on to new highs. Realize that you have made a rational choice to protect your capital from unlimited exposure. Your time and money will also be thankfully freed up to study and invest in other market opportunities. It is tempting to get caught up in sophisticated fundamental and technical arguments with yourself about why a stock is not moving in your favor; I have been there. But you can always go back in after you get out. If you stay in, on the other hand, you have no control over what happens. So when in doubt, stay out.

By setting up a conditional exit list, you will never again have to ask yourself questions like, "Why isn't this stock doing what I thought it would do?" Your selling will be mechanical. Remember that trading is the tip of the iceberg compared to your other preparations for extracting money out of the market, and setting up a conditional exit list should be part of those preparations. So leave your analysis of a trade for the times when you are out of the market. Once in the trade, do not argue with the market; react to it. You may win once or twice arguing with the market in the short term, but you will eventually lose either your money or your confidence going down this road. Businesspeople and lawyers draw up contracts all the time so that they know exactly how to act in complex human situations involving money. A conditional exit list is a contract you make with your-self, so be sure to follow through on it.

POSITION SIZING

Target Heat

I use the term "heat" to refer to the risk to you (the trader) on an individ-ual equity position—at the time that you enter it. The use of the term "heat" in a risk management context, to the best of my knowledge, was coined by futures trend followers Ed Seykota and David Druz.[5] In equity trading, I consider the heat of an individual position to be the gross per-cent of capital (in a segregated portion of your portfolio originally con-taining cash) that you would lose if you liquidated a new position at its stop price immediately after you have entered it.

For example, imagine that your portfolio has $10,000 in cash and nothing else. If you invest all of this cash in stock ABCD at $40, and use a $30 stop, your heat on the position is $(1 - \$30/\$40) = 25$ percent because if you immediately sell at $30, you will lose 25 percent of $10,000, or $2,500. Note that $(1 - \$30/\$40) = 25$ percent is also your dollar risk to price ratio, or R:P ratio, in the stock.

However, what if you want to risk *only* 5% of your cash on the posi-tion if your $30 stop is hit? I define the 5 percent of your capital that you *want* to risk on the position as your "target heat" (see box).

To reconcile your 5 percent target heat with the 25 percent R:P ratio of the stock (which is based on where you place your stop), divide target heat by the R:P ratio, which yields 5 percent/25 percent = 1/5 = 20 percent. This 20 percent is the fraction of your portfolio that you should invest in stock ABCD, so that you lose no more than 5 percent of your capital if your stop is triggered.

Let's do the math backward. If you invest 20 percent of $10,000 in stock ABCD, this means an investment of $2,000 in the stock (leaving $8,000 of your portfolio in cash). Since your R:P ratio is 25 percent, if you lose 25 percent of $2,000 this means a loss of $500. This loss of $500 repre-sents 5 percent of your original $10,000 capital.

Thus, you have successfully sized your position so that you will lose your target heat of 5 percent if the stock drops 25 percent. If target heat exceeds the R:P ratio, you would invest 100 percent of your capital in the stock (unless you wish to use margin).

There are two ways that you can use target heat in an equity portfolio to define your initial acceptable risk on a position:

1. Specify target heat separately in different portions of your portfolio, whose activity you track separately from each other.

2. Specify target heat for your entire portfolio at once, provided that you intend to make a whole portfolio trade in which you go long all portfolio positions simultaneously after having the whole portfolio in cash.

In a cash equity account, you can easily be prevented from taking on additional risk if you have existing dollar exposure to stocks. The reasons why this is true highlight major differences between equity and futures trading. First of all, you tie up no cash when you enter a futures contract, and have considerable flexibility in the amount of leverage you can take on. In fact, maximum permissible leverage for many exchange traded futures contracts exceeds 10:1. In stocks, however, your maximum leverage is 2:1, and in addition to this you tie up actual cash when you buy individual stocks. Furthermore, you must also pay interest on money that you borrow to increase your leverage past 1:1. Due to some of these limitations, you will be unable to take on the kinds of risk that you could in the futures market.

In futures trading, due to the availability of very high leverage, you may often be able to specify a very high target heat for a position in advance, and then pick a position size that corresponds to this target heat based on your chosen stop level, no matter what *else* is in your portfolio. For example, let's say that you start a futures account with $600,000 cash, which you use to buy 100,000 MMBtu of natural gas futures at $6/MMBtu (a market value that represents all the cash you initially place into the account). A year later, the natural gas contracts you own are trading at $10/MMBtu, meaning that your account's market value is now $1,000,000 (on a mark-to-market basis). At this point, you decide to buy some crude oil contracts, which are trading at $70/barrel. You want to go long crude oil futures, initially risking 3 percent of your total account capital of $1,000,000, but risking $4/barrel on the *price* of the crude oil futures contract itself. Since your account capital is $1 million, this means that you want to risk $30,000 (i.e., 3 percent of it) on a $4/barrel move in crude oil futures. To do this, you would have to own ($30,000) / ($4/barrel) = 7,500 barrels. Checking in reverse, if you own 7,500 barrels, and lose $4/barrel, you will lose $30,000, that is, 3 percent of your capital. In futures, it would be no problem to put on this additional crude oil position, which has a market value of 7,500 barrels × $70/barrel = $525,000. But in a cash equity account (i.e., with no margin) this would not be possible at all.

Let's imagine an analogous situation in stocks. You put $600,000 cash into a new cash equity account, and use it to buy 100,000 shares of a $6 stock. The stock runs up to $10, meaning you are sitting on an open profit of $400,000. Can you now buy 7,500 shares of a $70 stock? The answer is NO. In fact, you cannot buy *a single share* of any other stock because all your money is tied up! Even the $400,000 open profit is irrelevant; no money is free to be used at all. Note also that in a stock margin account, overnight leverage is limited to 2:1, and since you still tie up cash in your positions, you can easily run into limitations on position sizes you may want to take. Thus, in stocks you cannot simply specify a target heat in advance and then count on having the free cash to enter into a future position with exactly the position size that you want. As a result, you must structure your portfolio in a specific way that ensures that you will have the available cash to enter into future investments that you may be currently contemplating.

To explain how to do this, I first define a "subaccount" or "bin," which is simply a portion of a larger equity account that is segregated from the rest of the account on paper. (See box.) My rules are:

- A subaccount is used to trade one stock individually or a basket of stocks simultaneously, so you alternate in the subaccount between being partially or fully invested in stocks and being fully in cash.
- Target heat in a subaccount specifies the maximum percentage of the subaccount's cash that you are willing to place at risk *when you initiate* a new position (based on where you plan to stop yourself out in the worst case).
- You can specify actual heat only *individually* for each subaccount in a portfolio, and not for multiple subaccounts in aggregate. Adding the actual heat percentages of multiple subaccounts together, which may hold positions initiated at different times, does not produce a consistent total measure of risk.
- A subaccount must be 100 percent completely in cash *before* you can use target heat to size a new position.
- Your heat in a subaccount is then defined as the maximum percentage of the preinvestment cash in a subaccount that you would lose if you liquidated *a newly initiated position* at its stop price.
- Note that a subaccount can contain both cash and stock, that is, you do not have to invest 100 percent of the cash in a subaccount if you buy a stock.

Because of the way I define heat, it *cannot* be used as a measure of your instantaneous risk based on the mark-to-market value of your portfolio (or some other more sophisticated means). To calculate your risk in that sense, you would need to know the percentage of the portfolio's mark-to-market value that you would lose if you instantaneously liquidated all positions at their stop prices. Since the market value of each portfolio position constantly changes, and especially if you use trailing stops, this can be a complex calculation to perform. For example, for a subaccount containing *only* stock ABCD and cash, you can calculate the percentage of the subaccount's mark-to-market value that you are risking by using the following formula:

Percentage of a subaccount's mark-to-market value that you are risking based on your stop level = (mark-to-market value of stock ABCD)

$$\times \frac{\big[1 - (\text{highest confirmed stop price} / \text{market price of ABCD})\big]}{(\text{cash in the subaccount}) + (\text{mark-to-market value of stock ABCD})}$$

So for example, if you are trading stock ABCD with both a fixed stop and a stop based on an external pilot signal, the fixed stop price would be your highest confirmed stop price, since the pilot signal is not 100 percent correlated to stock ABCD (and thus you can't estimate a confirmed stop in stock ABCD based on it without going into some serious math). If you are trading stock ABCD with a trailing stop alone, the trailing stop price would be your highest confirmed stop price. This equation assumes that you will automatically be stopped out exactly at your highest confirmed stop price if the stock drops below it, which is of course not always a realistic assumption. The equation is applicable to a single subaccount containing only one stock; calculating the same value for your entire portfolio would be even more complex.

A "subaccount" is a portion of your portfolio that you segregate and treat separately from the rest of your portfolio as if it were its own individual account. Dividing your portfolio in this manner is a logical way to set aside money to trade other stocks that you may be interested in trading in the future.

I later go into more detail about structuring your equity portfolio into subaccounts, which I call "bins" going forward for simplicity. The process entails dividing a cash account into segregated (on paper) subaccounts and then separately accounting for the trading activity in each bin.

The following scenario illustrates the logic of why I require a bin to be fully in cash before using target heat to size a new position, rather than sizing a new position based on the mark-to-market value of my overall portfolio. Imagine once again that you start a cash equity account with $600,000. You use $300,000 of this (i.e., one half) to buy stock ABC, and leave the other $300,000 in cash. You are currently monitoring stock DEF as a buy candidate, and decide that you will risk losing a maximum of 5 percent of your *future* portfolio capital on a trade in it. You are waiting for a technical buy signal to occur in DEF before buying it, however. Visualize the following two scenarios:

Scenario A: Stock ABC doubles in price in six months, making your account value (stocks plus cash) equal to $300,000 (2) + $300,000 = $900,000. Your buy signal in stock DEF then occurs. Risking 5 percent of total capital at this point would mean risking 5% × (900,000) = $45,000.

Scenario B: Stock ABC halves in price in six months, making your account value (stocks plus cash) equal to $300,000 (1/2) + $300,000 = $450,000. Your buy signal in stock DEF then occurs. Risking 5 percent of total capital at this point would mean risking 5% × ($450,000) = $22,500.

What if in Scenario A you had bought stock ABC and are holding for a one-year period, with a fixed stop of 5 percent of the portfolio's *original* cash value (i.e., $600,000 × 5% = $30,000)? That is, your plan was to liquidate the position if you lost $30,000, but instead the stock ran up dramatically, leaving you with a $300,000 open profit after six months. You still have another half a year left, though, in which the entire open profit could evaporate and you could even end up losing an additional $15,000, for example. Is it appropriate to risk $45,000 on the position in stock DEF? And how much risk would this really entail since you still intend to hold the former position for another half year, and thus are not really treating your existing open profit as real yet?

Since you do not know where the former position will be valued in either a half year or a full year, if you size the position in stock DEF in half a year based on the mark-to-market value of your *entire* portfolio, you may be sizing it either too large or too small. Sure, the way you size it may make sense based on where your portfolio happens to be valued at the midyear mark, but as you have zero intention of liquidating the position in stock ABC at that point, what use is that? In truth, the only sensible thing to do is to size the position in stock DEF based on the original cash in your account reserved to invest in it (i.e., $300,000). According to this measure, if you risk $45,000 on the latter position, this would represent a whopping 15 percent of the original capital reserved to invest in that position! That is 50 percent higher than your $30,000 initial risk on the former position. So you might choose to initially risk 10 percent of your capital in that portion of the portfolio (as you did with the former position), which represents $30,000. Your target heat on both individual positions would thus be 10 percent, *respectively*.

"Heat" is the percentage of the *preinvestment* cash in a subaccount that you would lose by liquidating a *newly initiated* position at its stop. "Target heat" is the maximum percentage of a subaccount's preinvestment cash value that you are willing to initially risk on a trade. In practice, you want to choose a position size that gives you a heat less than or equal to your target heat when sizing a new position (see box).

> Thus, target heat is simply a value that you define before entering the market that instructs you how to size new positions. Heat in turn represents the initial risk that you actually take on when you enter a new position.

Heat is an *initial* measure of risk that you have when you enter a position, and can thus be discarded once you are in a position. Once the position is initiated and the stock's price (and possibly your stop price) starts to float, heat is no longer a very accurate measure of the risk of a sub-account based on its mark-to-market value. However, it is good to know, for example, that you will not risk any more than 10 percent of the preinvestment cash in a bin, no matter what the value of your portfolio happens to be.

My definition of heat means that you can accurately specify a target heat only for individual bins in a portfolio. To maintain consistency across your portfolio, you may use the *same* target heat (i.e., the target heat that you plan to size a future position with) for each bin. You may also choose to treat your entire portfolio as one giant bin, entering and exiting all stocks in it simultaneously. I discuss this possibility later.

Estimating Volatility When Placing Stops

Donchian Bands   There is a whole host of methods of estimating volatility. Let me state here that none of them are particularly right for trading, because they all use *past* data to estimate how volatile a stock is likely to be in the *future*. As an equity trader, it is useful to estimate volatility first because it is important to give a position a reasonable amount of room to fluctuate as it hopefully drifts in your favor. Second, a volatility estimate enables you to decide how much capital to allocate to a position based on how much you are willing to risk. Unless your profitability directly depends on very accurate volatility forecasting, your volatility estimate does not have to be perfect; an objective estimation method that you can use with all stocks that you are trading should suffice. Also keep in mind that the more stocks you intend to have in your portfolio, the more complicated your trading procedures will be. Thus, for simplicity, you may want to choose a consistent technical method of stop placement for all stocks in your portfolio, so you can concentrate more time on gaining an edge and less time on dealing with the minutiae of trading.

One such consistent method of stop placement for long-only trading is to set your stop level in each stock at:

Stop level = Entry Price × (N-day lowest price/N-day highest price)

Note that N-day lowest price and N-day highest price represent the lower and upper Donchian band values, respectively. If you wish, the N-day lowest price and N-day highest price that you use to set your stop level can include the current day's data in their calculation and can be measured at your time of entry. This would incorporate any price gaps that occur on your entry day into your stop level calculation. This is an incredibly simple stop placement method that is equivalent to setting your R:P ratio on a long position at:

$$R{:}P\ ratio = 1 - \frac{N\text{-day low}}{N\text{-day high}}$$

Note that your R:P ratio with this method is independent of your entry price, and based entirely on the ratio of the stock's N-day lowest price to its N-day highest price. Using this R:P ratio gives you room on a trade to lose the same percentage of your invested capital that you would lose by buying a stock at the highest price of the past N days and immediately liquidating your position at the lowest price of the past N days.

Is this formula a reasonable estimate of the downside volatility you are likely to encounter if you hold a position? It depends on your time horizon for the position and/or the technical exit method you are using. For example, if you set your stop at

$$Stop\ level = market\ price \times \frac{40\text{-day lowest price}}{40\text{-day highest price}}$$

without using any other exit method, it is quite unlikely that you will be stopped out within two days. On the other hand, it is a lot more likely that your stop will be triggered if you hold the stock for 200 days with no other exit method, because the price range that a stock traces out generally increases over time (see box).

> I view the quantity [1 – (N-day lowest price/N-day highest price)] as *a very rough estimate* of the maximum open loss I am likely to encounter in a stock *over the next N days.*

Of course this is not 100 percent accurate. It is somewhat like estimating today's price range to be equal to yesterday's price range. On some days the estimate will be nearly true, and on other days it will be quite a bit off. But at least it should be in the ballpark.

Note that if you don't want to include daily high and low data in your stop level calculation with this method, you may use the N-day highest open and the N-day lowest open in your stop level calculation instead, which would still allow you to take overnight gaps into account when trading.

I should also point out that this method of calculating your stop level does not mean that you are required to always enter a stock at the upper Donchian band; it is simply a consistent and quick method of stop placement that is applicable to any stock you happen to be trading at any price. Setting stops in a consistent manner should make planning your trades a little simpler. Thus, even if you enter a stock while it is in the middle of its Donchian bands, or closer to its lower Donchian band, your R:P ratio would still be 1 – (N-day low/N-day high), which can never exceed 100 percent by definition. I show an example of setting a stop in this manner in Figure 5.2. You may also place your stops at fractions of the distance from your entry price indicated by the stop level formula presented earlier. Even though there are other more sophisticated methods of volatility estimation, this method is simple to calculate and consistent across all stocks.

An alternative method of stop placement is to set your stops on long positions at:

$$\text{Entry price} - (\text{N-day high} - \text{N-day low})$$

Of course, (N-day high – N-day low) is the N-day Donchian bandwidth. This formula thus means that your dollar risk in a stock is equal to the N-day Donchian bandwidth, making your R:P ratio:

$$\text{R:P ratio} = \frac{\text{N-day Donchian bandwidth}}{\text{entry price}}$$

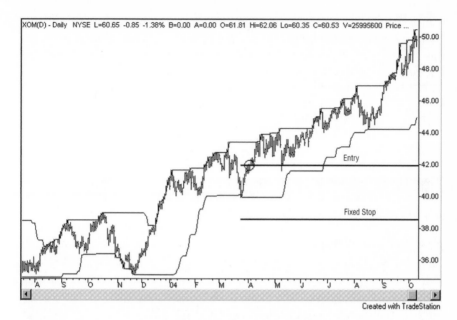

FIGURE 5.2 Entering a stock at a price in between its Donchian bands, and set-ting a fixed stop at Entry Price* (low band/high band), which in this case would end up below the lower Donchian band. (*Source:* © TradeStation® 1991–2006. All rights reserved.)

The only possible problem with this method is that the R:P ratio might sometimes exceed 100 percent. For example, imagine a $1 stock that has dropped to a $1 low price from a high price of $3 within the past 40 days. Imagine also that your stop level is [Entry price – (40-day high – 40-day low)]. If you buy the stock at $1, this would make your stop level $1 – ($3 – $1) = ($1 – $2) = –$1, which is a negative price. You'd thus have to cap the R:P ratio you come up with using this method at 100 percent in actual use.

Standard Deviation (of Closing Prices)

You may also calculate your stop level on a position by using the standard deviation of a series of closing prices. With this method, for example, you might set your stop level on a long position at:

[Entry price – (N-day standard deviation of closing prices)]
with a minimum stop level of 0

You may also use multiples or fractions of the N-day standard deviation to adjust your stop placement for longer or shorter time frames, respectively. An alternative method of stop placement based on the standard deviation of a price series is to set your stop on a position at:

$$\text{Entry price} \times \frac{\text{lower Bollinger band value}}{\text{upper Bollinger band value}}$$

The upper and lower Bollinger bands are separated by four N-day standard deviations of price, and setting a stop with this method ensures that you will never calculate a negative stop value.

Average True Range

Average true range (ATR), a volatility measure conceived of by Welles Wilder, requires daily high, low, and closing prices to calculate. A stock's daily range is simply its daily high minus its daily low. Its true daily range, on the other hand, would be the daily range it would have if you count the previous day's closing price as part of the current day's price data. Thus:

True range is:[6]

(The higher of today's high and yesterday's close)

minus

(the lower of today's low and yesterday's close)

Average true range is simply a moving average of the series of true range values, taken over some number of days. You may again use multiples or fractions of ATR to make volatility estimates in different time frames.

Converting ATR to a Percentage

The dollar volatility measures I have mentioned in this chapter, such as average true range, Donchian bandwidth, and Bollinger bandwidth can all be converted to percentages. This prevents you from calculating negative stop levels based on them. For example, imagine that you use a 10 ATR stop in a $1 stock which has an ATR of 12 cents. Well, in this case, 10 ATR would be $1.20, which would take you to a negative stop price. You could of course place your stop at a zero price (i.e., no stop), but there is another way to convert ATR into a percentage, which I give here.

In the preceding example, a 1 ATR drop of 12 cents would represent a

12 percent decline in a $1 stock. So 10 subsequent 12 percent declines in the stock would lead to a price of:

$$\$1 \times (100\% - 12\%)^{10} = \$1 \times (88\%)^{10} = \$1 \times (0.2785) = \$0.28$$

$0.28 is of course a positive value. This is one way to arrive at a reasonable nonzero number. An alternative way to calculate an ATR-related volatility measure is to take the average of each day's true low to its true high over a certain time period. If you subtract the percentage value you arrive at from 1, you will obtain an alternative, percentage based form of average true range.

That is, your R:P ratio for a 1 ATR stop, with ATR calculated over 40 days will be:

$$1 - \left[40\text{-day average of} \left(\frac{\text{true low}}{\text{true high}} \right) \right]$$

This yields a percentage form of ATR. If you lose this percentage on a trade, the new value of your portfolio *as a fraction of its original value* will be:

$$\left[40\text{-day average of} \left(\frac{\text{true low}}{\text{true high}} \right) \right]$$

If you lose an identical percentage on your portfolio N days in a row, your portfolio's new value as a fraction of its original value will be:

$$\left[40\text{-day average of} \left(\frac{\text{true low}}{\text{true high}} \right) \right]^{N}$$

This quantity must be positive.

Note that ATR can be used as a consistent volatility measure no matter at what price you enter a stock.

R-Multiples and Other Methods of Studying Trading Performance

Since a preplanned stop is an integral component of any trade, it is useful in some circumstances to think of any locked-in gains or losses as multiples of the *maximum gross amount* that you were willing to risk (i.e., before commissions and slippage). This is known as expressing P&L in terms of R-multiples, a term commonly used in systematic trading. Thus, if the maximum gross amount you are willing to risk on a trade is $1, but you end up making $2 net, you have made $2/$1 = 2 R-multiples. If your maximum amount risked is $1, but you end up losing $0.50 net, you have lost $0.50/$1 = 0.5 R-multiples. Clearly you want your wins to be massive R-multiple trades, but due to the unpredictability of the market, and the fact that your exit method must be preplanned, you will generally have little control over whether this actually occurs. R-multiples are useful for comparing trades in which identical percentages of your capital, like 1 percent, were risked on all trades.

However, I hope you realize that, especially if you are a discretionary rather than systematic trader, you will not always risk identical percentages of capital on each trade. You may have a trade where you lose 1 R-multiple, but risked 10 percent of your capital, for an overall loss of 10 percent. Contrast this with a trade where you make 5 R-multiples, but risked only 1 percent of your capital, for an overall gain of 5 percent. Clearly, the overall effect to your portfolio of the +5 R-multiple trade and the –1 R-multiple trade will be a net loss.

An alternative method of organizing your trade data is to simply rank all your trades by their individual dollar returns, and sort them into bins as well. If you are not trading with a purely systematic method in which percentage risk on each trade is approximately the same, this method of analyzing your trade performance, illustrated in Figure 5.3, may make more sense. However, you can also do this visually, by scanning through your trades for the ones that cost you the most and made you the most money (both of which should be imprinted on your psyche anyway).

By periodically sorting the net dollar proceeds of your trades over rolling periods (for example, rolling three-month periods), you can observe weak and strong areas in your trading. For example, do you have many small profits that are offset by a few large losses? Sorting your trades by their net dollar returns helps you to focus on what is really important—extracting money from the market! In the final analysis, all you care about is making net profits; your win percentage and your trade returns expressed in R-multiples are less important to your overall profitability than the net sum of your aggregate winnings and losses. However, R-multiple returns are a useful normalized measure of the efficiency of individual trades.

To sort your net dollar returns into several bins, you may use the following method. Subtract your worst single trade loss over a period you want to examine from your greatest win, and divide the resulting range into equal partitions. For example, if your greatest win was $5,300 and your worst loss was $3,700, your range of trade values was $5,300 –

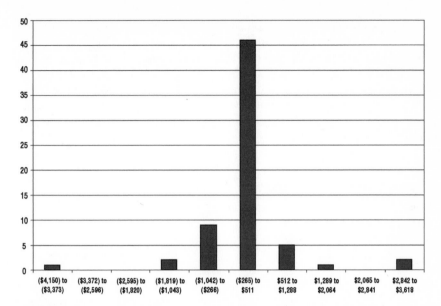

FIGURE 5.3 A sample dollar return distribution for a group of trades.

(−$3,700) = $5,300 + $3,700 = $9,000. You would then divide $9000 by N if you intend to sort your trade results into N bins. *Please note that this is a different use of the word "bin" from my use of it as a subsection of your portfolio.*

Let's say you want 10 bins. Then you would divide $9,000 by 10 which yields $900, the width of each bin. To find out the dividing values between bins, start with −$3,700, and add $900 a total of 10 times, which will yield the values: −$3,700, −$2,800, −$1,900, −$1,000, −$100, +$800,+$1,700, +$2,600, +$3,500, +$4,400, and +$5,300.

Your *barriers between bins* will of course be the same numbers, excluding the highest and the lowest values. That is: −$2,800, −$1,900, −$1,000, −$100, +$800,+$1,700, +$2,600, +$3,500, and +$4,400

Simply sort all the trades that fall in between these barriers into the respective bins. The lowest bin contains all trades with dollar returns less than −$2,800, the bin immediately to its right contains trades with dollar returns between −$2,800 and −$1,900, and so on until the highest bin, which contains all trades with dollar returns greater than +$4,400. So using these bin barrier values, if one of your trades made $2,800 and another made $3,400, you would put them both into the bin with barriers of +$2,600 and +$3,500, counting two trades in that bin. If another of your trades lost $2,100, you would place it into the bin with barriers of –$2,800 and –$1,900, counting one trade in that bin.

Besides looking nice on a chart, reviewing your dollar returns for individual trades in this manner, for example, on a rolling basis, can help you to monitor where your money is made and lost from a fresh perspective. Are you making less overall than you should because of large losses that fall into the lower bins? Are the bulk of your wins coming from a few very profitable trades?

CHAPTER 6

Structuring a Trend Trading Portfolio

PORTFOLIO STRUCTURING

Using Bins

Although many books talk mostly about trading individual stocks, in real life you will likely be managing a portfolio of multiple stocks, which requires a more advanced set of risk management tools. In this section I discuss in more detail how "heat" and the "R:P ratio" can be used to structure a cash equity portfolio in a logical manner.

First, back to basics. Let's first imagine an all cash portfolio in which we are going to buy only one stock, and want to lose no more than 10 percent of the portfolio value. The value 10 percent is thus our target heat, the maximum percentage of capital in the all cash portfolio that we are willing to risk at initiation of a position. We need to ensure that our risk to the whole portfolio will never exceed the target heat, no matter which dollar risk to price ratio we choose. To do this, divide the target heat by the R:P ratio (see box).

Both target heat and the R:P ratio are percentages, and dividing one by the other will yield another percentage—the percentage of the portfolio's cash that you should invest in the stock.

153

So for example, let's say you want to buy a $50 stock with a stop level of $42, meaning your dollar risk is $8 and your R:P ratio is $8/$50 = 16 percent. You have $100,000 cash in your account and want to risk only 10 percent of your capital on the trade (i.e., your target heat is 10 percent). What percentage of your overall capital do you invest in the stock? The answer is:

$$\begin{array}{l} \text{Percentage of portfolio capital} \\ \text{to invest in stock} \end{array} = \frac{\text{target heat}}{\text{R:P ratio}}$$

$$= \frac{10\%}{16\%}$$

$$= 62.5\%$$

To find the number of shares of the $50 stock you would actually have to buy, divide the dollar amount that you will invest in the stock by the stock's price.

In this example, this means that you would buy 62.5% × ($100,000) / $50 = 1,250 shares. Checking in reverse, 1,250 shares × $50 = $62,500, which is 62.5 percent of $100,000. Our dollar stop is at $42/share, and if it drops there we will lose $8/share on a position of 1,250 shares, for a total loss of $10,000. Of course, $10,000 is 10 percent of $100,000. Thus, we will lose our target heat of 10 percent of the original cash in the portfolio if stopped out at $42 (even though the stock has dropped $8/$50 = 16%, which is more than 10%).

Commit this calculation process to memory by testing it out by hand with different scenarios. It should be clear to you at this point that: *No matter where you place your stop in a stock, you can adjust your position size properly so that you do not lose a higher percentage of your preinvestment cash than your target heat.*

What if you run into the scenario where your R:P ratio is less than your target heat? For example you may have an R:P ratio of 7 percent with a target heat of 11 percent. This would imply that you should invest 11%/7% = 157% of your total capital in the stock. Clearly you cannot do this in a cash account, although you can do this in a margin account if you choose to do so. For cash accounts, you must thus add an additional caveat to the equation determining the percentage of your total capital to invest in a stock. The equation then looks like:

$$\begin{array}{l} \text{Percentage of portfolio} \\ \text{cash to invest in stock} \\ \textit{(up to a maximum of 100\%)} \end{array} = \frac{\text{(target heat)}}{\text{R:P Ratio}}$$

This is a fancy way of saying that if target heat *exceeds* the R:P ratio in a cash equity account, you would invest 100 percent of your portfolio cash in the stock. Once again, to use target heat properly to size a position, the segregated section of your portfolio that you are applying it to must be all in cash before you initiate that position.

Well, so much for our hypothetical one-stock portfolio. Let's move on to more realistic situations. Let's say you have a cash account and decide in advance to hold a portfolio consisting of a certain number of stocks, for example four stocks. You divide your starting capital into four equal sub-accounts or bins, before putting on any trades. You then proceed to treat each bin as if it were an entirely separate account, although the cash and stock positions across the various bins are all commingled in your overall account.

You may use bins within the context of a larger trend trading strategy that I call a "campaign." For example, let's say that the Semiconductor Index's (symbol: SOX) P/E just fell below 10 for the first time in several years. You feel that this makes the sector very undervalued, and so decide to buy four semiconductor stocks (e.g., stocks ABC, DEF, GHI, and JKL) to take advantage of this. Your trading plan, including conditional exit statements, is as follows:

1. Buy all four stocks, ABC, DEF, GHI, and JKL, immediately.
2. If any of the stocks drops 10 percent from your respective entry price in it, then exit that stock immediately.
3. If the SOX Index's P/E moves above 20, then exit *all* positions immediately.
4. If the SOX Index's P/E is below 15, *and* you get stopped out of an individual stock, then reenter that stock if it rallies back to your original entry level (provided that the SOX Index's P/E is still below 15).
5. Treat any reentered stock as if you had just entered it in step 1.

Note that Statement #4 is a reentry condition. As long as the SOX Index P/E remains below 15, you need to specify how you will get back into the market if you get stopped out of a stock. Why? Because you consider any period when the SOX Index has a P/E below 15 to be a window of opportunity. You feel yourself fortunate enough to have gotten a great bargain by entering the market with a SOX Index P/E below 10, but if the SOX Index rises to a P/E of 11 or 12, you would still consider it a great bargain, as long as it is still below a P/E of 15. Once its P/E is above this, though, you do not believe that the potential reward is worth the risk, and so are content to stay out of the market if you are stopped out. By confining each stock to a separate bin, and trading in each bin separately within the context of a larger portfolio campaign, you are making sure that you have adequate capital to reinvest if you get stopped out of the market in a particular stock.

A lot to think about, isn't it? And I still haven't mentioned *how much* of each stock we would actually be buying. This is where the concept of bins comes in handy. Since you want to trade four stocks separately for the duration of your trade campaign, separate your original capital into four separate bins. The easiest way to keep track of the process is to make a worksheet containing one column for each bin. On this worksheet, journal the total amount of cash and stock in each bin each time you make a trade in any bin. So let's say you start a portfolio with $80,000 in cash on January 2, 2006. On that date, each bin would contain $80,000/4 = $20,000, and would be treated on your worksheet as a separate account going forward. Bin #1 would be used to trade stock ABC exclusively, bin #2 would be used for stock DEF, bin #3 for stock GHI and bin #4 for stock JKL, as illustrated in Table 6.1.

Since you treat each bin as a separate account, you would then assign a target heat to each bin, which specifies the maximum percentage of bin capital that you are willing to risk on any new trade. For simplicity's sake, you can assign an identical target heat to each bin. Note also that if you get stopped out of a stock in a particular bin, you do not reinvest the cash you have raised from the sale unless your trading plan tells you to reenter that particular stock.

After splitting our $80,000 capital into four bins of $20,000 each, let's say that we fully invest the cash in each respective bin in stocks ABC (bin 1), DEF (bin 2), GHI (bin 3) and JKL (bin 4) simultaneously, on January 3, 2006. Stock ABC has a $20 entry price, Stock DEF a $40 entry price, Stock GHI a $50 entry price and Stock JKL a $100 entry price, meaning that we buy 1000 shares, 500 shares, 400 shares, and 200 shares of each, respectively. For simplicity's sake, let's also say that the R:P ratio of each stock is equal to your target heat for the bin it is in, that is, 30 percent. On April 3, 2006 (three months after your entry), you are stopped out of stock JKL (in bin 4) at $70 with a 30 percent loss, but you still own ABC, DEF, and GHI, which are above their respective stop levels. You have now lost 30 percent on your $20,000 investment in bin 4, leaving $14,000 in cash in that bin.

TABLE 6.1 An $80,000 portfolio split into four equal-sized bins, each set aside for the trading of one stock.

	Bin 1 (ABC)	Bin 2 (DEF)	Bin 3 (GHI)	Bin 4 (JKL)
Stock (1/2/06)	0 shares	0 shares	0 shares	0 shares
Cash (1/2/06)	$20,000	$20,000	$20,000	$20,000

You would leave this money in cash unless you get a reentry signal in stock JKL. So let's say you do get a reentry signal in JKL, on July 3, 2006, at $50. You buy 280 shares with the $14,000 cash in bin 4. All other stocks remain above their respective stop levels during this entire time, and your target heat in each bin remains at 30 percent. If you get stopped out again for a 30 percent loss on October 3, 2006, at $35, you will now have $9,800 left in bin 4. This entire process is illustrated in Table 6.2.

The process continues like this, with your treating bin 4 as if it were a completely separate account that trades only stock JKL. Note that you may often run into a situation where you are sitting in cash in several bins simultaneously. You would still treat the bins as separate in this case. Furthermore, note that although your target heat in an individual bin might be 30 percent, you can lose more than 30 percent of the original cash in the bin if you allow yourself to reenter an individual stock after you are stopped out. In this example, you lose a total of $10,200 in bin 4 after 2 trades (i.e., 12.75% of the portfolio's original cash value). If losses of the same magnitude occurred in each of the portfolio's four bins, you would end up losing 51 percent of your portfolio's original cash value, which is significantly greater than 30 percent.

TABLE 6.2 A sample bin worksheet for a cash equity portfolio.

	Bin 1 (ABC) Target Heat 30%	Bin 2 (DEF) Target Heat 30%	Bin 3 (GHI) Target Heat 30%	Bin 4 (JKL) Target Heat 30%
Stock (1/2/06)	0 shares	0 shares	0 shares	0 shares
Cash (1/2/06)	$20,000	$20,000	$20,000	$20,000
Stock (1/3/06)	1,000 shares	500 shares	400 shares	200 shares
Cash (1/3/06)	$0	$0	$0	$0
Stock (4/3/06)	1,000 shares	500 shares	400 shares	0 shares
Cash (4/3/06)	$0	$0	$0	$14,000
Stock (7/3/06)	1,000 shares	500 shares	400 shares	280 shares
Cash (7/3/06)	$0	$0	$0	$0
Stock (10/3/06)	1000 shares	500 shares	400 shares	0 shares
Cash (10/3/06)	$0	$0	$0	$9,800

Although my example shows the simplest scenario where you are always fully investing the money in each bin, you can of course imagine other scenarios. In real life, your target heat for each bin and your R:P ratio for a stock that you are trading in that bin will not always be the same. You can fix it to be this way by using percentage stops, but percentage stops have some disadvantages that I mentioned earlier (especially in cheap stocks with wide spreads).

Let's imagine again that you have just started an account on January 2, 2006, with $80,000 cash, which you split into four equal bins of $20,000 each. In these bins, you once again intend to trade stocks ABC (bin 1), DEF (bin 2), GHI (bin 3) and JKL (bin 4). This time, however, your target heats in bins 1, 2, 3, and 4 are 10 percent, 20 percent, 30 percent, and 40 percent, respectively. The R:P ratios that you choose for the stocks in bins 1, 2, 3, and 4 are 30 percent, 30 percent, 30 percent, and 30 percent, respectively (e.g., fixed percentage stops of 30%). Finally, stock ABC has a $20 entry price, stock DEF a $40 entry price, stock GHI a $50 entry price, and stock JKL a $100 entry price. You enter each stock on January 3, 2006, after calculating your position sizes.

1. In bin 1, which has a 10 percent target heat and 30 percent R:P ratio, you invest 10%/30% = 33.33% of the $20,000 cash in the bin (i.e., $6667) in stock ABC, leaving $13,333 in cash.

2. In bin 2, which has a 20 percent target heat and 30 percent R:P ratio, you invest 20%/30% = 66.67% of the $20,000 cash in the bin (i.e., $13,334) in stock DEF, leaving $6,666 in cash.

3. In bin 3, which has a 30 percent target heat and 30 percent R:P ratio, you invest 30%/30% = 100% of the $20,000 cash in the bin (i.e., $20,000) in stock GHI, leaving $0 in cash.

4. In bin 4, which has a 40 percent target heat and 30 percent R:P ratio, you invest 100 percent of the $20,000 cash in the bin (i.e., $20,000) in stock JKL, leaving $0 in cash. Since the target heat exceeds the R:P ratio in this case, you invest the maximum of 100 percent of the cash in the bin.

I show this process in Table 6.3.

Once again, if you are using a cash portfolio and the R:P ratio is less than the target heat at your time of entry, you will invest 100 percent of the money in the bin. However, if the R:P ratio exceeds the target heat at your time of entry, you will invest the fraction (target heat/R:P ratio) of the capital in the bin.

One possible disadvantage of using bins in a *cash* account, in which your R:P ratios in individual stocks are not equal to the respective target

	TABLE 6.3	How to make journal entries into your bin worksheet if you assign varying target heats to each bin (R:P ratios are assumed to be fixed at 30%).

	Bin 1 (ABC) Target Heat 10%	**Bin 2 (DEF)** Target Heat 20%	**Bin 3 (GHI)** Target Heat 30%	**Bin 4 (JKL)** Target Heat 40%
Stock (1/2/06)	0 shares	0 shares	0 shares	0 shares
Cash (1/2/06)	$20,000	$20,000	$20,000	$20,000
Stock (1/3/06)	333 shares	333 shares	400 shares	200 shares
Cash (1/3/06)	$13,333	$6,666	$0	$0

heats of the bins they are in, is that you may often not be fully invested. Depending on how you set your stops, some bins may have less than 100 percent of their capital invested, while others may theoretically require you to have more than 100 percent of capital invested. With the latter group you can invest only 100 percent of the capital in the bin. This asymmetry means that you may not be investing as much as you would like to theoretically in some bins even though you will do this in others. One way to get around this is to use margin, with which you can borrow in cash up to 100 percent of the value of a stock you are purchasing, but will have to pay interest on your borrowings. In this case, you would use margin simply to get yourself to the theoretical risk level you are willing to be. Of course, when using margin you would once again record the share amount of a stock that you buy. For example, if you have $14,000 cash in bin 4, and buy $28,000 worth of stock JKL at $100 by borrowing $14,000 on margin, you would write 280 shares in stock and $0 in cash in the Bin Journal column for bin 4. After you have sold the JKL position, you then journal all the cash that you have raised (after all fees and costs) into the next level of rows of your worksheet, in the bin 4 column, and update the bin 4 stock position to 0 shares.

R:P Ratio Averaging

R:P ratio averaging is an advanced position sizing method that you can use to determine position sizes for a group of positions if you want to make a portfolio trade. For example, rather than tracking each stock's progress separately using bins, you may instead decide to enter your entire portfolio of chosen stocks at once, and later exit the entire portfolio at once. R:P ratio averaging can be useful for trading situations like these. One such situation may be to use R:P ratio averaging to time a whole portfolio trade under the guidance of an external pilot signal. You may choose to use the pilot signal with stops in individual stocks, or alternatively you may use a fixed dollar stop for the entire portfolio. Due to the likelihood of high correlations among stocks in the portfolio, make sure that you are comfortable losing not only the percentage of your preinvestment portfolio cash represented by your target heat, but also *more than* that percentage if you choose to reenter the market after being stopped out.

How would you use a fixed dollar stop on an entire portfolio? You would buy your portfolio of stocks on one date and set a dollar loss limit at which you would liquidate the entire portfolio. For example, let's say you buy $100,000 worth of stock (i.e., multiple positions) using a pilot signal to time your trades. In addition to the pilot signal, you tell yourself that if you lose $10,000 on paper (based on the portfolio's closing values each day), you will liquidate the entire portfolio on the open the next day. Using this method, you would simply monitor your total account value after each day's close, and if it dips below ($100,000 – $10,000) = $90,000, you would liquidate the entire account the next trading day. Otherwise, if the *pilot signal* tells you to liquidate (and your portfolio hasn't yet dropped below a value of $90,000), you would liquidate the entire portfolio, hopefully for a profit.

Regardless of whether you use a fixed dollar stop, you still want to size your positions properly based on logical volatility estimates. In reality, the portfolio volatility you encounter will be a function of the correlation of different stocks with one another, the historical volatility of the different stocks, your position sizes, and a host of other factors. However, by using a simple, normalized volatility measure for each stock, you can at least attempt to make a ballpark estimate of the downside volatility that you may encounter while holding these stocks. This is where R:P ratio averaging becomes useful.

As I discussed, a simple, normalized estimate of a stock's maximum N-day downside volatility is:

$$\left[1 - \left(\frac{\text{N-day lowest low}}{\text{N-day highest high}} \right) \right]$$

This is also equal to a stock's R:P ratio *if you set your initial stop in the stock* at:

$$\text{Entry price} \times \left(\frac{\text{N-day lowest low}}{\text{N-day highest high}} \right)$$

For simplicity going forward, let's define the quantity (N-day lowest low/N day highest high) as the "normalized stop ratio":

$$\text{Normalized stop ratio} = \frac{\text{N-day lowest low}}{\text{N-day highest high}}$$

Therefore, a stop price of:

$$\text{Entry price} \times \left(\frac{\text{N-day lowest low}}{\text{N-day highest high}} \right)$$

$$= \text{Entry price} \times (\text{normalized stop ratio})$$

If you invested 100 percent of your account capital into a single stock, and liquidated at the preceding stop price, the *percentage of your original capital remaining* would thus be:

$$(\text{original account value}) \times (\text{normalized stop ratio})$$

Analogously, if you invest in an equally weighted portfolio of stocks that all have stops at entry price × (normalized stop ratio) you can liquidate if your account value drops to the value that your portfolio would be if all your stops were simultaneously hit (i.e., if each stock was immediately stopped out at its respective stop price).

For example, let's say you have a portfolio of five stocks. To determine a sensible dollar stop for the entire portfolio, you would:

1. Calculate the normalized stop ratio of each stock in your target portfolio individually.

2. *Average* the normalized stop ratios of all stocks in the portfolio, to come up with an *average normalized stop ratio* for the portfolio.

3. Subtract this average normalized stop ratio from 1 to determine an average R:P ratio for the portfolio.

4. Divide your target heat (since you are treating the entire portfolio as one bin) by this *average R:P ratio* to determine the percentage of your portfolio capital to invest. If the resulting fraction is greater than 1, invest 100 percent of portfolio capital.

5. Once this percentage of portfolio capital to invest is determined, invest it in your target portfolio by splitting it into equal portions and investing *equal dollar amounts* in each stock.

This deserves an example, so let's imagine that the respective normalized stop ratios for the five stocks are 0.91, 0.86, 0.75, 0.81, and 0.93. Your average normalized stop ratio would then be 0.852. In turn, your average R:P ratio would be $1 - 0.852 = 0.148$. If you have a target heat of 10 percent, you would then invest $10\%/14.8\% = 67.6\%$ of your total portfolio capital into the five stocks, meaning an investment of $67.6\%/5 = 13.5\%$ of your capital in each respective stock. In other words, you do not want to lose more than 10 percent of your original account capital when stopping yourself out, and so you adjust the percentage of capital that you invest to ensure that if you do in fact lose 10 percent, you will have given each stock a reasonable amount of room to fluctuate based on a *normalized* volatility measure.

An alternative way of calculating your average R:P ratio is to start with R:P ratios derived from your normalized stop ratios by simply subtracting each of the respective normalized stop ratios from 1. You would thus have R:P ratios of $(1 - 0.91)$, $(1 - 0.86)$, $(1 - 0.75)$, $(1 - 0.81)$, and $(1 - 0.93)$. This is equivalent to R:P ratios of 0.09, 0.14, 0.25, 0.19, and 0.07, respectively, and once again yields an average R:P ratio of 14.8 percent.

Since you size the amount of portfolio capital you invest based on your target heat *and* your average R:P ratio, you would stop out your portfolio if your open losses exceed the dollar amount of your portfolio represented by your target heat. For example, a target heat of 10 percent on an $80,000 portfolio would represent $8,000. You would thus stop out your portfolio if open losses exceed $8,000 (which would mean that its value has dropped below $80,000 - $8,000 = $72,000$).

Keep in mind that it may only make sense to employ R:P ratio averaging when trading a portfolio with the use of an external pilot signal, or over a fixed time interval such as the first quarter of the year. If you use a whole portfolio stop, some positions will cause more volatility to your portfolio than others during your holding period, and occasionally you may have to stop yourself out of the entire portfolio, so make sure that your target heat is a percentage that you're comfortable with. If you are more daring, you may decide to trade completely under the guidance of an external pilot signal and avoid the use of a portfolio stop altogether. However, this may expose you to an occasional large loss if you happen to be holding some stocks whose downside volatility dramatically exceeds your volatility estimate based on your R:P ratio in them at your time of entry. If you trade with a cash account (as opposed to margin), hopefully the damage from such events can be somewhat limited. Furthermore, diversification across multiple sectors can also help to alleviate downside volatility in your portfolio, although diversification may also take away upside volatility.

Volatility Matching

Every once in a while you may choose to hold a position or positions for a fixed time interval (with or without stops), and exit at the end of that time interval (in other words, you may choose to trade with a time stop). As I said before, a *very rough* estimate of the downside volatility that you may encounter over the N days after you enter the position is (1 − N-day low/N-day high). However, let's say that you make this calculation in stock ABCD for a prospective 16-month holding period and obtain a 40 percent result. However, you are unsure of what target heat to use to size your position. How can you know what is a reasonable downside volatility to expect when holding stocks for that time interval, so that you can in turn choose an appropriate target heat to size your position in that stock?

My suggested remedy is to make the same calculation for a major market index (e.g., the S&P 500) and see what the result is. For example, if

$$\left[1-\left(\frac{\text{S \& P 500's 16-month low}}{\text{S \& P 500's 16-month high}}\right)\right] = 20\%$$

then you know that ABCD was about twice as volatile as the benchmark (very roughly) during the time interval in question. If the same calculation yields 60 percent, ABCD was only about two-thirds as volatile as the benchmark during the time interval in question. This information can aid you in your choice of a target heat for the time interval you are interested in holding.

For example, let's say that the preceding calculation based on S&P 500 prices yields 30 percent. You may then choose to *match* the volatility of the ABCD position to that of the benchmark, by picking a target heat equal to 30 percent. Since the same equation applied to ABCD's prices over the past 16 months yields 40 percent, this means that the percentage of capital you invest in ABCD would be equal to:

$$\frac{[1-(\text{S \& P 500's 16-month low}/\text{S \& P 500's 16-month high})]}{[1-(\text{ABCD's 16-month low}/\text{ABCD's 16-month high})]}$$

In this way, you expose yourself to an amount of volatility that you consider reasonable for holding stocks for your intended holding period—reasonable because your estimate is based on the volatility of the broader market. Of course, this method is not an academic method of matching volatility, and so on, but it is a quick and dirty method that you may find useful.

This is of course the simplified case with a single stock, stock ABCD. However, you may also volatility match an entire portfolio of stocks that you want to trade in a campaign. Let's say you have a basket of stocks that you want to hold for 24 months, and you want to match its volatility to the S&P 500. To do this, you would:

1. Find the value (1 – 24-month low/24-month high) for each stock individually, that is, an approximate volatility measure.
2. Average these values together to find an average for the entire portfolio.
3. Find the value (1 – S&P 500's 24-month low/S&P 500's 24-month high), that is, an approximate volatility measure calculated in the same manner as in step 1.
4. Divide the results of step 3 by the results of step 2 to determine the percentage of portfolio capital to invest (up to a maximum of 100 percent).
5. Invest the resulting percentage of portfolio capital in stocks, equally weighting each stock position (i.e., investing the same dollar amount in each stock).

For example, imagine three stocks, ABC, DEF, and GHI. After applying the instructions in step 1 to these three stocks, you get values of 0.21, 0.24, and 0.27. You then average these three numbers together, as step 2 requires, and get 0.24. You find after applying step 3 to the S&P 500, that your result is 0.21. You then divide 0.21 by 0.24 to determine your percentage of capital to invest, which in this case is 87.5 percent.

Using Official Volatility Measures for Volatility Matching   An alternative possibility for matching the volatility of a stock position to that of a benchmark is to find the historical or implied volatility of a stock, and compare this to the same value for some benchmark index or ETF. Volatility measures for certain stocks are available on Web sites such as www.Ivolatility.com. This allows you to pick one number for all time frames you wish to hold for, rather than having to calculate different numbers for different prospective holding times. So for example, let's say that you choose to use an 11 percent measure of implied volatility for the S&P Depositary Receipts (symbol: SPY) in your calculation. For stock ABCD, which you wish to buy, you use a measure of implied volatility of 22 percent in your calculation. Your goal is to size your position so that you are exposed to the loosely similar volatility you would have in an SPY position (regardless of the holding period), so you would divide 11 percent by 22 percent, which would yield 50 percent. This 50 percent means that you would invest 50 percent of your capital in stock ABCD, to experience roughly the same volatility as a SPY position. To estimate your portfolio risk and size your positions with more precision, I suggest reading more on subjects like volatility, correlation, and value at risk.

Pareto Allocations

An interesting tactic that you may use to manage your portfolio's volatility is a method I call Pareto allocating. The Pareto principle, coined from the name of Vilfredo Pareto, is also known as the 80-20 rule. For example, 80 percent of a company's revenues may come from 20 percent of their customers. Similarly, by carefully selecting the volatilities of a few stocks that make up a fraction of an otherwise low volatility portfolio, you may be able to increase its overall volatility substantially.

For example, let's say you want a target heat of 10 percent in your portfolio. You may decide to hold 80 percent of your assets in stocks with 7 percent R:P ratios, and 20 percent of your assets in stocks with 22 percent R:P ratios. This gives you an average R:P ratio for your portfolio of 10 percent (for which you can set a whole portfolio dollar stop). However, since stocks are unbounded on the upside, if a runaway bull market occurs, your *hope* in doing this is that the 20 percent of your assets in higher volatility stocks will overcompensate you for the additional percentage risk you are taking on in them. For example, a $2 stock may run to $8 while the market advances 50 percent. I have not quantified this idea, but I point out that there have been many instances, such as in 2003, of lower priced stocks doubling, tripling, or more in value in response to powerful, sustained bull market action. Use caution with this approach, however, as the hopes you have placed in the higher volatility stocks generating outsized returns for your portfolio may not always come true.

Of course, Pareto allocations do not have to be confined to 80-20 splits. For example, let's say that the NASDAQ 100 has a normalized stop ratio of 92 percent (e.g., based on the ratio of its 40-day low to its 40-day high), which means an R:P ratio of (100% − 92%) = 8%. You may be able to mimic this volatility by investing 25 percent of your money in a basket of low priced tech stocks with an average R:P ratio of 32 percent, and placing the other 75 percent of your money in cash. Of course there will not be 1 for 1 correlation with your portfolio and the NASDAQ 100, and you may also underperform the NASDAQ 100. However, with up to 75 percent of your portfolio in cash, you are guaranteed not to lose more than 25 percent of your portfolio value.

One note of caution when using normalized volatility measures to structure a portfolio is that they assume a strong degree of correlation between the stocks you intend to hold. In other words, these methods are a crude estimate. There are much more sophisticated methods of analyzing your portfolio's risk, for example if some stocks happen to be negatively correlated to each other, but a proper exploration of these methods is beyond the scope of this book. However, note that if you diversify your portfolio well, your actual risk may well be less than that implied by my approximations, which may mean that you can take larger position sizes.

The exact volatility measures you use, the target heats you choose, and so on, will be largely based on your own preferences. There is no one right answer, but what is important is that you are comfortable with the money management protocols you are using, and understand them thoroughly.

Weighting by Market Cap

Several major market indices weight by market cap, a method of weighting that is loosely representative of the relative size of investment opportunities out there. Of course, this weighting method does not take liquidity into account, as a company may have a high market cap but may be very illiquid. Also, if you happen to hold one high market cap stock like General Electric (GE) in your portfolio, along with a number of very low market cap stocks, the weighting method will place the bulk of your money in the high market cap stock. In any case, you can still weight a basket of stocks by market cap if you specify a target heat for your portfolio in advance. Here is an example of how you might do this:

1. Start with an all-cash portfolio.
2. Find the individual market cap of each stock in the basket that you intend to buy.
3. Find the total of all stock market caps in your intended basket.
4. For each individual stock, divide its market cap by the total market cap of all stocks in your intended basket, to determine its relative weighting.
5. For each individual stock, multiply this (individual market cap / total market cap) ratio by a volatility measure for that stock. A volatility measure might be [1 – (32-day low/32 day high)] in the stock, for example. The value you come up with for each stock after this step is that stock's adjusted R:P ratio.
6. Add all the adjusted R:P ratios to determine the weighted R:P ratio of your overall portfolio.

7. Divide your portfolio's target heat by this weighted portfolio R:P ratio, to determine the fraction of portfolio capital to invest. For example, if your portfolio's target heat is 8 percent and your weighted R:P ratio is 10 percent, you would invest 80 percent of portfolio capital in stocks and leave 20 percent in cash.

8. Divide the portfolio capital allocated for investment into the fractions indicated by the relative weightings in step 4, and invest the respective amounts in each of the relevant stocks.

This example demonstrates sizing your positions for a portfolio trade based both on market cap and volatility. If all of your stocks come from the S&P 500, which is weighted by market cap, you may thus be loosely mimicking holding a small piece of the S&P 500.

Suggestions for Using Rankings and Watch Lists

So far I have discussed portfolio structuring methods that you would use if undertaking a trade campaign, for example, putting on a whole portfolio trade based on the price action of an external index. You may alternatively choose, as did Nicholas Darvas, to trend-follow in individual ideas as they come along. To trade in this manner, you must maintain a constant, ranked watch list of buy candidates, in addition to any portfolio positions you have. This watch list need not be ranked by purely objective criteria, but you must be personally comfortable with each of its picks and their relative rankings. You should thus always be able to answer the question, "If I need to pick N stocks right now to buy, what would they be, and how would I rank them?" You would then trade each stock that you buy from the watch list independently, based on its individual price action. Note that the use of a watch list does not necessarily mean that if you sell a stock in your portfolio, that you immediately enter into the number one stock on the watch list. Rather, it means that if you liquidate a stock, creating space in your portfolio, that you will buy a stock on the watch list if it exhibits features that make it compelling to buy.

Darvas bought stocks that made *all-time highs* after exhibiting a certain form of technical price action. The companies he chose also often had products that he thought would excite the public imagination, and stocks that had shown a marked increase in volume, both criteria that are highly subjective. Whereas he scaled into individual stocks making as many as five prints (individual trades) sometimes, there is no reason to do this. Since an all-time high will be a high on all time frames, you may simply choose an appropriate lower Donchian band to serve as your stop. For example, you may choose to buy a new all-time high and sell if the stock breaks below its lower 32-day Donchian band. Alternatively, you may choose to use a trailing percentage or trailing dollar stop, a ratchet stop, an N-day trough exit or numerous other methods to time your exit and size your positions.

Here is one such method that illustrates the incorporation of a watch list into a trading plan:

1. Buy the number one stock on your watch list as soon as it makes a new all-time high.

2. Set a fixed stop level at 96 percent of your entry price, and size your position accordingly based on your target heat.

3. Liquidate the position if price breaks down through your fixed stop level.

4. Otherwise, liquidate the position if price makes a new 32-day low, and cancel the other stop.

5. Reenter the stock if it makes a subsequent new all-time high and is not outranked on your watch list by another position at the time.

This method allows you to enter a strong upward momentum stock with a relatively close fixed stop, but then to occasionally exit using a trend following method with considerably more leeway.

Periodically Rebalancing Bins to Equal Weight

If you split a cash portfolio into equally sized bins, based on the number of positions you intend to hold, some bins will grow dramatically larger than others after you invest, and you may occasionally want to rebalance so that the sizes of the bins are approximately equal again. If you think that the trading and money management methods given here are complex to back-test, imagine how complex it must be to simulate portfolio rebalancing on top of the trading methods. In any case, here is an example of a rebalancing method for your consideration.

Periodic Equal Weight Bin Rebalancing *without* Reinvestment of Cash Proceeds

1. Leave bin sizes as they are following each of your individual trades, but then periodically (e.g., quarterly or annually) rebalance the portfolio as follows.

2. During rebalancing, make each bin size equal weight by redistributing cash from the larger-sized bins (through position liquidation if necessary) to the smaller-sized bins.

3. First, divide the portfolio's mark-to-market value on your rebalancing day by the number of bins.

4. Then make each bin equal weight through a combination of position liquidations and journal entries that make the respective market values of each bin equal to one another.

5. Note that the fact that *you do not reinvest the cash proceeds* from position liquidation means that you will not increase the sizes of any positions, whether winning or losing. However, it may mean that you decrease the sizes of winning or losing positions.

Let's look at an example of this method. Imagine a simple three-bin portfolio, starting in cash with equally weighted bins containing 33.33 percent of this cash. You buy three stocks simultaneously, investing 100 percent of the cash in each bin in a respective stock. A year later, on the day you decide to rebalance, stock 1 (in bin 1) has halved, stock 2 (in bin 2) remains unchanged, and stock 3 (in bin 3) has doubled. How would you go about rebalancing with this method?

Based on your original portfolio value, on the day you decide to rebalance, each bin will have:

Bin 1 (16.67% stock, 0% cash).

Bin 2 (33.33% stock, 0% cash).

Bin 3 (66.67% stock, 0% cash).

This means that your portfolio is 16.67 percent + 33.33 percent + 66.67 percent = 116.67 percent of its original value. To rebalance each bin to equal weight, each bin must now have 116.67%/3 = 38.89% of the portfolio's original value. This means that some of the stock in bin 3 must be liquidated to provide cash in the other bins so that *each* has a total weighting of 38.89 percent of the portfolio's original value. Thus, 27.78 percent of the portfolio's original value must be converted to cash through liquidations of the stock in bin 3 (i.e., 66.67% – 38.89% = 27.78%). This requires you to sell 41.67 percent of your stock position *in bin 3* (i.e., 41.67% × 66.67% = 27.78%). The cash proceeds are then distributed by a journal entry into bins 1 and 2, making the final bin weightings:

Bin 1 (16.67% stock, 22.22% cash).

Bin 2 (33.33% stock, 5.56% cash).

Bin 3 (38.89% stock, 0% cash).

Thus, for example, if you liquidate the stock in bin 1 the next day, and then subsequently want to invest all the cash in bin 1 in a new stock, you should have a less skewed amount of cash for your new investment.

Compounding

Compounding is a subject that should need little mention. The bottom line is that you must try to think of your portfolio position sizes and returns in percentage terms, and not dollar terms. Thinking in percentage terms allows you to trade in a consistent manner regardless of whether you are trading with a small or a large amount of capital. As a bin's size grows, you invest larger amounts in subsequent positions. As a bin's size falls, you invest smaller amounts in subsequent positions. Since you invest percentages of your capital rather than fixed cash amounts, you can compound your losses to cushion their impact on your portfolio. For example, six compounded losses in a row of 10 percent each in a bin would not lead to a loss of 60 percent, but rather to a loss of $1 - (0.9)^6 = 46.86\%$. On the other hand, six compounded gains in a row of 10% each would lead to a gain greater than 60%, of $(1.1)^6 - 1 = 77.16\%$. In yet another instance, three gains of 10 percent each, respectively, and three losses of 10 percent each, respectively would not lead to a loss of 0 percent, but rather a loss of $1 - (0.9 \times 1.1)^3 = 2.97$ percent.

It is imperative to keep the amounts that you risk on individual trades to a manageable level, because large losses can require substantial gains to return to breakeven. If your portfolio's value as a percentage of its original value is less than 1, you must make *the inverse of its new value minus 1* to break even. That is, if your portfolio's original value is V, and its new value is W, with W < V, you have to make a return of (V/W − 1) to break even.

So if your portfolio drops to 80 percent of its original value (a loss of 20 percent), you must make a (1/0.8) − 1 = 25% return to break even. If it drops to 75 percent of its original value (a loss of 25%), you must make a (1/0.75) − 1 = 33.33% return to break even. A loss of 33.33 percent requires a gain of 50 percent to break even. A loss of 50 percent requires a 100 percent gain to break even. The moral of the story is to keep your losses manageable and compound profits and losses on your trades.

CHAPTER 7

Out of the Box: Further Possibilities

I have talked a lot in this book about planning how you will trade specific situations in advance. The purpose of this chapter is to open up your mind to new areas in which you can consider applying trend trading techniques and to suggest methods of charting that aren't commonly discussed. Many books talk exclusively about applying technical analysis to the trading of single stocks, that is, rotating between stocks and cash. I want to take the different step of suggesting other areas that you may be able to apply technical trading in or look for an edge in the markets. As a result, this section is primarily theoretical, but should provide excellent food for thought. Let's first examine charting methods for long-long equity pairs.

LONG-LONG EQUITY PAIRS

Charting Methods

In order to trade a basket of stocks, you need a reliable indicator of the basket's price behavior to be able to time your trades. Earlier in the book, I mentioned stochastic averaging as a possible method of timing your trades in multiple stocks at the same time. Stochastic averaging indicates to you the average trending state of a basket of stocks based on price behavior during a rolling period of the past N days. You can use the stochastic average as a pilot signal for timing your exits (or entries) in the basket of stocks. You can size your positions in the individual stocks by setting

(1 minus the ratio of each stock's N-day low to its N-day high) as your R:P ratio for that stock. You can then use R:P ratio averaging in conjunction with target heat to size your position in the basket of stocks simultaneously.

Stochastic averaging, however, gives you a signal that may be very distorted compared to the price signals of the stocks you are charting. In other words, stochastics take stock prices, which have a lower bound of 0, and an unlimited upper bound, and convert them into a signal that is lower bounded by 0 and upper bounded by 100. So a stochastic can be used as a pilot signal, but is obviously not a very direct indicator of how your P&L on a particular trade will behave. Therefore, if you want to trade more than one stock by using *a simple* price related signal that will more accurately track the behavior of your P&L, you can use the methods in this section.

There are several reasons why you might want to make a trade in a long-long pair or a tiny basket of stocks rather than an individual stock. You might have a hunch about a directional move in the industry, but don't want to concentrate your risk exposure in one company or experience the volatility associated with holding an individual stock position, so you diversify, enabling you to trade a signal that's smoother than a single stock but more volatile than an index.

Charting the Price Behavior of Multiple Stocks Simultaneously Using Simple Addition   When you are trading a pair of stocks in which you are long both positions (i.e., a long-long equity pair), it's prudent to chart it properly to ensure that you are trading off a signal that is reasonably related to the price behavior of both stocks. In the case of a long-long equity pair (or mini-basket), you can of course add the prices of both stocks together. In this case, the resulting sum will be a new price signal, actually a tiny price weighted index, which you can use to trade. So for example, a $20 stock and a $50 stock would have a combined price of $70. The Dow Jones Industrial Average is calculated in a similar manner, and is considered a price based index. If you intend to combine the prices of stocks in this manner, you must also have a plan for how you will adjust the value of the sum (e.g., in the case of stock splits). To accomplish this, you may use a multiplier to ensure that the overall price of the average is not altered due to splits. For example, let's say that one of the two stocks in your mini-index that add up to $70 (due to individual stock prices of $20 and $50) has a split. One day the sum closes at $70 and then the $50 stock splits 2:1 overnight, giving it a price of $25 and making the index's price $20 + $25 = $45. The sum of the index would automatically gap down to $45, even though no real loss in value has occurred. That is, the $50 stock is now worth $25, but each prior owner of one share now has two shares, meaning no change in market value. Multiplying this new sum of $45 by

$70/$45 (and maintaining this multiplier going forward) would restore the sum of the two stocks to its original value of $70. Alternatively, you could choose to adjust the price of only the stock that split, by multiplying its price by 2. In short, if you trade using a sum of prices as a price signal, you will have to make sure that you are adjusting properly for events like splits. Furthermore, it also makes sense to be aware of when splits occurred in the past, since many stock charts automatically adjust all prices on the chart after splits have occurred. If you don't do this, any price data that you try to study in the past may be thrown off a bit. For example, you might run a study on a day in the past when you think the sum of two stocks was $20 + $50 = $70. However, it may actually be true that on that particular day, the $20 stock was actually priced at $40, and later had a 2:1 split that is reflected in the adjusted chart. Thus, instead of the $20 stock having a weight of 20/70ths of your mini-index's value on that day, its true weighting at the time should have been 40/90ths. This fact may have made you trade the long-long pair differently on that particular day.

Since a simple long-long pairs chart using this method is a summation of equity prices, the chart's behavior should mimic the price of a single stock in many ways, and thus technical trading methodologies should also be applicable to trading it, similar to an index. I show an example of charting a summation of equity prices in Figure 7.1.

As I mentioned earlier, Livermore in his book *How to Trade in Stocks* actually used the price sum of two major stocks in a particular industry as a trading indicator, which he called the "key price."[1] There is no reason that the same money management and timing techniques that you use on a single stock should not be applicable to the trading of a long-long pair or larger basket of stocks. The combined prices of the two stocks will still register N-day highs and N-day lows, and all methods of technical analysis should be applicable to the sum, just as they can also be applied to larger indices such as the Dow.

To size your position in a long-long pair, which you monitor by tracking the sum of two stock prices, you would once again set a target heat (for the bin in which you intend to trade the pair) and then determine an R:P ratio based on the behavior of the pair. For example, you may choose a target heat of 20 percent, and find that 1 minus the ratio of the pair's 40-day low to its 40-day high is 25 percent, which you use as your R:P ratio. You would then invest 20%/25% = 80% of bin capital into the long-long pair position. Keep in mind that when you buy the pair, your share position in both stocks will be the same. So you can use the combined price of the two stocks to calculate the share position that you must purchase in both stocks. For example, let's say you have $10,000 in a bin, and have determined that you will invest $8,000 of this in a pair of stocks. You are watching a pair composed of a $30 stock and a $10 stock, which currently sum

FIGURE 7.1 Ford Motor Company stock (symbol: F) and General Motors stock (symbol: GM) charted separately, and also with a sum of their prices. (*Source:* Stock price data from Yahoo! Finance.)

up to $40. You divide $8,000 by $40, and determine that you must buy 200 shares of the pair, which means 200 shares of the $30 stock *and* 200 shares of the $10 stock, which is equivalent to buying 200 shares of the $40 sum of the two stocks.

Note that if you study a sum of two stock prices, you have no way of knowing, unless you track the sum on a continuous basis throughout time, what the intraday high and intraday low of the sum on any particular day were. Thus, your understanding of the intraday volatility of the pair will be somewhat limited. To get a better feel for intraday volatility, you may choose to chart the sum of the two stocks using intraday price data, for example the last price of each five-minute bar, and then take a look at the rolling N-period range over some period of time. Since the archive of five-minute bar data is likely to be limited in your charting software (compared to daily bar data), this method of estimating intraday volatility will limit how far back you can study. An alternative method is to use both daily open and close data when calculating the sum. With this method, chart the sum of the opening prices of the individual stocks as the opening price of the sum, and the sum of the closing prices of the individual stocks as the closing price of the sum (which you would normally do anyway). However, for example if you chart with Microsoft Excel, you will also have to specify high and low prices for each day (that is, four data points per day). Thus, you will have to define each day's high as the *higher* of that day's open and close. You will then define each day's low as the *lower* of that day's open and close. The resulting bars will be candlestick bodies without shadows. This method of course assumes that both stocks open and close simultaneously, which may not always be accurate, for example if one of the stocks is halted overnight and opens at noon the next day. However, by being able to chart both the opening and closing prices of each bar in a sum of several prices, you can gain a better understanding of the extent of intraday movement than you would be able to by looking only at the daily closing prices of the sum.

Although charting a pair of stocks by adding their prices is reasonably useful, it has its own issues. If one stock is trading at $200 and the other stock at $2, the daily movements of the $200 stock will nearly swamp out the daily movements of the $2 stock. Stochastic averaging helps to alleviate this issue by indicating the position of a stock's price relative to its high and low over some number of days (a method of volatility normalization of price behavior). However, stochastic averaging cannot give you a great indication of how your P&L behaves over time. To achieve a different balance in your charting of multiple stocks, you can use the following method.

Another Method of Charting a Long-Long Pair: Assuming Daily Equal Weight Rebalancing   Another method of *charting* the behavior of long-long equity pairs is the following, in which you assume that you balance your funds equally between the two stocks in the pair immediately after the close (or alternatively the open) of each trading day. For example, if you had $5,000, respectively, invested in two stocks, for a total of $10,000, and one stock increased 20 percent in a day (to $6,000) while the other stock stayed flat (at $5,000), the market value of your two-stock portfolio would increase to $6,000 + $5,000 = $11,000, a gain of 10 percent. You would then *instantaneously* sell $500 worth of the stock with a $6,000 market value and invest that $500 in the stock with the $5,000 market value at the closing prices (assuming no costs). This would leave you with an equal amount of $5,500 invested in both stocks.

If instead, one stock had increased 20 percent (from $5,000 to $6,000) while the other decreased 20 percent (from $5,000 to $4,000), you would sell $1,000 worth of the stock with the $6,000 market value, and invest it in the stock with the $4,000 market value. This would leave you with a market value of $5,000, respectively, in both stocks. On the other hand, if one stock had increased 20 percent (from $5,000 to $6,000) and the other had increased 40 percent (from $5,000 to $7,000), you would sell $500 worth of the stock with the $7,000 market value and invest it in the stock with the

$6,000 market value. This would leave you with a market value of $6,500, respectively, in both stocks.

The reason you would theoretically rebalance daily is so that each day's *average* percentage change in both stocks will be the actual percentage change of a hypothetical pairs position over that same day. However, in order to compound each *daily average percentage change* as time moves forward, you would need to have an equal amount of money invested in each stock directly after the close of each day. For example, imagine that you have a $10,000 portfolio split equally between two stocks (i.e., into two $5,000 portions). If one stock goes up 10 percent one day, and the other stock goes up 20 percent on the same day, you can say that your average percentage change was (10% + 20%)/2 = 15% on $10,000 over that day. However, if you had different amounts in the two stocks at the beginning of the day, for example $6,000 and $4,000, you could not get the average percentage change of the $10,000 total by taking a simple average of 10 percent and 20 percent. You would have to weight the average by the size of the dollar position in each stock, which would add new complexities.

By assuming that you rebalance your positions so that you are equally weighted in each stock right after the close of each day, you enable yourself to track the price movements of the two stocks with reasonable accuracy. Of course, you can't rebalance in practice each day exactly at the closing prices of both stocks with no costs, so you may still have to use the combined price signal as a pilot signal for real life trading (i.e., it would not track the percentage changes in your P&L 100 percent accurately). However, day-to-day percentage changes would stay the same if a stock's prices are altered to reflect a split, so using this method requires less maintenance in some instances than the simple summation method of charting a long-long pair.

In short, this method (see Figure 7.2) assumes that you repeatedly rotate money from the better performing stock over the previous period to the worse performing stock, which might of course lead to some problems if you don't use proper money management and one of the stocks in the pair happens to drop like a rock during your holding period. Rebalancing on the daily close in this manner is also not precisely achievable in actual practice because the close is not known in advance (and thus the amount you will have to shift between stocks to rebalance them is also not known in advance). If you want to actually attempt daily rebalancing, so that your P&L tracks the P&L indicated by the signal more closely, you might choose to rebalance directly after each day's open, or rebalance less frequently than daily in order to save on commission and slippage costs. You might also use opening prices for your percentage change calculations instead of closing prices, and choose to make rebalancing trades right after both stocks have opened. In short, although this method of

FIGURE 7.2 Charting a long-long pair assuming daily equal weight rebalancing. (*Source:* Stock price data from Yahoo! Finance.)

charting a long-long pair may provide better information about the combined percentage returns of the pair than a stochastic average, the method cannot show you what your true P&L would be because it cannot take into account commissions and slippage losses from daily rebalancing.

Here is how you would chart a long-long pair of stock A and stock B in this manner:

1. Take the ratio of today's close to yesterday's close for stock A and stock B, respectively. For example, today's ratio for stock A might be 1.06 and that for stock B might be 0.96.

2. Average these two ratios to get the current day's "average ratio." Using the above example, this would yield (1.06 + 0.96)/2 = 1.01. This is equivalent to an average percentage change for that day of 1.01 − 1.00 = 0.01 = 1%.

3. Multiply today's average ratio by the current value of the plot, beginning with a starting value of 1 on a day of your choosing, which I call the starting date. (You may also begin the plot with a value of 100, or any other initial value.) Then, multiply the initial value of 1 by the next day's "average ratio" to get the next day's plot value. Then, multiply the next plot value by the subsequent day's average ratio to get that day's plot value, and so on.

Let me give an example with numbers. Table 7.1 gives two series of hypothetical daily price ratios of today's close to yesterday's close, and the value of the plots that you would see for each individually, and then the two averaged together. Time flows forward in a downward direction on the table.

Note that the plot values of an individual stock will be different depending on the day you choose to start the plot. For example, if you start the "A Plot" one day later than I have shown on Table 7.1, the 103.00 value would be 100.00 instead (i.e., the starting value). However, the-day-to day *percentage changes* going forward will be identical (to those of the original plot) although the actual plot values will differ due to the different starting dates. Note also that if you replace the starting value of 100.00 in the A Plot with the closing price of Stock A on that date, the resulting A Plot will have the same values as the stock's price series (by definition). Using this method of plotting, the plot values will of course never fall below zero, and are unbounded on the upside as well.

Clearly, your plot values will depend on the starting date and starting value that you choose. If you use your daily equal weight rebalancing plot as a pilot signal, you can expect that your P&L behavior will differ from the percentage returns shown on the table, whether due to your using a different rebalancing frequency than daily, or due to the impact of commissions and slippage. Thus, you may choose, for example, to set a fixed dollar stop on a long-long pairs position and use infrequent rebalancing, and also to size your positions and time your exits based on the behavior of the average plot.

TABLE 7.1 Averaging daily price ratios.

Day	Stock A Ratio of Consecutive Closes	A Plot	Stock B Ratio of Consecutive Closes	B Plot	Average Ratio	Average Plot
1		100.00		100.00		100.00
2	1.03	103.00	0.96	96.00	0.995	99.50
3	1.08	111.24	0.94	90.24	1.010	100.50
4	0.94	104.57	1.06	95.65	1.000	100.50
5	1.02	106.66	1.03	98.52	1.025	103.01
6	0.99	105.59	1.01	99.51	1.000	103.01
7	0.97	102.42	0.95	94.53	0.960	98.89
8	1.01	103.45	0.98	92.64	0.995	98.39

One possible method of sizing your position in the pair is to subtract the ratio of the Average Plot's N-day low to its N-day high from 1 to get an R:P ratio. Using a personally defined target heat, you would then figure out the fraction of capital in a bin that you will invest in the pair of stocks. When you then invest, make sure to invest an equal dollar amount in each stock.

Although this method may be used to chart the price behavior of a long-long pair, you can see that it may also be used to chart the price behavior of a larger basket of stocks (as can the simple summation method). To do this, simply average the respective ratios of today's close to yesterday's close across a larger number of stocks than two, and use the resulting values to plot a new function.

A Quick Word on Long-Short Pairs

Long-short pairs add a host of additional complications if you want to trade them with technical methods, but in theory technical trading methods for timing your exits should also be applicable to them, provided that your reasons for entering the pair are sound. The standard method of trading a long-short pair involves first mathematically establishing a relationship between the stocks in the pair, and betting on a contraction (expansion) of the spread when it expands (contracts) to a different level from where you have estimated its fair value is.

However, if you have an advantageous entry idea with a long-short pair, you may also be able to successfully time your exit with technical trading methods. For example, perhaps you have an opinion from simple fundamental research that General Motors (GM) stock will outperform Ford stock on a percentage basis at least over the next quarter, and don't have the sophistication to create a mathematical model to time your trades in the spread. Using a technical exit method may come in handy in this case.

Out of a universe of N stocks, there are $N(N - 1)/2$ unique pairs that can be traded. Most people bother only modeling the price behavior of small universes of stocks, for example, within the same industry. For example, if you follow 20 stocks within an industry, and you want to pick a single pair to trade, you have $20(19)/2 = 190$ possibilities to choose from. However, if you look at a larger universe of, for example, 100 stocks across multiple industries, you then have $100(99)/2 = 4,950$ unique pair possibilities (although a great deal of the possible pairs may not have any strong relationship to each other). If you choose one pair and remove these two stocks from your universe, you then have 98 other stocks to choose a pair from, leading to $98(97)/2 = 4,753$ possibilities, and so on. You have many more pairs choices if you choose from a larger universe, but it may be considerably more difficult to model the behavior of pairs that are not closely related, especially if you lack sophisticated resources.

Some factors to keep in mind when trading a long-short pair include the fact that your risk on the short side of the trade is potentially unlimited, while your potential reward on the long side of the trade is also unlimited. If the stocks in the pair are highly correlated, however, your risk in practice can be quite low. Just as you can manage your open position P&L on a long-long pairs trade using technical trading techniques, you should also be able to do the same with a long-short pairs trade. You will have to choose your own method of charting and/or analyzing the pair. No matter what methods you ultimately use, the principles of sound money management remain the same.

EQUITY CURVE TRADING AND TRADING DIFFERENT PRICE BAR TIME FRAMES

Mutual Funds

Just as technical trading methods can be applied to the trading of individual stocks and baskets, they can also be applied to the trading of mutual funds or other funds where net asset values (NAVs) are published less frequently than that of a stock. This makes sense because the price chart of a stock is essentially an equity curve for a portfolio that holds one share of that stock. A portfolio that holds any other combination of shares will look different. Keep in mind, though, that with actively managed funds you will not necessarily be able to know the instantaneous portfolio composition or the strategy being used. Also, there are often additional fees involved with mutual funds that are not present with stocks, as well as minimum investment amounts for many funds and dividend payments that may not show up on a NAV chart. With some funds such as hedge funds there may even be a lockup period, so timing of equity curves may not always be as simple as entering and exiting a stock.

However, the same technical tools that are used to size positions and plan trades in individual stocks can theoretically be used to trade the equity curves of mutual funds, closed end funds, and so on. For example, a bin can be isolated for the purpose of investing in such a fund. If NAV data is published on a closing basis only, you would simply follow the same protocols for trading that you did with a single stock for which closing data only is published.

Imagine, for example, that you decide to enter a value based mutual fund that has just dipped 15 percent, risking a maximum of 10 percent of your capital. You have already set aside cash to invest and intend to invest more than the fund's minimum in the fund. Here is a sample strategy that you might use:

1. Percentage of bin capital to invest = target heat / R:P ratio. Set target heat at 10 percent, and set the R:P ratio equal to 1 minus (the fund's lowest NAV of the past 32 day divided by the fund's highest NAV of the past 32 days). Invest a maximum of 100 percent of bin capital.

2. Set a fixed stop loss level at the last NAV times (the lowest NAV of the past 32 days divided by the highest NAV of the past 32 days). If the fund's NAV closes below this level, liquidate your entire position the next day.

3. Set a trailing stop of the 32-day lowest low of the fund's NAV. If the fund closes at a new 32-day low, liquidate your entire position the next day.

4. Liquidate your entire position when either stop is triggered, and cancel the other stop.

Of course, if you are going to plan your trading of mutual funds with trend trading techniques, it is a good idea to be cognizant of the strategy that the fund is using or the trading philosophy of its managers.

Trading with Long-Term Price Bars

You may also wish to trade a regular stock using the price data from weekly or monthly bars rather than daily bars. If you are using a simple Donchian exit strategy, that is, exiting a stock if it makes a new N-day low, this enables you to adjust your stops directly after the end of each bar period, rather than monitoring prices on a more frequent basis. For example, you may choose to substitute an 8-week Donchian strategy for a 40-day Donchian strategy. Since you will be monitoring only eight bars of price data, it stands to reason that you should use the open, high, low, and close of all these bars in making your trading decisions (as opposed to only the closing prices, for example). Here is a sample strategy:

1. Buy a stock at the market price based on proprietary criteria. For illustration purposes, imagine that the stock is in between its high price and low price of the past six weekly price bars (rather than breaking out).

2. Size your position by dividing your target heat by (1 minus the ratio of the lowest price of the past six weekly bars to the highest price of the past six weekly bars), and investing that fraction of your allocated capital in the stock.

3. Set a fixed stop at your entry price multiplied by (the ratio of the lowest price of the past six weekly bars to the highest price of the past six weekly bars). This fixed stop will hold until triggered or replaced by another one.

4. After the close of each week's trading, check the low price of the past six weekly bars. If it is higher than your most recent fixed stop price, raise your fixed stop price to this level and cancel out any previous fixed stops. If it is lower than your most recent fixed stop price, leave your fixed stop price as it is.

One thing to be aware of when trading with weekly bars is that large overnight gap ups or gap downs that occur during the period of the bar will appear as *continuous price movement* on a weekly bar. So you should beware of assuming when looking at the bar that you could have traded at all prices between its high and low. Some of those prices may not have been accessible in reality because of gaps.

STRATEGY ROTATION

Mixing It Up

Rather than simply trading in and out of individual stocks, you may choose to rotate between different trading styles based on some technical timing method for the broader market. For example, based on the Best Six Months Switching Strategy mentioned in *The Almanac Investor* by Hirsch and Brown,[2] you may decide to hold growth stocks (long-only) during the better performing November 1 through April 30 period, and use a long-short trading strategy (rather than going into cash) during the worse performing May 1 through October 31 period. In this manner you will continually have long exposure to the stock market, but will be at least partially hedged during periods that you consider to be less favorable for investing.

You may also want to consider rotating from one asset class to another. For example, are there periods in which the action of the ratio of the QQQQs to the TLTs (a long-term Treasury bond exchange-traded fund) might give you clues for holding one ETF versus another? What about using the price action of the TLT to rotate between holding the TLT (in TLT uptrends) and holding the SHY (a short-term Treasury bond ETF) in TLT downtrends?

What sort of performance would you have if you rotate between having half of your portfolio holding the S&P in a buy and hold fashion, and the other half in the NASDAQ Composite in a simple Donchian trend following (i.e., long/flat) strategy? The two indices are pretty strongly correlated, but this would give you upside exposure to the more volatile one while limiting your downside in it. When you are not in the NASDAQ Composite, you would be partially invested in the S&P 500. What about using a pilot signal based on the NASDAQ Composite's price to vary your leverage in the QQQQs? For example, if the NASDAQ Composite enters an uptrend, you go 150 percent long in the QQQQs. If the NASDAQ Composite enters a downtrend, you cut back to 100 percent long in the QQQQs. This would be a rather volatile strategy, so what about other exposure combinations like rotating between 100 percent long and 25 percent long in the QQQQs? Clearly, there is a world of simple but unusual investment ideas that can be explored without having to resort to heavy mathematics. Regardless of what strategies you ultimately choose to use, I hope this book has made clear that a sound trade planning strategy is a necessary first step.

Rotations versus a Benchmark Index: Can You Beat the Market Temporarily Rather Than Permanently?

The various rotation ideas that I listed earlier lead into the final idea I discuss. So far in this book I have mostly talked about technical trading as a stand-alone style of trading. In other words, when you are not in the market based on the technical trading signals you are following, you spend your time sitting in cash. This is a very basic method of applying technical analysis, and it is easy to see why it may be difficult to beat the broader market's performance over the long term if you trade like this, as the efficient market hypothesis seems to imply. In short, your technical trading in this manner must be good enough to beat the market's long-term upward drift *both* while you are in the market *and* while you are out of the market. This means you have to use pretty high-powered strategies, which will not just be sitting there on the surface advertising themselves to you. In addition to this, if you use a completely canned trend following strategy, with which you are chasing prices on both the upside and the downside, you may also run into some pretty serious whipsaws that can rapidly erode your capital.

However, what if you do not think you can beat the market at all times, but are pretty sure that you can occasionally beat it for limited time periods? This agrees with Livermore's assertion that:

> *A man may beat a stock or group at a certain time, but no man living can beat the stock market! A man may make money out of indi-*

vidual deals in cotton or grain, but no man can beat the cotton market or the grain market.[3]

In this case, why not just hold the broader market portfolio when you are not trying to beat the market with a technical strategy, in place of cash? This entails considerably more risk, but also exposes you to the market's upward drift during periods when you are not trading on an investment insight. In a very simple example, perhaps you are very sure that you can beat the S&P 500's monthly return by 1 percent each January, by buying and holding stock ABC during that month. Then you could simply be 100 percent invested in the S&P 500 Depositary Receipts (symbol: SPY) for all months of the year except January (I assume here that the SPY's return is identical to the S&P 500's return). On the last day of each year, you would dump your SPY position and immediately buy stock ABC with the proceeds, trading both on their closing prices. You would then hold stock ABC until the last day of January, on which you would dump it and rotate back into full investment in the SPY. For each January, you would beat the S&P 500 by 1 percent, increasing your overall annual return.

If you applied the January strategy on its own and sat in cash the rest of the time, however, you would most likely not beat the market. For example, imagine that the average January return of the S&P 500 is 2 percent a month. Applying this strategy would yield you an average January return of 3 percent, which would also work out to 3 percent for the year, since you would sit in cash for the rest of the year. This would not beat the S&P 500's long-term return. However, if you sit in the S&P 500 rather than cash for the other 11 months of the year, you would beat the S&P 500's long-term return by consistently beating the S&P 500 in the month of January only! Contrast this with searching for a technical strategy that must beat the market's return of roughly 10 percent compounded annually because you spend all of the time when you're not in the market sitting in cash. Which is more difficult to find? The moral of the story is that if you can beat the market consistently over the short term, you can still beat the market over the long term simply by holding the market portfolio when you are not trading with a special technical strategy.

Let's look at another hypothetical example. Imagine that you are trend following an index ETF (ETF XYZ) that is highly correlated to the S&P 500 and makes approximately twice the percentage change of the S&P 500 each day. You decide to go long or stay long ETF XYZ when it makes a new 32-day high, but when ETF XYZ makes a new 32-day low, you rotate into full investment in the S&P 500. In this way, instead of trying to beat the S&P 500 at *all* times, you limit yourself to trying to beat the S&P 500 *occasionally*, that is, only during your holding period of ETF

XYZ. So the question you ask yourself whenever you want to make a trade in this manner is:

Do I think I can beat the S&P 500 for the duration of this trade?

The same question asked another way is:

Do I think the S&P 500 will underperform the instrument I want to hold for the duration of this trade?

This is much simpler than asking yourself whether you can beat the S&P 500 over the long term with some canned technical strategy. An alternative way of asking the same question regarding a canned strategy that you happen to be using is:

Do I think that this strategy can outperform the S&P 500 during the holding periods that it indicates for me to be in the market?

If the answer to either of these questions is yes, you may still be able to beat the S&P 500 long term by simply holding the S&P 500 *when you are not trading another strategy*. However, note that since you are fully invested in the S&P 500 when holding it, you are theoretically allowing yourself to risk up to 100 percent of your capital each time you do this (assuming no use of margin). In practice, however, it is probably extremely unlikely that the S&P 500 will drop to zero, or even close to it, especially given its historical upward drift. So by working on trying to outperform the S&P 500 (or some other broad market index) in the short term and settling for matching performance otherwise, you simplify your job over that of a pure long/flat technical trader.

Furthermore, for example if you alternate between holding a diversified ETF like the iShares MSCI Japan (symbol: EWJ) and holding the S&P 500, you have the benefit of continuous portfolio diversification. By being continually in stocks, you also get the benefit of any dividends that might be paid out due to your continuous holding. You can reinvest these dividends and earn a greater total return than that implied by the basic price charts. Now, holding the S&P 500 at all times when you are not trading with a technical strategy can be dangerous. At the very least, you may be exposed to events like the crashes of 1987 or 2000 if you happen to be holding the S&P 500 when they occur. You may also be exposed to sustained bear market drops such as the drop of 2002, so you must take the good with the bad. However, if you can occasionally trounce the market over the short term, the effects of these infrequent capital erosion periods will be reduced, especially after the effects of compounding.

For example, imagine that you hold the S&P 500 for a year, and make 25 percent in the first half of the year and then lose 20 percent in the second half of the year, returning you back to breakeven. That is, your portfolio's value as a percentage of its original value would be (1 + 0.25)(1 – 0.20) = 1.00 if you hold the S&P 500 for the full year. Now, imagine instead that you employ an alternative strategy for the first half of the year that makes you 30 percent, and then you switch into the S&P 500 for the second half of the year, losing 20 percent. Your portfolio value as a percentage of its original value would then be (1 + 0.30)(1 – 0.20) = 1.04 after the full year. By beating the market by 5 percent for one-half of the year, you beat the market by a whopping 4 percent for the entire year, even though there is a massive crash in the second half of the year.

In the next year, the S&P 500 might crash by 30 percent for the first half of the year and then rebound by 50 percent, taking it to an annual gain of 5 percent, and a two-year gain of 5 percent. If you trade with a strategy that loses you *only* 25 percent in the first half of the year, and hold the S&P 500 in the second half, making 50 percent, you make 12.5 percent for the entire year, outperforming the S&P 500 by 7.5 percent. Over two years, your return thus becomes (1.04)(1.125) – 1 = 17%, versus the market's (1.00)(1.05) – 1 = 5%. You achieved this theoretical trouncing of the S&P 500 by beating it over two half-year periods and equaling its return for the other half-year periods in which it drifted up by a small amount, even though there was considerable volatility in between. If you had employed your strategy by itself, holding cash otherwise, you would have made (1.30)(0.75) – 1 = –2.5%, a small loss, versus the S&P 500's return during the same periods of (1.25)(0.70) – 1 = –12.5%, and its two-year return of (1.00)(1.05) – 1 = 5%. In the periods where you sat out of the market, you would then miss out on a return of (0.80)(1.50) – 1 = 20%. In short, see box.

> If you hold a proxy for the S&P 500 at all times when not trading, you need only to outperform the proxy during the holding periods of your trades to beat its long-term performance (before commissions and taxes). You do not even have to make money on all your trades to accomplish this.

In the preceding example, the net result of your two trades was *a loss* of 2.5 percent, but being exposed to the market's drift in the periods when you were not trading rocketed you to a two-year gain of 17 percent. You can thus outperform the market by *occasionally* losing less during periods when it loses, or making more during periods when it gains. This does not have to occur during every period when you substitute one group of stocks for the market portfolio. You just have to win enough to outperform overall. This is a double-edged sword, in that you can of course make less of a return when the market gains or lose more when it drops. The market's long-term upward drift may also not continue forever. However, if you rotate between a technical strategy and cash rather than a technical strategy and the S&P 500, your strategy has to be absolutely spectacular to trounce the market's total return over all periods

Now back to my ETF XYZ example. If ETF XYZ makes twice the daily percentage move of the S&P 500, then for the periods when you hold ETF XYZ, your portfolio volatility will be higher. If the signal that you use to time your entries and exits into ETF XYZ is a quality signal, then you *hope* that the extra volatility you will be exposed to will remain mostly on the upside. It is much more preferable to experience additional upside volatility in your portfolio than additional downside volatility. Also, if you run into a series of whipsaws, you will be rotating out of ETF XYZ into the S&P 500 rather than into cash, which should dampen the effects of the whipsaws compared to if you rotate out of ETF XYZ directly into cash. Of course you will sometimes run into sustained drawdowns in the S&P 500, but remember that those drawdowns are part of being able to participate in the index's long-term performance. Drawdowns are also a feature of a long/flat trend following strategy—you will experience them in all strategies.

The good news is that if you trade in a cash account, you will be unable to lose more money than you originally placed into the account, so although you may experience a lot of volatility based on your trading style, there is something of an element of safety. Use of leverage, however, requires borrowing and may theoretically expose you to a loss of more than your account's value on the downside.

Let's examine the results of a basic 32-day Donchian, long-only trend following strategy on the NASDAQ Composite. That is:

1. IF the NASDAQ Composite's close today exceeds the highest close of the past 32 days, THEN invest 100 percent of your capital in the NASDAQ Composite on tomorrow's close.

2. IF the NASDAQ Composite's close today is below the lowest close of the past 32 days, THEN liquidate your NASDAQ Composite position on tomorrow's close AND leave the proceeds in *cash*.

3. IF an existing NASDAQ Composite buy signal is in place and you have a position, THEN ignore subsequent buy signals until after a sell signal has occurred.

4. Repeat the process.

This is the simple case of leaving the proceeds from liquidation of your investment in cash. I also look at the more complicated case of investing 100 percent of your capital in the S&P 500 during periods when you would otherwise be in cash in the preceding strategy. That is, on the days when you liquidate your NASDAQ Composite position on the closing price, you immediately buy the S&P 500 on its closing price that same day. In this case, you would alter steps 1 to 3, and your strategy would be the following:

1. If the NASDAQ Composite's close today exceeds the highest close of the past 32 days, THEN liquidate any existing S&P 500 position on tomorrow's close AND invest 100 percent of your capital in the NASDAQ Composite also on tomorrow's close.

2. If the NASDAQ Composite's close today is below the lowest close of the past 32 days, THEN liquidate any existing NASDAQ Composite position on tomorrow's close and invest 100 percent of your capital in the S&P 500 on tomorrow's close.

3. If a signal based on statements 1 and 2 requires you to enter a position that you already have, simply ignore it and continue to hold that position until you have received a liquidation signal for that position.

4. Repeat the process.

Clearly in practice, you may for example use opening prices rather than closing prices in your calculations. You may then liquidate one position at the opening price, and enter the other with the proceeds immediately after the open, or use any other execution strategy you see fit.

Let's examine the trades produced by the Donchian strategy used solely on the NASDAQ Composite, over the approximately 10-year period from December 29, 1995, through December 23, 2005, inclusive. In the following summary, I show the return of holding the S&P 500 over the same periods that you would hold the NASDAQ Composite, as well as over the periods in which you would hold cash. Dividends are excluded.

- If the strategy is used by itself (with rotation into cash), it produces a return of 178.45 percent over the 10-year period.
- If the S&P 500 is held *in place of* the NASDAQ Composite during the times when you would have held the NASDAQ Composite, and you stay in cash otherwise, your return would be only 76.16 percent over the 10-year period. Thus, the strategy trounces the S&P 500 all by itself *during the time you use it*. Note that this is the same as trading the S&P 500 using the NASDAQ Composite as a pilot signal.
- If you buy and hold the S&P 500 for the overall 10-year period, you achieve a return of 105.97 percent.
- If you buy and hold the NASDAQ Composite for the overall 10-year period, you achieve a return of 113.80 percent.
- If you use the strategy with the NASDAQ Composite, and rotate into the S&P 500 *when you are not using the strategy*, you achieve a re-

turn of 225.58 percent over the 10-year period. This return soundly beats the return from buying and holding *either* index individually over the same time period. It also beats the return from using the Donchian technical strategy on its own and placing the investment proceeds in cash.

The performance of this strategy versus the performance of the S&P 500 index is illustrated in Figure 7.3. In this figure I show performance only after completion of trades in the indices, and thus straight lines are shown during the holding periods of individual trades. Since the rotation strategy rotates in between the NASDAQ Composite and the S&P 500, I check performance of the strategy versus performance of holding the S&P 500 after each trade in the strategy. I begin both the chart of strategy performance and the chart of S&P 500 performance at values of 1.

Although the strategy performs well on its own (even though it is quite volatile), and even better when you rotate between it and the S&P 500, we do have the luxury of knowing that the NASDAQ did well during the period in question, like looking in the rearview mirror. However, note

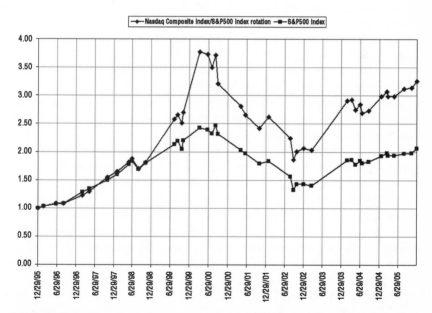

FIGURE 7.3 Hypothetical returns from rotating between the NASDAQ Composite index and the S&P 500 index (using a 32-day Donchian trend following strategy on the NASDAQ Composite and ignoring fees, taxes, and dividends), versus holding the S&P 500 over an approximately 10-year period. (*Source:* Stock price data from Yahoo! Finance.)

that the difference in performance between the NASDAQ and the S&P 500 over the nearly 10-year period was only 113.80% – 105.97% = 7.83%, so clearly the simple Donchian strategy used on the NASDAQ would have helped to lock in some of its upside movement while limiting the effects of some of its downside movement. When a technical strategy is combined with the exposure to the drift of the S&P 500 during the periods you are not applying the strategy, its long-term return can be impressive even excluding reinvestment of dividends. A negative is that your maximum downside during the periods where you hold the S&P 500 is not known in advance, so you can theoretically experience terrific downside volatility. A positive is that instead of having to beat the market's total return over *all* periods with your trading strategy (even though you are in the market only part of the time), you only have to beat the market's total return over finite time periods if you rotate back into the market portfolio when not using your strategy. At all other times you hold the market portfolio and your return thus equals the market return. Furthermore, rather than worrying about timing your trades in and out of the S&P 500, you concentrate only on timing your trades in the NASDAQ Composite strategy. Keep in mind also that full investment of the portfolio in a strategy is not required. If you want to invest a fraction of your portfolio in a strategy, you can do so and hold the balance of your portfolio in the S&P 500.

As of this writing, tech stocks still hold the public imagination quite strongly, although they are not as frothy as they were in 1999 or so. However, you can imagine that with results like this for the NASDAQ Composite, the results of trading some individual Internet stocks with the NASDAQ Composite as a pilot signal (in an attempt to reduce whipsaws), and then switching into the S&P 500 when not in those stocks, could have been significantly better, although you would have experienced a lot more portfolio volatility with Internet stocks.

In any case, we all know that the NASDAQ did pretty well over the past few years, but what if you were a believer in energy stocks, which have only really started to sizzle over the past few years? Let's take a look at the results of using the same 32-day Donchian strategy on the XOI Index (AMEX Oil and Gas Index) over the same period, which essentially went sideways during the six years 1997 through 2002 inclusive. I illustrate relative performance versus holding the S&P 500 in Figure 7.4. Did switching into the S&P 500 when not in the XOI Index help overall performance?

- If the strategy is used on the XOI by itself (with rotation into cash), it produces a return of 99.08 percent over the 10-year period.
- If the S&P 500 is held during the times when you would have held the XOI with the strategy, and you stay in cash otherwise, your return

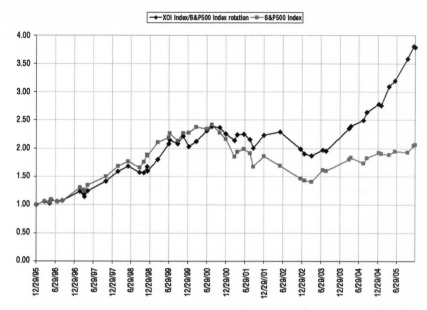

FIGURE 7.4 Hypothetical returns from rotating between the AMEX Oil and Gas index and the S&P 500 index (using a 32-day Donchian trend following strategy on the AMEX Oil and Gas index, ignoring fees, taxes, and dividends), versus holding the S&P 500 index over an approximately 10-year period. (*Source:* Stock price data from Yahoo! Finance.)

would be *only* 8.25 percent over the 10-year period. Thus, the strategy trounces the S&P 500 *during the time you use it.*

- If you hold the S&P 500 for the overall 10-year period, you achieve a return of 105.97 percent.
- If you hold the XOI for the overall 10-year period, you achieve a return of 212.26 percent.
- If you use the strategy, and rotate into the S&P 500 when not using the strategy, you achieve a return of 278.81 percent over the 10-year period. Rotating between the two indices thus beats holding either index individually over the same period, as well as using the technical strategy by itself.

"Wait a second," you may say. Both the NASDAQ Composite and the XOI Index beat the S&P 500 over the period in question (although the NASDAQ Composite did so only marginally). If you had just bought and held the NASDAQ Composite index *or* the XOI Index, you would *also* have outperformed the S&P 500. So let's look at an index that *underperformed* the S&P 500 (excluding dividends), the PHLX Utility Index (symbol: UTY).

Once again, we use a 32-day Donchian trend following strategy on the UTY, whose relative performance is illustrated in Figure 7.5.

- If the strategy is used on the UTY by itself (with rotation into cash), it produces a return of only 28.58 percent over the 10-year period.
- If the S&P 500 is held during the times when you would have held the UTY with the Donchian strategy, and you stay in cash otherwise, your return would be 9.61 percent over the 10-year period. Thus, the strategy beats the S&P 500 during the time you use it.
- If you hold the S&P 500 for the overall 10-year period, you achieve a return of 105.97 percent.
- If you hold the UTY for the overall 10-year period, you achieve a return of 55.52 percent. That is, the UTY Index underperforms the S&P significantly during the overall 10-year period (excluding dividends).
- If you use the strategy with the UTY, and rotate into the S&P 500 when not using the strategy, you achieve a return of 141.61 percent over the

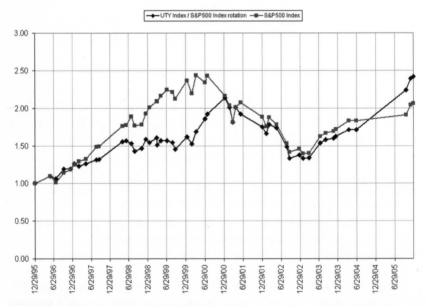

FIGURE 7.5 Hypothetical returns from rotating between the PHLX Utility index and the S&P 500 index (using a 32-day Donchian trend following strategy on the PHLX Utility index, ignoring fees, taxes, and dividends), versus holding the S&P 500 over an approximately 10-year period. (*Source:* Stock price data from Yahoo! Finance.)

10-year period. Rotating between the two indices thus beats holding either index individually over the same period, or using the strategy by itself.

Clearly, rotations versus a benchmark index (or even versus another index or stock) add a whole new dimension to technical trading.

MY ASSUMPTIONS IN THIS STUDY

The simple illustrations of technical rotation between an index and a benchmark index that I have used make some major, and very generous, assumptions, for simplicity.

- Use closing prices only to determine if a breakout or breakdown has occurred, and trade on the subsequent day's close in both the S&P 500 *and* the other index that you are timing technically.
- Invest 100 percent of your capital in each signal, with no commissions or slippage. I exclude dividends and the effects of reinvesting them, and I exclude the effects of taxes.
- Sample rotation strategies are illustrated here with indices rather than stocks, which you cannot truly invest in, although there are instruments now that closely mimic some of the major indexes.
- Exclude all data before the starting date of December 29, 1995, in your calculations of new 32-day highs and lows. That is, the first day on which a trade signal could occur is the thirty-third day of data under consideration, and the first day that a hypothetical trade could occur would be the thirty-fourth day of data under consideration.

DISCUSSION

Technical trading is derided by some because many strategies looked at all by themselves fail to beat the market's long-term return. However, my illustrations in this chapter are meant to show that technical trading can provide an extra boost to your portfolio if you use it to beat the market occasionally (especially based on a powerful underlying idea) rather than trying to beat the market over all time periods. All of the tools I present in this book can help in your studies in this area. Timing methods for trades such as the use of pilot signals, whole portfolio position sizing methods such as the use of R:P ratio averaging, and so on can all be applied. The only difference if you use a rotation strategy is that each time when you would normally put the proceeds of a single or multistock investment in cash with a pure technical strategy, you would instead rotate into the S&P 500 (or the benchmark index you are trying to beat).

If you want to be even more aggressive, you can invest each dollar that would otherwise be in cash, in the S&P 500. This would mean that if your position sizing criteria says that you should invest 80 percent of portfolio capital and leave 20 percent in cash, you might place the other 20 percent in the S&P 500 instead of holding it in cash. All of these methods would produce very different risk and equity curve profiles from using a pure technical strategy or from simply holding the S&P 500. Due to your constant exposure to stocks when employing a rotation method, the effects of whipsaws from a pure price chasing strategy (in which you sit in cash when not in stocks) can be reduced somewhat if the stocks you trade have reasonably strong correlations to the benchmark index. For example, if you sell a stock on a short-term low using a technical strategy, you may then be investing the proceeds into the S&P 500 around one of its own short-term lows. However, you can also be exposed to large market drawdowns in the S&P 500 if they occur.

Rotating from a stock to an index may also help to reduce slippage. Since your timing for trades in the S&P 500 are generally based on signals in the stocks, funds, or ETFs that you are trading technically (that is, rather than the S&P 500 itself), you will not always be chasing S&P 500 prices. If the stocks you are technically trading are closely correlated to the S&P 500, any slippage you experience when buying or selling these stocks may actually be offset by slippage in your favor when respectively selling or buying the S&P 500. With the tremendous number of ETFs and closed-end funds covering various asset classes, industries, and countries, you have a great deal of choice when deciding what to hold when not in the S&P 500.

Epilogue

You must know yourself when trading. Know your limits, understand how you react to pressure situations, and then take the time to plan out your trades in detail in a manner that makes sense to you. What kind of equity curve behavior are you willing to tolerate? Is your goal to beat the market outright with a technical strategy and spend the time when you're not using the strategy holding cash? Or are you content to hold a benchmark index ETF most of the time and occasionally try to beat the benchmark with a technical strategy? How much of your capital do you wish to allocate to various positions? Do you want to trade multiple stocks simultaneously or time your trades in each stock individually? Are you more comfortable trading a stock using its individual price action to time your trades or using the broader market's price action to time your trades? All of these questions and many more are ones that only you as an investor can answer.

In this book I have shown you

- Timing and money management tools for planning technical trades in detail.
- Unique methods of technical analysis that enable you to analyze the price behavior of multiple stocks simultaneously, such as stochastic averaging.
- Methods of timing trades in individual stocks using external indices or other stocks as a filter.
- Specialized ways in which you can apply technical trading, such as using it in an attempt to temporarily beat a benchmark index like the S&P 500 as opposed to always beating the benchmark.

Now that you understand position sizing and exit timing in detail, you can focus the bulk of your time on maximizing your edge through intelligent instrument selection and entry timing, rounding out your trade planning expertise. I hope that you have found my writings useful, and wish you the best of luck in your trading!

Trend Trading Worksheets and Checklists

USING NOTES IN THE TRADING PROCESS

Research Notebook/Notes

- Note brainstorms and original trading ideas in your Research Notebook.
- Make a list of situations to monitor based on your ideas, such as the price action of specific indices, overseas news headlines, special calendar dates, and so on.
- Note any additional research on your ideas, listing as many relevant facts and figures as possible.

Trading Diary

- Write out your trading plan in advance for situations that you intend to trade, from how you'll identify or have identified the trade setup, through your entry and conditional exit statements.
- Note how precisely you carry out your trading plan.
- Note any observations or doubts that you have before, during, or after each trade.

GENERAL POSITION SIZING FORMULAS FOR BINS IN A CASH EQUITY ACCOUNT

Note: Determine both target heat and stop levels.

$$\text{Dollar risk} = \text{entry price} - \text{stop price}$$

Dollar risk to price ratio (R:P ratio) in an individual stock

$$= \frac{\text{entry price} - \text{stop price}}{\text{entry price}}$$

$$= \frac{\text{dollar risk}}{\text{entry price}}$$

$$= 1 - \left(\frac{\text{stop price}}{\text{entry price}} \right)$$

Fraction of bin capital to invest (capped at a maximum of 100%)

$$= \frac{\text{target heat} \times \text{entry price}}{\text{dollar risk}}$$

$$= \frac{\text{target heat}}{\text{R:P ratio}}$$

POSITION SIZING FORMULAS USING A DONCHIAN BAND-BASED VOLATILITY MEASURE

Notes

- Determine target heat, but base stop price and thus R:P ratio on the stock's volatility and your entry price.
- Measure N-day lows and N-day highs at your time of entry.
- N-day lows and N-day highs can be determined from a series of single daily prices like closes only, or from a series consisting of all open, high, low, and close price data. It may include or exclude today's prices depending on your preference.
- The respective series of N-day lows and N-day highs (i.e., Donchian bands) that you use to size your positions can be replaced by low and high bands from a different band-based indicator such as Bollinger bands.

$$\text{Donchian dollar risk} = (\text{entry price}) \times \left[1 - \left(\frac{\text{N-day low}}{\text{N-day high}}\right)\right]$$

$$\text{Donchian R:P ratio} = \left[1 - \left(\frac{\text{N-day low}}{\text{N-day high}}\right)\right]$$

$$\text{Donchian stop level} = (\text{entry price}) \times \left(\frac{\text{N-day low}}{\text{N-day high}}\right)$$

$$\begin{array}{l}\text{Fraction of bin capital to invest} \\ \text{(capped at a maximum of 100\%)}\end{array} = \frac{\text{target heat}}{\text{Donchian R:P ratio}}$$

POSITION SIZING FORMULAS INCORPORATING AN ARBITRARY R:P RATIO SET BY TRADER

$$\text{Dollar risk} = \text{entry price} \times \text{R:P ratio}$$

$$\begin{array}{l}\text{Fraction of bin capital to invest} \\ \text{(capped at a maximum of 100\%)}\end{array} = \frac{\text{target heat}}{\text{R:P ratio}}$$

SAMPLE INDIVIDUAL TRADE WORKSHEET

Note: This information may be incorporated into your trading and research diaries.

Stock name and symbol: _____

Reasons for putting on the trade (Write here your fundamental and/or technical reasons for putting on the trade, as well as how you've come to terms with any doubts you may have):

_____

_____

_____

_____

Trading plan (Write here the technical details of how you will trade your idea. For example, you may mention pilot signals, Donchian bands, *conditional exit statements*, etc.):

_____

_____

_____

_____

_____

_____

TRADE VALUES

Pre-Trade Theoretical Values

Target Heat: _____

Initial Stop Level: _____

Entry Price: _____

Dollar Risk: _____

R:P Ratio: _____

Fraction of Bin Capital to Invest: _____

Dollar Amount of Bin Capital to Invest: _____

Actual Trade Values

Entry Date and Price: _____

Number of Shares Purchased: _____

Cost Basis: _____

Exit Date and Price: _____

Proceeds after Costs: _____

Net Profit or Loss of Trade: _____

Did you make a trading plan in advance of your trade? _____

Did you follow your trading plan? _____

What are your post-trade observations? _____

_____

_____

PORTFOLIO BIN WORKSHEET FOR ONE STOCK PER BIN

Starting cash in portfolio: _____

Total number of bins: _____

Respective starting bin weightings (if not equal weight):

_____

Intended rebalancing methodology (if applicable):

_____

_____

Individual Bin Worksheet

Before first purchase

Date of inception: _____

Bin number or name/description: _____

Starting cash in bin: _____

Percentage of mark-to-market portfolio value this starting cash represents: _____

After first purchase

Date of purchase: _____

Free cash in bin: _____

Symbol of stock in bin: _____

Shares of stock in bin: _____

After first bin liquidation / before second purchase

Date of liquidation: _____

Total cash in bin: _____

After second purchase

Date of purchase: _____

Free cash in bin: _____

Symbol of stock in bin: _____

Shares of stock in bin: _____

After second bin liquidation / before third purchase

Date of liquidation: _____

Total cash in bin: _____

Continue in a similar fashion for further use of the bin.

Abandoning use of the bin

Date you cease using the bin: _____

Reason for doing so: _____

_____

_____

PORTFOLIO CONTINGENCY CHECKLIST

Note: Don't let remote possibilities of bad things happening discourage you from trading. This list simply contains some general scenarios that you should be aware of.

What Are Your Protocols for If:

- Your computer or phone line goes down and you are unable to trade?
- Your broker's online systems or phones go down and you are unable to trade?
- Due to system problems, you cannot find out whether a trade that you tried to make has been received or executed?
- Your broker runs into a sudden liquidity or bankruptcy problem and your account is frozen?
- You intend to go on vacation and leave open positions in your account, or to travel with limited Internet or phone access?
- You make a trading error that is your fault (e.g., a wrong-sided trade, wrong symbol, or failure to cancel limit or stop orders)?
- Your broker makes a trading error that is your broker's fault?
- You have a dispute with your broker due to a poor fill, missed execution, or a misinterpretation of your instructions?
- A stock that you own has a catastrophic gap down that is well past your stop level?
- A stock that you are using as a pilot signal to trade another stock is halted?
- A stock that you own, or one that you are considering entering, is halted?

- Your broker has to reroute operations to a disaster recovery site? What about if a stock exchange has to do this?
- You suddenly need the money in your account for an emergency?
- Multiple positions in your portfolio suddenly become highly correlated and considerably more volatile on the downside than you had anticipated?
- You encounter sudden illiquidity when trying to enter or exit a position?
- You forget to make a trade and either miss an entry point or lose more money than you had planned to on an exit?
- You have an existing position with no exit plan in place?
- You lose 25 percent of your account's peak value? What about 50 percent or another value?
- You receive a margin call or are forced to liquidate a position?

How Do You Plan to

- Reinvest dividends received, if at all?
- Liquidate shares received as part of a spin-off?
- Liquidate a stock you own that has a takeover announced or is delisted?
- Invest additional cash that you want to add to your account among stocks that you already own?
- Rebalance bins or positions in your account, if at all?

Notes

Preface

1. William Shakespeare, David Bevington, ed., *Julius Caesar* (New York: Bantam Books, 1988).
2. Michael Covel, *Trend Following: How Great Traders Make Millions in Up or Down Markets* (Upper Saddle River, NJ: Financial Times Prentice Hall, 2004).
3. Edwin Lefevre, *Reminiscences of a Stock Operator* (New York: John Wiley & Sons, 1994 [1923]).
4. For example, the Web site www.originalturtles.org details a mechanical trading system previously used by some trend followers in the futures markets.

CHAPTER 1 Elements of an Edge

1. Robert Hagin, *Modern Portfolio Theory* (Homewood, IL: Dow Jones-Irwin, 1979), 12.
2. William Gallacher, *Winner Take All: A Brutally Honest and Irreverent Look at the Motivations and Methods of the Top Traders* (New York: McGraw-Hill, 1994), 54.
3. Roger Lowenstein, *When Genius Failed: The Rise and Fall of Long Term Capital Management* (New York: Random House, 2000).
4. Jim Puplava, from the article "The Golden Bull: I'm Bullish on 'Things,'" www.financialsense.com, access date 1/28/2006.
5. As quoted in Jack Schwager, *Market Wizards* (New York: HarperCollins, 1993), 286.
6. Edwin Lefevre, *Reminiscences of a Stock Operator* (New York: John Wiley & Sons, 1994 [1923]), 22.
7. Jesse Livermore, *How to Trade in Stocks* (Greenville, SC: Traders Press, 1991), 31.
8. Bruce Lee, John Little, ed., *The Tao of Gung Fu* (Boston: Tuttle Publishing, 1997).
9. Gallacher, *Winner Take All*, 178.
10. Roger Bacon's thoughts on intelligent turf speculation, outlined in his outstanding book *Secrets of Professional Turf Betting*, have been helpful to me in my understanding of probabilities of winning and stock speculation.

CHAPTER 2   What Can an Equity Trader Learn from a Futures Trend Follower?

1. Michael Covel, *Trend Following: How Great Traders Make Millions in Up or Down Markets* (Upper Saddle River, NJ: Financial Times Prentice Hall, 2004), 16–19

2. Edwin Lefevre, *Reminiscences of a Stock Operator* (New York: John Wiley & Sons, 1994 [1923]), 69.

3. Lefevre, *Reminiscences*, 91.

4. For example, see Lois Peltz, *The New Investment Superstars* (New York: John Wiley & Sons, 2001), 148.

5. William Eckhardt, as quoted by Jack D. Schwager in *The New Market Wizards* (New York: HarperBusiness, 1992), 111–112.

6. Covel, *Trend Following*, 93–94.

7. For example, see Jack D. Schwager, *Market Wizards* (New York: HarperBusiness, 1993), 164 and Covel, *Trend Following*, 93.

8. For example, Covel, *Trend Following*, 48.

9. Covel, *Trend Following*, 228.

10. Robert Rotella covers this subject in excellent detail in *The Elements of Successful Trading* (New York Institute of Finance, 1992), 435–439.

11. Van K. Tharp, *Trade Your Way to Financial Freedom* (New York: McGraw-Hill, 1999) 38–39.

12. Todd Lofton, *Getting Started in Futures*, 5th ed. (Hoboken, NJ: John Wiley & Sons, 2005), 159–162.

13. Lefevre, *Reminiscences*, 130–131.

14. Covel, *Trend Following*, 25–83.

15. Lois Peltz, *The New Investment Superstars* (New York: John Wiley & Sons, 2001), 145–161.

16. Lefevre, *Reminiscences*, 89.

17. Ibid., 70.

18. For example, Yale Hirsch and Jeffrey A. Hirsch, *Stock Trader's Almanac 2006* (Hoboken, NJ: John Wiley & Sons, 2006).

19. Jeffrey A. Hirsch and J. Taylor Brown, *The Almanac Investor: Profit from Market History and Seasonal Trends* (Hoboken, NJ: John Wiley and Sons, 2006).

20. I discuss Darvas's trading in more detail in the next chapter.

21. Nicholas Darvas, *How I Made $2,000,000 in the Stock Market* (New York: Lyle Stuart, Kensington Publishing Corporation, 1986), 60–61.

CHAPTER 3   Equity Trend Following in Action

1. Robert D. Edwards and John Magee, *Technical Analysis of Stock Trends*, 5th ed. (Boston: John Magee Inc., 1966).

2. Edwards and Magee, *Technical Analysis of Stock Trends*, 11. Also see Richard Russell, Dow Theory Letters Incorporated Online, "*The History of the Dow Theory*," www.dowtheoryletters.com, Access date 1/28/2006.

3. Edwards and Magee, *Technical Analysis of Stock Trends*, 12.
4. Ibid., 13.
5. Ibid., 13–15.
6. Ibid., 15–16.
7. Ibid., 17–19.
8. Ibid., 19.
9. Ibid., 19–20.
10. Ibid., 20.
11. Ibid., 20–21.
12. Ibid., 13.
13. Ibid., 45.
14. Ibid., 13–15.
15. Ibid., 13.
16. Ibid., 13-14.
17. Ibid., 16.
18. Ibid., 17–19.
19. Robert D. Edwards and John Magee (W.H.C. Basseti, ed.), *Technical Analysis of Stock Trends*, 8th ed. (Boca Raton, FL: St. Lucie Press, CRC Press LLC, 2001), 49–51.
20. Richard Russell, Dow Theory Letters Incorporated Online, "The History of the Dow Theory," www.dowtheoryletters.com, Access date 1/31/2006.
21. For a much more detailed analysis of Livermore's speculative wisdom, refer to Adam Hamilton's excellent series of essays on the "Wisdom of Jesse Livermore," on his Web site www.zealllc.com.
22. Edwin Lefevre, *Reminiscences of a Stock Operator* (John Wiley & Sons, 1994 [1923]), 5.
23. Lefevre, *Reminiscences* (Foreword by Jack Schwager), 7.
24. Ibid., 186.
25. For example, Lefevre, *Reminiscences*, 12.
26. Lefevre, *Reminiscences*, 14.
27. Ibid., 68.
28. Ibid., 66.
29. Ibid.
30. Ibid., 69.
31. Ibid.
32. Ibid.
33. For example, Jesse Livermore, *How to Trade in Stocks* (Greenville, SC: Traders Press, 1991), 68.
34. Nicholas Darvas, *How I Made $2,000,000 in the Stock Market* (New York: Lyle Stuart, Kensington Publishing Corporation, 1986).
35. Nicholas Darvas, *Wall Street: The Other Las Vegas* (New York: Lyle Stuart, Kensington Publishing Corporation, 2002 [1964]).
36. Darvas, *Wall Street*, 148–149.
37. Ibid., 149.
38. Ibid., 158.
39. Darvas, *How I Made $2,000,000*, 79.
40. Ibid., 66.

41. Adam Hamilton, "The Great Commodities Bull of the 00's," http://www .zealllc.com/commentary/commbull.htm, Access date 1/28/2006.

42. See for example a Jim Puplava article titled "The Golden Bull: I'm Bullish on 'Things'" http://www.financialsense.com/stormwatch/oldupdates/2003/0329.htm, Access date 1/28/2006.

CHAPTER 4 Three-Dimensional Technical Analysis

1. Edwin Lefevre, *Reminiscences of a Stock Operator* (New York: John Wiley & Sons, 1994 [1923]), 61.

2. Michael Covel, *Trend Following* (Upper Saddle River, NJ: Financial Times Prentice Hall, 2004), 77–79.

3. Steven B. Achelis, *Technical Analysis from A to Z* (New York: McGraw-Hill, 2001), 265.

4. Ibid., 321.

5. Ibid., 324.

6. Larry R. Williams, *How I Made One Million Dollars . . . Last Year . . . Trading Commodities* (Brightwaters, NY: Windsor Books, 1979), 69.

7. For example, see Charles Mackay, *Extraordinary Popular Delusions and the Madness of Crowds* (New York: Barnes and Noble, 1989), 89–97.

8. Recall that Edwards and Magee mention in *Technical Analysis of Stock Trends* that part of Dow Theory comprises a description of public sentiment at various stages of bull and bear markets.

9. Jesse Livermore, *How to Trade in Stocks* (Greenville, SC: Traders Pess, 1991), 68.

10. Ibid.

11. As quoted in Jack Schwager, *Market Wizards* (New York: HarperCollins, 1993), 161.

12. Ibid.

CHAPTER 5 Structuring a Trend Trade

1. Todd Lofton, *Getting Started in Futures*, 5th ed. (Hoboken, NJ: John Wiley & Sons, 2005), 31.

2. For example, Michael Covel, *Trend Following* (Upper Saddle River, NJ: Financial Times Prentice Hall, 2004), 46. See also www.iasg.com for profiles of managed futures funds.

3. Robert Rotella, *The Elements of Successful Trading* (New York: New York Institute of Finance, 1992), 564.

4. William Gallacher makes this excellent point in his book *Winner Take All* (New York: McGraw-Hill, 1994), 160–161.

5. See Ed Seykota and David Druz, "Determining Optimal Risk," *Trader's Magazine* 11:3, 122–124.

6. An equivalent formula is given in: Steven B. Achelis, *Technical Analysis from A to Z* (New York: McGraw-Hill, 2001), 68.

CHAPTER 7   Out of the Box: Further Possibilities

1. Jesse Livermore, *How to Trade in Stocks* (Greenville, SC: Traders Press, 1991), 68.
2. Jeffrey A. Hirsch and J. Taylor Brown, *The Almanac Investor* (Hoboken, NJ: John Wiley & Sons, 2006), 83.
3. Edwin Lefevre, *Reminiscences of a Stock Operator* (New York: John Wiley & Sons, 1994, [1923], 131.

Bibliography

Achelis, Steven B. *Technical Analysis from A to Z*, 2nd ed. New York: McGraw-Hill, 2001.

Bacon, Robert. *Secrets of Professional Turf Betting*, 6th ed. Brattleboro, VT: Amerpub Corporation, 1961.

Covel, Michael. *Trend Following: How Great Traders Make Millions in Up or Down Markets*. Upper Saddle River, NJ: Financial Times Prentice Hall, 2004.

Darvas, Nicholas. *How I Made $2,000,000 in the Stock Market*. New York: Lyle Stuart, Kensington Publishing Corp., 1986.

Darvas, Nicholas. *Wall Street: The Other Las Vegas*. New York: Lyle Stuart, Kensington Publishing Corp., 2002 (1964).

Edwards, Robert D., and John Magee. *Technical Analysis of Stock Trends*, 5th ed. Boston: John Magee Inc., 1966.

Edwards, Robert D., and John Magee. *Technical Analysis of Stock Trends*, 8th ed. Boca Raton, FL: St. Lucie Press, CRC Press LLC, 2001.

Gallacher, William R. *Winner Take All: A Brutally Honest and Irreverent Look at the Motivations and Methods of the Top Traders*. New York: McGraw-Hill, 1994.

Hagin, Robert. *Modern Portfolio Theory*. Homewood, IL: Dow Jones-Irwin, 1979.

Hirsch, Jeffrey A., and J. Taylor Brown. *The Almanac Investor. Profit from Market History and Seasonal Trends*. Hoboken, NJ: John Wiley & Sons, Inc., 2006.

Hirsch, Yale, and Jeffrey A. Hirsch. *Stock Trader's Almanac 2006*, Hoboken, NJ: John Wiley & Sons, 2006.

Lee, Bruce. *The Tao of Gung Fu*. Edited by John Little. Boston: Tuttle Publishing, 1997.

Lefevre, Edwin. *Reminiscences of a Stock Operator*. New York: John Wiley & Sons, 1994 (1923).

Livermore, Jesse. *How to Trade in Stocks*. Greenville, SC: Traders Press, 1991 (1940).

Lofton, Todd. *Getting Started in Futures*. Hoboken, NJ: John Wiley & Sons, 2005.

Lowenstein, Roger. *When Genius Failed: The Rise and Fall of Long Term Capital Management*. New York: Random House, 2000.

Mackay, Charles. *Extraordinary Popular Delusions and the Madness of Crowds.* New York: Barnes & Noble Books, 1989 (1841).

Peltz, Lois. *The New Investment Superstars.* New York: John Wiley & Sons, 2001.

Rotella, Robert. *The Elements of Successful Trading.* New York: New York Institute of Finance, 1992.

Schwager, Jack. *Market Wizards.* New York: HarperBusiness, HarperCollins Publishers, 1993.

Schwager, Jack. *The New Market Wizards.* New York: HarperBusiness, Harper-Collins Publishers, 1992.

Shakespeare, William. *Julius Caesar.* Edited by David Bevington. New York: Bantam Books, 1988.

Tharp, Van K. *Trade Your Way to Financial Freedom.* New York: McGraw-Hill, 1999.

Williams, Larry R. *How I Made One Million Dollars . . . Last Year . . . Trading Commodities.* Brightwaters, NY: Windsor Books, 1979.

Recommended Reading

Goodspeed, Bennett. *The Tao Jones Averages: A Guide to Whole-Brained Investing*. New York: Viking Penguin, 1984.

Kuhn, Thomas S. *The Structure of Scientific Revolutions*. Third edition. Chicago: The University of Chicago Press. 1996 (1962).

Niederhoffer, Victor. *The Education of a Speculator*. New York: John Wiley and Sons, Inc., 1997.

O'Neill, William J. *How to Make Money in Stocks*. Third edition. New York: McGraw-Hill, 2002.

Rogers, Jim. *Hot Commodities: How Anyone Can Invest Profitably in the World's Best Market*. New York: Random House, 2004.

Schwager, Jack. *Stock Market Wizards*. New York: HarperBusiness, HarperCollins Publishers, 2003.

Shiller, Robert J. *Irrational Exuberance*. Princeton, NJ: Princeton University Press, 2000.

Soros, George. *The Alchemy of Finance*. Hoboken, NJ: John Wiley & Sons, 2003 (1987).

Sun Tzu. *The Art of War*. Edited by James Clavell. New York: Delta Trade Paperbacks, 1983.

Additional Resources

RECOMMENDED WEB SITES

www.financialsense.com The unparalleled, generally value oriented commentary of Jim Puplava, as well as valuable commentary from numerous other sources.

www.kirkreport.com The highly intelligent insights of Charles E. Kirk, a self-made, often intermediate-term trader.

www.iasg.com Institutional Advisory Services Group, a repository of managed futures fund profiles and performance data.

www.zealllc.com Adam Hamilton's excellent, often contrarian commentary on investment ideas and the art of speculation itself.

finance.yahoo.com Yahoo! Finance—An invaluable resource for stock price and fundamental data, news, ETF profiles, and much more.

www.streetstories.com Profiles of and quotes made by some of the world's greatest investors, across a wide variety of styles.

RECOMMENDED NEWSPAPERS

Investor's Business Daily

Barron's

The Wall Street Journal

The Financial Times

Index

Almanac Investor, The, 182
  best six months switching
    strategy, 182
Altera Corporation (ALTR), 110
AMEX Oil and Gas Index (XOI), 71,
  72, 110, 190, 191
AMEX Gold Bugs Index (HUI), 70,
  72
Arbitrage:
  versus speculation, 13
Arch Coal Inc. (ACI), 107, 109
Average (equity index), *See* Index
Average plot, 177–179
Average ratio, 177–178
Average directional movement
    index, 78
Average true range, 148–149
  related volatility measure, 149

Back-testing, 27, 115
  equities versus futures, 121
  as follow-up research to market
    insights, 55
  limitations of, 27, 37–40
Barron's, *See* Darvas, Nicholas,
    reading of *Barron's*
Basket (of stocks), 164, 171–172
Bins:
  as sub-accounts of a larger equity
    account, 141, 153–155
  definition, 142

rebalancing to equal weight,
    168–169
  for sorting net dollar returns,
    150–152
Black-box strategy, 39, 40,
    113–115
  on use in a single asset class,
    114
Bollinger bands, 86–87, 99, 148
  construction, 86
  and Donchian bands, 86–87
Bollinger, John, 86
Buffett, Warren, 41
Bull Market, *See* Market, bull

Campaign, *See* Portfolio, trading
    campaign
Candlestick:
  Japanese, 112
    and long-long pairs charting,
    174–175
Canned strategy, *See* Black box
    strategy
Casino, 17–18
Choppiness, *See* Market, choppy
Chevron Corporation (CVX),
    110
Commodities,
  bull market, 71–72, 77
  comparisons to stocks, 117–121
  stocks, 66–73

Commodity trading advisor(s)
(CTA), 26, 27, 31, 49, 115
and portfolio diversification, 114,
119
Compounding, 170
Correlation:
among portfolio stocks, 119, 160,
166
between a pair of stocks, 180
Costs, trading, 16, 20–23, 177,
178
Covel, Michael, 49
Crowd:
behavior, 52, 92, 100, 119
herd effect, 92, 100
Crude oil futures, 140
Curve:
price-time exit, 134–135
forward (for crude oil futures),
93
and backwardation, 93
and contango, 93

Darvas, Nicholas, 52, 53, 63–66, 89,
167
boxes, 63–65
buying of all-time highs, 167
reading of *Barron's*, 53
stock selection method, 63
techno-fundamentalist theory,
63
trailing stop method, 63–64
Degrees of freedom, 39
Diagnosis of a trading opportunity:
qualitative method, 26, 59
quantitative method, 26, 59
Diary, trading, 53–55
Discipline, 40, 50
trade planning, 49
Dollar loss limit, 160
Dollar risk, 125, 128–130, 131, 133,
146
to price ratio, *See* R:P ratio

Donchian bands (channels), 78–82,
86–87, 98, 128, 146–147,
167–168, 183
construction, 78–82
relationship to the stochastic,
85
trend identification with, 97–99
use as a volatility measure,
144–147
Donchian, Richard, 78, 83
Dow, Charles, 57–60, 94, 100
Dow Jones Industrial Average, 93,
100, 173
Dow theory, 57–60, 62, 96, 97
bear market, 58–60
bull market, 58–60
description, 57–58
principle of confirmation, 60
and trend following, 58
trend descriptions,
minor, 57–59
primary, 57–59
secondary, 57–59
Dow Jones Transportation
Average, 60, 100
Downtrend:
market:
Donchian, 97
stochastic, 99–100
Drawdown, 51, 114, 138, 187
Druz, David, 139

Earnings, 133, 134
Edge, 16, 26, 49, 58, 124
Edwards, Robert D., 57
Efficient market hypothesis, 3, 97
Emotion, 15, 35
Entry, 122
price, 130, 156, 158, 160
timing, 24, 44, 51, 53
trend following versus others, 32
Equity curve, 11
trading, 180–181

Exit, 122
  conditional, 125–126, 128, 133,
      134
    list, 123, 126, 137–139
  timing, 24, 32, 44, 51
  plan, 35, 123, 135–137
Exxon Mobil (XOM), 130

Filter:
  double trend identification, 100
  Dow Theory, 60
  for identifying buy candidates,
      38
Ford Motor Company (F), 174, 179
Foundation Coal Holdings (FCL),
      107
Frenzies:
  in markets, 94–95
Futures,
  contract description, 117–118
  comparisons to equities,
      117–121, 140
  trading characteristics, 117–118

Gallacher, William:
  on risk to trading equity, 20
  on trend lines, 7
General Electric (GE), 166
General Motors (GM), 174, 179
Gold, 67–71
  bear market, 68
  bull market, 69–70
  mining companies, 67–69
  price, 69
Group:
  behavior, *See* Crowd, behavior

Hamilton, William, 57
Heat, 139–142, 153
  definition, 144
  in a subaccount, 141
  target, *See* Target Heat
Henry, John, 49

Herd, *See* Crowd
Hirsch, Yale, 52
Hirsch, Jeffrey A., 52
Holy grail, 42, 51

Illiquidity, 126
Index, 109, 112
  alterations in the composition of,
      28
  multipliers, 106
  rebalancing, 106, 107
  and stock splits, 106
  use as a pilot signal, 101–105, *See
      also* Pilot Signal
  weighting, 106
    by market cap, 166
    by price, 112
Indicators
  and simplicity, 78
Institutional Advisory Services
      Group, 49, 119
Instrument selection, 24, 51, 53
Intel Corporation (INTC), 127–128
Investing:
  from the long side, 28
Investment:
  climate, 52
  themes, 14
Investor's Business Daily (IBD),
      52
  IBD 100, 39
iShares Lehman 1-3 Year Treasury
      Bond Fund (SHY), 182
iShares Lehman 20+-year Treasury
      Bond Fund (TLT), 121,
      182
iShares MSCI Japan Index Fund
      (EWJ), 185

Keltner channels, 89
Kepler, Johannes, 56
KLA-Tencor Corporation (KLAC),
      102, 103, 128

Lane, George:
  invention of stochastic indicator,
      82, *See also* Stochastic
Leverage, 28, 140–141, 183, 187
Liquidity, 13, 126, 127
Livermore, Jesse, 17, 33, 34, 49,
      61–63, 65, 100, 173, 183
  and bucket shops, 61
  and trend following, 62
  use of price-weighted index, 112,
      173
  "Old Man Partridge" story, 62
  on charting, 78
Lofton, Todd, 118
Long Term Capital Management, 12
Loser averaging, 137
Loss:
  aggregate losses, 20
  average gross, 20–22
  catastrophic, 12
  compounding, 170
  open, 50, 124, 137, 146, 162
  probability of consecutive
      losses, 45–47

Mackay, Charles, 94
Magee, John, 57
Margin, *See* Leverage
Mark-to-market, 142, 143, 169
Market:
  bear, 58, 59, 62, 100
  bull, 58, 59, 62, 100
    1990s, 66
    runaway, 95
  cap, 166–167
  choppy, 44, 122
  downtrend, *See* Downtrend,
      market
  drift, 15, 26, 184–185
  drops,
    October 1987, 120
    October 1997, 120
  emerging markets, 14

entry, *See* Entry
  extreme conditions, 127
  psychology, 60
  randomly walking, 15, 20
  uptrend, *See* Uptrend, market
Massey Energy Company (MEE),
      107
Microsoft (MSFT), 38
Minimum value fluctuations:
  on equities versus futures
      exchanges, 120
Money management:
  comfort with protocols, 166
Moving average, 88
  crossover, 122
  exponential, 89
Mutual fund, 80, 180

NASDAQ Composite Index, 97–98,
      101–103, 105, 165, 188–191
  2000 crash, 67–68
NASDAQ 100 Trust Shares
      (QQQQ), 110, 120, 182–183
Natural gas futures, 140
Negativity:
  public, toward an industry, 95
Net asset value (NAV), 180
New York Stock Exchange (NYSE),
      69
Nineteen nineties (1990s):
  stock market euphoria, 95
Normalized stop ratio, 161–162

Overbought, 83
Oversold, 83

P/E ratio, 133, 134
Pairs (long-long):
  charting methods, 171–179
    daily equal weight
        rebalancing, 175–179
    simple addition, 172–175
  on the intraday volatility of, 174

Pairs (long-short), 179
Pareto allocating, 165
Patience, 16–17, 40–42
Pattern:
  peak, 89–90, 92, 122
  trough, 89, 91, 122, 131
    exit, 168
Peltz, Lois, 49
PHLX Utility Index, 191–192
Pilot signal, 122, 127, 128, 135, 100,
    101, 104–106, 110, 142, 171,
    176, 190, 193
Portfolio:
  diversification, 162
  dollar loss limit, 160–162
  managed futures, 119
  rebalancing, 35, 36, 168, 169
  structuring, 117, 153–159
  target heat, 161, 162, 165–167
  volatility, *See* Volatility, portfolio
Position:
  losing, 43
  open, 138
    P&L, 32
Position Sizing, 24, 43, 51, 65, 120,
    139–144
  on the portfolio level, 153–170
Price:
  breakdown, 82
  chasing, 50, 82
  information, 33
  on weekly and monthly bars,
    181, 182
  peak price, 90
  stop, *See* Stop(s)
  target price, 47, 132, 138
  trough price, 91
  using a snapshot to trade, 88
Price-time exit curve, 134–135
Profit:
  actual, 24
  aggregate, 35
  average net, 20

  limit, 43
  open, 50, 54, 137
  potential, 24
Psychology, 49, 92
  psychological pain, 53
Public sentiment, 52
Puplava, Jim 14, 67, 70

R multiples, 149–150
R:P ratio, 125, 140, 145–147, 149,
    153–160, 166–167, 172,
    173
R:P Ratio Averaging, 159–162, 165,
    172, 193
Random walk:
  on the lack of a trading edge in a
    random market, 15
  on similarities between
    randomly generated and
    real price data, 4–7
Ratio oscillator, 112–113
  and momentum indicator, 113
Reentry, 122, 156–157
*Reminiscences of a Stock
    Operator*, *See* Livermore,
    Jesse
Research:
  notebook, 55
Reuters/Jefferies CRB Index, 71
Rhea, Robert, 57
Risk:
  estimate, 123
  management, 139
  perceived, 86
Rogers, Jim:
  on patience, 16
Rotations, 171, 176, 193–194
  strategies, 182–194
Rotella, Robert, 121
Roulette wheel, 17
  and statistics, 17–18
Russell, Richard, 60
Russell 2000 Index, 39

S&P 500 Index, 14, 28, 29, 39, 163,
167, 182–191, 194
S&P Depositary Receipts (SPY),
164, 184
Schaefer, E. George, 57
Semiconductor:
Index (SOX), 155
industry, 134
Sentiment, investor, 66
Seykota, Ed, 114, 139
Signal:
buy, 39
pilot, See Pilot Signal
Silver, 67, 70
bull market, 70
Slippage, 16, 20, 50, 80, 101, 104,
126, 177, 178, 194
Soros, George, 41
Standard deviation, 86, 147–148
Stochastic, 82, 84–85, 99–100, 106,
122, 129, 172
and Donchian bands, 85, 99
and fixed floor stops, 128
fixed time intervals, 84
market,
uptrend, 99
downtrend, 99–100
NASDAQ Composite Index's, 103
snapshot, 84
trigger level, 84–85
Stochastic averaging, 106–107,
171–172, 175, 177
computing, 109–111
definition, 106
and threshold levels, 111
as a trending state indicator, 107,
110–111
use of a stochastic average as a
pilot signal, 109–112
Stop(s), 122–124
adjustment, 126
fixed (or fixed floor), 105,
127–129, 134, 135, 138

fixed dollar, 160
level, 145
percentage, 122, 126–127, 133
and a stock's minimum price
variation, 126
placement, 145, 148
ratchet, 129–131, 138, 168
time, 133, 138, 163
trailing, 63, 86, 128, 134, 142
continuous, 128
dollar, 168
streetTRACKS Gold Shares (GLD),
121
Sub-account, See Bins
Subjectivity:
chart scale related, 7–9

Target Heat, 139–142, 144, 153–159,
162–163, 165, 166–167, 172,
173
Technical Analysis, 4, 60, 63, 92, 93,
183
predictive versus reactive use,
4
two-dimensional, 77–92
three-dimensional, 92–113
and market momentum, 101
definition, 93
Time frame, 50, 99, 148
short-term, 77
Time stop, See Stop(s), time
Trading:
on the challenges of using
technical strategies, 183,
193
costs, See Costs, trading
diary, See Diary, Trading
flat periods, 51
on long-term discipline and
patience, 40–42
overtrading, 12
paper trading, 11
studying performance, 149–152

strategies:
  back-testing, *See* Back-testing
  risk-reward profiles of, 47–49
  on trading plans, 12, 24, 25, 34,
    42, 55, 122
  on the usefulness of technical
    strategies, 23, 27
  on using simple indicators and
    rules, 10, 78
  winning percentage, 20–23
Trend:
  binary identification methods,
    96–105
  down, *See* Downtrend
  on secular market trends, 15,
    66–73
  up, *See* Uptrend
Trendlines, 4–7
Trend following:
  competition among trend
    followers, 115
  and Dow theory, 57–60
  and Jesse Livermore, 61–63
  long-term example, 66–73
  and natural human instincts,
    42–44
  and Nicholas Darvas, 63–66
  philosophy, 32–35
  strategy, 43, 64, 78, 101, 131
    coping with the realities of,
      49–56
    definition, 31
    indicators, 78–85
    long/flat, 187

Triggers:
  and technical indicators, 84–85
  fundamental, 133
  price, 131–132
  time, 133

Uptrend:
  market:
    Donchian, 96–99, 101, 102,
      105
    stochastic, 99, 100, 103,
      104

Volatility, 11, 53, 100, 101, 103,
    144, 167
  implied, 164
  in open losses, 36
  in open profits, 36, 51
  portfolio, 114, 119, 160–168
  using a normalized measure,
    160–162, 166
Volatility Matching, 163–165
Volume, 50, 132

Whipsaws, 44, 51, 88, 94–95,
    101–103, 110, 114, 183, 187,
    194
Wilder, Welles, 148
Williams, Larry:
  %R indicator, 82, 85
Winnings:
  aggregate, 20

Yield Curve, 93